The Healthy Heart Gourmet

Timely Nutritional Guidelines
And Gourmet Quality, Heart-Safe Recipes
For Healthier Living

641. 563
H 434 H
1994

Published by

The Healthy Heart Gourmet, Inc.

Recipes by Tom and Arlene Mills

Nutritional Guidelines by Cecilia Hennig, R.D.

Medical Foreword by Kenneth V. Adams, M.D.

THE HEALTHY HEART GOURMET

is endorsed by

HEART AND LUNG INSTITUTE
At St. Vincent's Medical Center
Jacksonville, Florida

Copyright 1994
Thomas and Arlene Mills
All rights reserved

ISBN --0-9620896-1-3

To order additional copies of **THE HEALTHY HEART GOURMET** cookbook, write to:

THE HEALTHY HEART GOURMET
3716 North A-1-A
Vero Beach, FL 32963
MC/VISA 1-800-444-2524

Printed in the United States of America
by
Moran Printing Company
Orlando, Florida

First Edition
First Printing: 1988
Second Printing: 1989

Second Edition – Updated and Revised
First Printing: 1994

Cover: an original oil on linen, 18½ x 24 - by Steve Mills

---

* *"I am absolutely thrilled with your 'Healthy Heart Gourmet'. I didn't know healthy food could taste so good."*- M.G., Ithaca, MI

* *"Everything tastes great and I'm losing weight too!"* - J.H., Greensboro, NC

* *"An intelligently and beautifully done cookbook."* - J.B., Wilmington, DE

* *"We love the heart-safe deviled eggs!"* - M.T., Baltimore, MD

* *"We don't feel we are being deprived of anything."* - B.B., Ft. Lauderdale, FL

* *"This is an especially well written cookbook."* - Nancy Nessa, **Cookbook Review**

* *"The Healthy Heart Gourmet will show you how to enjoy wonderful heart-safe foods that taste like great gourmet meals rather than bland baby food."* - **Great Cookbooks #7** - Simmer Pot Press

* *"Fooling the taste buds is the secret of the recipes."* - Trent Rowe, **New York Times** Regional Food Writer

* *"This book has all the flavor and pizzazz of classic favorites without the use of butter, cream and other dietary culprits."* - Janet Groene, **Cooking on the Go**

* *"This is the ultimate cooking guide for people with cardiovascular problems and those who wish to avoid them."* - Dr. Walter Smithwick, III, **Cardiovascular Surgeon**

ACKNOWLEDGEMENTS

Thomas P. Mills - Co-Author and Heart Patient, Graduate of New England Conservatory of Music, Boston, MA, with degrees in Church Music, Music Education and Conducting. Music Teacher, Organist/Choirmaster and Experimental Chef.

Arlene M. Mills - Co-Author, Graduate of Albany Business College, Albany, NY, in Clerical Administration. Homemaker, Clinical Chef.

Kenneth V. Adams, M.D. - Cardiologist, Graduate of University of Miami, School of Medicine. Affiliated with St. Vincent's Medical Center. Past affiliation with Cleveland Clinic, Cardiology Department, Cleveland, OH.

Cecilia Hennig, R.D. - Co-Author, Graduate (magna cum laude) Florida State University in Dietetics and School Food Services. A.D.A. Dietetic Internship, New York Hospital - Cornell Medical Center, New York, NY. Clinical Dietitian at St. Vincent's Medical Center, Jacksonville, FL.

Steve Mills - Artist/Illustrator, Graduate (magna cum laude) Bridgewater State College, Bridgewater, MA. Internationally recognized realist artist.

Michelle VanDoren, M.S., R.D. - Consultant, Graduate B.S. (cum laude) State University College at Buffalo, NY. M.S. Rutgers University. Dietitian for The Heart & Lung Institute at St. Vincent's Medical Center, Jacksonville, FL.

The following companies have given permission to use their trade names in
THE HEALTHY HEART GOURMET

CUMBERLAND PACKING COMPANY, Brooklyn, NY - **BUTTER BUDS**

GENERAL MILLS, INC., Minneapolis, MN - **BAC*OS** (bacon flavored bits)

GALAXY FOODS CO., Orlando, FL - **FORMAGG CHEESE ALTERNATIVES**

FOOD ANALYSIS

In analyzing the food values for this book, we considered only the Calories, Total Fat, Saturated Fat and Cholesterol.

The analysis was realized through the use of **THE DIET BALANCER - Version 2** computer program - a product of the **Nutridata Software Corporation, P.O. Box 769, Wappinger Falls, NY 12590**

The analysis was reviewed by The Heart and Lung Institute at St. Vincent's Medical Center, Jacksonville, FL.

Today, cardiologists and cardiovascular surgeons have a host of advanced tools and techniques for the diagnosis and repair of the effects of heart disease. They agree, however, that many cases could be prevented if people changed their pattern of daily living, such as diet, exercise and smoking habits.

Whereas, it is very simple for physicians to instruct their patients to become vegetarians, I suspect compliance is oftentimes zero. I am extremely proud of this book and the way Tom and Arlene Mills and Cecilia Hennig have designed it to offer information and recipes. They have put together a system of low-fat, low-cholesterol recipes that I recommend for use daily and for entertaining your friends and colleagues.

Education is the key to reducing the incidence of heart disease. I believe this book contains a vital message about heart-healthy nutrition and offers its readers an opportunity to make changes that can potentially add years to their lives.

The Heart and Lung Institute welcomes your comments on this book. Any modifications or recipes you would like to have reviewed for inclusion in future books can be forwarded to THE HEALTHY HEART GOURMET, Inc.

On behalf of the Board of Trustees of The Heart and Lung Institute at St. Vincent's, Inc., this book is recommended as a resource for years to come.

Walter Smithwick III, M.D.
Cardiovascular/Thoracic Surgery, St. Vincent's Medical Center
Founding Chairman of the Board/The Heart and Lung Institute

TABLE OF CONTENTS

THE HEART AND LUNG INSTITUTE
AT ST. VINCENT'S, INC.

The Heart and Lung Institute at St. Vincent's, Inc. is dedicated to research, education and patient care for heart and pulmonary disease. Established in 1985, The Heart and Lung Institute is the first and only facility of its kind in the Southeast. The Institute consists of physicians and allied health professionals from a variety of medical specialties who have a particular interest in research and the advancement of cardiac and pulmonary care.

Through its three-pronged approach of research, education and patient care, The Heart and Lung Institute is totally committed to the fight against heart and lung disease.

The research program of the Institute is a collaborative effort between the medical staff of St. Vincent's Medical Center, the local and state public health departments and universities. Contacts with the National Institutes of Health are ongoing to explore the mutually beneficial resources for research activities in both cardiovascular and pulmonary disease.

Besides research, The Heart and Lung Institute offers a variety of programs, support groups and classes, cardiopulmonary resuscitation (CPR) classes, cardiovascular exercise programs, biking and walking events to promote healthy living. Cholesterol and high blood pressure screenings are also offered at various times throughout the year.

The Institute provides local, regional and national seminars and conferences for physicians and allied health professionals on cardiovascular disease prevention and treatment. Visiting physicians, professors and eminent clinical practice health professionals provide a broad range of educational offerings.

The education of the public regarding cholesterol has been a major goal of The Heart and Lung Institute. This book serves as a comprehensive healthy guide to prevent heart disease through nutritional information and excellent recipes. This book represents the commitment of the Institute to coordinate efforts with the National Cholesterol Education Program of the National Heart, Lung & Blood Institute, and with the American Heart Association to communicate the message about cholesterol to the American public.

PREFACE

A WORD ABOUT THIS BOOK - WHY AN UPDATE?

A cookbook based on proper nutritional guidelines, using food alternatives for flavor, finds itself in a very tenuous arena. Weekly, new products arrive on the market. Some are found to have little value. Many, however, are proving to be a boon to healthy eating. Therefore an update was absolutely necessary. We have introduced many of these new products, computerized the food analysis and trimmed many recipes of excess oils and fat.

THE HEALTHY HEART GOURMET has a reputation as a cookbook with great-tasting recipes. We merely made it healthier! We retired a few recipes and replaced them with new. We included two cream soups offering safe alternatives for your casseroles.

We have meals to serve on your best china and those to place in a bun on a paper plate. (Check out "Pork" Barbeque on page 159.) Our variety of recipes allows you to open new and healthier doors to the world of good eating. Most of these recipes are easy to prepare, using products found in local supermarkets. All are analyzed for total fat, saturated fat, cholesterol and calorie content.

The NUTRITIONAL section states that your intake of fats should be no more than 30% of your calories, averaged daily. Also be sure to use only poly-unsaturated or mono-unsaturated fats, **AND ONLY THEN IN MODERATION!** Keep animal and saturated fats to a minimum!

The oil used in this cookbook is canola oil. This oil contains the least saturated fat of any oil presently on the market. For a particular flavor, in some recipes, we use extra-virgin Italian olive oil. In revising **THE HEALTHY HEART GOURMET** we found most recipes lost nothing by reducing the oil to lower levels. In some cases ⅔ less oil was used.

The suggested daily limit for cholesterol is 300 milligrams. If you have an egg for breakfast this means you have already consumed 213 milligrams of cholesterol. Plan the rest of the day accordingly. Red meat and all **REAL** dairy products contain many milligrams of this artery-clogging substance, and it is advisable to eat these foods in moderation. Your heart will thank you!

Take extra time for meal planning. Plan lunch and dinner meals a week at a time. (See pages 252-256.) Shopping once a week will also drastically lower chances for impulse buying. Remember, the food industry thrives on tricking people into buying unplanned items.

We have friends who prepare their week's meals on the weekend, freeze them in individual containers, and enjoy the convenience of quick meal preparation throughout the week, without the worry of excess fats and sodium one finds in store-bought frozen foods.

You may ask, "If this book is called **THE HEALTHY HEART GOURMET**, is it truly gourmet?" What is gourmet? The dictionary defines the gourmet as one who likes the delicacies of the table. We would add to that: the gourmet cook is one who creates and experiments with combinations of foodstuffs, searching for a meal that excites the taste buds, pleases the eye and brings on the ooh's and ah's from family and guests. These meals do not have to be *"served under glass"* and/or swimming in exotic sauces. The simplest of meals can be gourmet. **THE HEALTHY HEART GOURMET** cookbook has over 270 easy to prepare recipes, all great tasting.

You might argue, "If I want to eat fancy foods, I can always eat out!" This is true, and some restaurants now offer *"heart-safe"* meals, but our personal feeling is that few restaurants can match the meals we cook in our own kitchen. By eating at home we know exactly what ingredients are used. Most restaurants tend to over-season their foods with salt, sugar and fats to counteract the numbed taste buds of smokers and those having too many cocktails. When we do eat out, it is merely to let someone else do the planning, cooking and cleaning up. By using this book you too can match or better those meals found in many restaurants. Your home-cooked meals will be far healthier and much less expensive.

When looking through your book, examine carefully the process for making liquid <u>Butter Buds</u> on page 48. This is a key ingredient used throughout the book. It offers real butter taste with low fat and no cholesterol. What more could you want?

From **APPETIZERS,** amaze everyone by presenting Deviled Eggs with zero cholesterol, or Hot Sausage in Sour Cream with only a trace of fat. How do we keep the fat so low? The book will tell you!

There are enough recipes in **BRUNCHES AND LUNCHES** to keep you going for weeks without repeating any. No further need to serve monotonous breakfasts and lunches in your home.

In **BREADS**, check out Jamaican Corn Muffins or Beer Bread. In **SOUPS** how about a great Mexican Gaspacho, or New England Clam Chowder? In the **SALAD** section, a Cole Slaw or Potato Salad with only 2% fat is truly remarkable **AND** delicious.

Check carefully the chapter on **MEAT SUBSTITUTES**. Some of these quasi-red-meat dishes are international classics. You won't believe your taste buds when sampling "Sosaties" from the Near East, "Veal" Marsala from Italy or "Veal" Oscar from France.

In **POULTRY** try the Broccoli Chicken Stew. This is not just "another" stew, but leans toward a poultry Bouillabaisse, - **and** - talk about nutritious. This may be better for you than grandma's chicken soup.

SEAFOOD, wonderful heart-healthy seafood. Crab Imperial, from the Chesapeake Bay region, a cinch to prepare, is a must for company. Blender Salmon Mousse works as either an entree or an appetizer.

Nutritrionists say nothing is better for your health than **VEGETABLES.** Therefore, we offer a variety large enough to satisfy all possible tastes. We even have a low-fat version of Southern Style Collard Greens. How about a reborn German Sauerkraut with added vegetables, or a single giant Stuffed Zucchini for four?

The crowning glory is the chapter on **SAUCES**. Discovering how to adapt these sauces, in a heart-safe manner, was the catalyst needed to put **THE HEALTHY HEART GOUR-MET** in the spotlight. Just check out the figures in the following comparisons:

BEARNAISE SAUCE, ¼ cup

REAL	**THE HEALTHY HEART GOURMET**
Calories - 196	Calories - 55
Total Fat - 20.6g	Total Fat - 3.9g
Saturated Fat - 11.9g	Saturated Fat - .3g
Cholesterol - 129.5mg	Cholesterol - 0

HOLLANDAISE SAUCE, ¼ cup

REAL	**THE HEALTHY HEART GOURMET**
Calories - 256	Calories - 79
Total Fat - 27.5g	Total Fat - 5.2g
Saturated Fat - 15.8g	Saturated Fat - .4g
Cholesterol - 172.5mg	Cholesterol - 0

If these dramatic figures lead you to believe the flavor must be missing, try them. Serve the Bearnaise over grilled salmon or turkey medallions and the Hollandaise over asparagus or other green vegetables. You will soon find out what we mean. Great taste without any heavy, fatty afterfeeling.

There are **DESSERTS** you won't believe. Chocolate Cake, Custard, scrumptious pies, Cheesecake, etc., all in a *"heart-safe"* mode.

Two finicky gourmand friends of ours said, while sampling a recipe from Meat Substitutes, *"we don't feel we are missing anything!"* That's the real point of this book. Fool your palate - Save your heart! You **CAN** have all the great tastes you are looking for. You will miss nothing - except perhaps some clogged arteries and a few unwanted pounds.

We know you will enjoy cooking and eating the meals prepared from **THE HEALTHY HEART GOURMET** and benefit from the improved health which will surely follow.

Tom & Arlene Mills
Co-authors

FOREWORD
DIETARY PREVENTION OF HEART DISEASE
A MEDICAL PERSPECTIVE

FIRST IMPRESSIONS

This is a book for people who are interested in the preparation of gourmet quality meals of sufficient food value to be considered "healthful" from the standpoint of prevention of heart disease. Most people, I believe, are well aware of the common perception that "everything that's good for us tastes bad." This book represents the committed efforts of a heart patient and his wife, both gourmet cooks, to adapt a collection of delicious recipes to meet the needs of other health-conscious food lovers. Their efforts represent the best possible approach to the problem of providing Americans with a truly palatable alternative to our deeply-ingrained tradition of eating the wrong kinds of foods. This part of the book is supplied to provide insight into the rationale for dietary manipulation with respect to cardiovascular well-being.

ATHEROSCLEROSIS: WHAT IT MEANS

Initially, let's understand what is meant by the generic expression "heart disease." Atherosclerosis is a pathological term doctors use to define the process that is more popularly known as "hardening of the arteries." Medical students and doctors in training spend more time than they care to remember examining the defective anatomic machinery that led to the demise of departed souls. Those people unfortunate enough to have died of heart disease exhibit a defect that is quickly recognizable by anyone who cares to observe. The heart musculature is supplied by a network of arteries running along its outer surface. Healthy coronary arteries have a diameter ranging from 3 to 7 mm so that a BB could roll freely from the opening of the artery almost to its end before it branches out into smaller vessels. Coronary patients, on the other hand, have arteries that exhibit several abnormalities all at once. First, the arteries themselves are hard to the touch and feel as though they were made of porcelain rather than the rubbery texture of healthy arteries. The reason for this is that the interior arterial surfaces have developed a diffuse ingrowth of waxy chalklike material called plaque which reduces the arterial diameter throughout the entire coronary tree. This problem is aggravated by the development of focal areas of even more plaque growth which may only be a couple of millimeters in length but which act as plugs to limit, and finally cut off the supply of the rich arterial blood which the heart requires to function and survive. If one of these plaque areas should become inflamed, a clot may form, cutting off the blood supply to a portion of the heart muscle. That portion of the muscle is then destroyed, and this event is specifically what is meant by a "heart attack" or "myocardial infarction." Progressive hardening of the arteries may be associated with the development of chest pains in many cases. However, a large number of people may develop critical coronary obstructions without any inkling of what is going on until it is too late to do anything meaningful about it. It's not that these people are stupid or stubborn, but they appear to have a defective pain sensory system which reduces their ability to detect cardiac pain. Thus the heart's cry for lifegiving oxygenated blood is muted, and so the machinery must eventually break down.

This process is commonly understood to be responsible for 25 to 40 percent of the deaths in the United States, many of which occur in people who are otherwise seemingly healthy and in their peak productive years.

CARDIAC RISK FACTORS

It is possible to produce a statistical probability that an individual may be likely to develop coronary disease based on a limited number of cardiac risk factors. These factors are 1) elevated blood fats or cholesterol, 2) high blood pressure, 3) diabetes, 4) cigarette smoking and 5) positive family history of premature cardiovascular disorders. Most other popularly perceived risk factors such as sedentary lifestyle, stressful environment, "Type A" (aggressive or compulsive) personality, et cetera, have not held up well as statistically meaningful predictors of cardiac risk, although the final word has undoubtedly not been written in this regard.

It is gratifying to note that the prevalence and mortality of coronary disease has declined significantly in the last 10 years by about 15 percent. There are many possible explanations for this happy observation. Cigarette smoking has declined to its lowest level in the population since World War I, although, disturbingly, it appears to still be on the increase among adolescents and women. Cardiac disease, once diagnosed, can certainly be treated with a host of effective medications and therapeutic procedures such as cardiac catheterization, coronary bypass surgery, balloon angioplasty and other measures. Hundreds of thousands of people with known coronary artery disease are today outliving their natural years primarily because of the proliferation of heart-saving diagnostic and therapeutic techniques.

The other side of the coin, unfortunately, is that health care expenditures are rising at a rate much faster than the pace of inflation, and no end is in sight. Furthermore, there is a certain risk to any and all medical interventions which must be factored into a consideration of the total risk of the atherosclerotic process.

Better control of diabetes and hypertension, along with some degree of improved dietary awareness, have also had an impact in the improved cardiovascular outlook for our nation toward the end of the Twentieth Century.

SOCIO-CULTURAL FACTORS

It's fair to say that atherosclerotic heart disease should be considered "a disease of prosperity." Research psychologists have described certain animals as being unable to curb their appetite for food, so that if given an unlimited supply, they will predictably eat themselves to death. Humankind appears to suffer from a similar affliction except that instead of gorging ourselves into oblivion at one sitting, we prolong the period of excessive ingestion over several decades with a resultant severe and significant reduction in our potential allotted lifespan. Coronary disease was not generally appreciated as a common ailment as recently as 100 years ago in Europe, although detection methods were limited to *post mortem* studies at that time. However, the symptom complex that we describe as angina has been recognized by physicians for centuries. Nevertheless, I believe that we are in the midst of a prolonged pandemic of atherogenic dietary consumption with devastating individual and public health consequences.

The People's Republic of China (PRC) offers a superb example of the cultural and dietary underpinnings of coronary heart disease. The Chinese have an entire hospital in Beijing devoted entirely to cardiovascular disorders. The hospital directors made a tour of the United States in 1982, giving a presentation concerning the types of heart disease most prevalent in China. It was their finding that coronary atherosclerosis is considered so unusual as to be treated as a curiosity when it appears in the PRC. The cardiac disease that the Chinese see most is rheumatic heart disease as well as hypertensive, congenital and cardiomyopathic disorders which have nothing to do with the atherosclerotic process. These last catagories, while not at all rare in the United States, are decidedly less common than coronary atherosclerosis. However, the Chinese doctors made one more very interesting observation. They found that when Chinese nationals move to Western countries, their incidence of atherosclerotic heart disease increases to approach the incidence of the native population of Westerners. Certainly, other factors could potentially come into play, but it is probable that change in the diet plays an enormous role in this dramatically increased prevalence in this population group.

SPECIFIC ADVICE FOR THE CHOLESTEROL-CONSCIOUS

It has been known since the 1950s that high blood cholesterol is a devastating cardiac risk factor. That much has been determined by the Framingham Study as well as by many other similar evaluations. However, the medical community has been slow to take an organized stand on what should be done about the problem. One reason for this is the difficulty in creating a scientifically-meaningful study that would encompass thousands of individuals over the years of dietary surveillance and modification with resultant analysis in comparison to control groups. However, research interest has accelerated in the '80s to such an extent that in the last two years the National Heart, Lung and Blood Institute has promulgated a formal recommendation that all hypercholesterolemic adults undergo a formal program for the purpose of cholesterol reduction and disease avoidance.

The medical community recently set guidelines for classifying blood cholesterol levels. They advise that a total cholesterol level less than 200 mg/dl is "desirable" for adults - above the 200 mg/dl the risk of coronary heart disease steadily increases. The classifications of total blood cholesterol in the following chart are related to the risk of developing heart disease.

DESIRABLE	BORDERLINE-HIGH	HIGH
Less than 200 mg/dl	200-239 mg/dl	240 mg/dl and above

If, for example, a person has a cholesterol level of 250, they are considered to be at "high" risk of developing premature atherosclerosis. That's not to say that he or she will probably drop dead soon, but does imply a significant increased probability of disease development over the years. Additional evaluation helps your physician determine more accurately your risk of coronary heart disease and make decisions about your treatment. Specifically, your doctor will probably want to measure your low density lipoprotein (LDL) cholesterol level - since LDL-cholesterol more accurately reflects your risk for developing coronary heart disease than a total cholesterol level alone. Additionally, the HDL or high-density cholesterol, a protective factor, is also measured, along with triglycerides, or vegetable fat. After evaluating your LDL-cholesterol level and other risk factors for coronary heart disease, your physician will determine your treatment program. It's never really too early to start checking cholesterol, and children of patients with known severe hyperlipidemia should also be screened. Once a baseline level has been established, we can identify the population that needs to concentrate on cholesterol reduction.

We have at our disposal two general methods of lowering blood fats. The first and most important matter of concern is dietary modification. I have found in my practice that many people have difficulty achieving this goal on their own, even though they insist that "I know what I should and shouldn't eat." Unfortunately, general appreciation of the problem does not seem to be adequate in promoting people's willpower. Most of the time, seriously obese individuals require the services of a registered dietitian to tailor a diet to the individual. Dietitians are specially-trained health professionals who, in the course of a single one-hour session, construct a realistic, realizable diet that fits an individual's preferences, specific needs and ideal body weight. Thus as a physician, I can conveniently prescribe a "low lipid weight reduction diet" with the assurance that my patient will come away with an understanding of the types and quantities of foods that he or she considers desirable. Of course, the fattiest foods must be severely curtailed or eliminated. If the dietitian has done his or her job well, and the patient sticks to these recommendations, he or she has a better than 50 percent chance of experiencing a significant reduction in weight and cholesterol over a period of several months. Moreover, these patients seem to sustain their weight and cholesterol reduction over a longer period of time than do the people who prefer not to use a dietitian's services. If they go off their diet for a long period of time, a repeat visit to the dietitian is often welcome.

It is obvious from the foregoing remarks that the whole business of cholesterol reduction is now being taken very seriously. The practical reason for this is that the research community and government have now given the go-ahead (in the form of a formal recommendation to treat) to the use of a large number of cholesterol-lowering drugs. These medications are indicated for patients who are unable to lower their blood lipids to normal levels by dietary management alone. This recommendation has an enormous impact on our society from the standpoint of the possible good that it may do. Two recently-published reports have found significant mortality reduction and disease regression in high-cholesterol heart patients treated with these drugs compared to matched control groups of similar patients. However, there is an economic price to be paid, along with the fact that many otherwise healthy people find it objectionable to take expensive medications that don't make them feel better and may even have side effects. This reluctance is understandable, but I mention the medications only to underscore the crucial importance that must be given to serious dietary modification. A person who wants to change his or her lifestyle is ideally given about a year to try to bring the weight and blood fats down to acceptable levels with a combination of diet and exercise. If these conservative measures fail, however, patients must expect that they will be advised that medication is necessary. These are the same people who may also need medications for hypertension and diabetes, and these associated conditions are similarly highly amenable to dietary control in the well-disposed patient. I would vastly prefer my patients achieve control of their objectionable metabolic tendencies by means that do not require the use of drugs. However, the blueprint is laid out pretty much as described and the choice is up to every individual.

We are left with a mandate for radical restructuring of our internal environments if we are to avoid the ravages of self-inflicted disease. Few people wish to be condemned to a lifetime of bland uninteresting food and that is the point where this volume comes into play. We are all in desperate need of learning to fix the right kinds of foods in the right way. The satisfaction to be achieved is both immediate and long-lasting and available to everyone who cares to take a few simple steps in the right direction. I join the authors of this book in wishing our readers a healthy and long-lived experience in culinary delight.

                                                            Kenneth Adams, M.D., Cardiologist

INTRODUCTION

A low-fat, low-cholesterol eating plan has been a part of coronary heart disease treatment for many years. More recently, this concept has graduated to the realm of coronary disease prevention. Indeed, the general recommendations to decrease consumption of cholesterol and fat (especially saturated fat) pertains to everyone over the age of two years.

With a wider acknowledgement of the importance of dietary habits, we've seen some positive changes in the marketplace. Leaner meats, more nonfat dairy products, and lower-fat bakery goods are readily available to the consumer. However, label reading and interpretation continue to be essential in deciding how new products fit into our personal dietary plans.

Recipes and cookbooks are also changing to meet the consumer's desire for heart-healthy, good-tasting menu ideas to serve family and friends. This revision of **THE HEALTHY HEART GOURMET** has refined many of the original recipes to meet the latest recommendations for heart-smart dining. Leaner and tastier, you are encouraged to try, taste, and most definitely enjoy the new **HEALTHY HEART GOURMET** treats.

Michelle VanDoran, R.D.
Consultant

IMPROVING YOUR NUTRITIONAL PROFILE
FOR A HEALTHY HEART

What should you eat to stay healthy? Hardly a day goes by that we are not exposed to a new miracle diet, the wonder cures of megavitamin doses, the cure for acne, the wonders of kelp-lecithin and many more claims for better health. We eagerly listen to the newest, and then decide if we will invest our time and money to test its credibility.

Unfortunately, people fail to realize there are no miracle cures, no "magic effortless cure-all" diets to meet our body's needs. Our own health depends on many things, including our diet, lifestyle, personality traits, mental health and attitudes, heredity and our own environment. There are no specific guidelines which can guarantee health or well-being. But, educated food choices based on sound nutrition can be learned and incorporated into your daily diet.

Heart-healthy eating habits enhance your chances for overall good health, and, in fact, can reduce your risk factors for heart disease. There is much scientific evidence that coronary disease begins early in life. The American Heart Association recommends moderate reductions in cholesterol, fat and sodium for healthy children over the age of two with emphasis on substitution and modification rather than elimination of food groups to assure nutritional adequacy.[1] Forming good habits, especially eating habits in the early years, helps keep the whole family on the healthy heart track.

In an effort to develop a framework for good eating habits, eating for a healthy heart will be incorporated into the Dietary Guidelines for Americans.[2] These guidelines were established in 1977 by the Senate Select Committee on Nutrition, revised in 1985, and later adapted by the U.S. Department of Agriculture and the U.S. Department of Health and Human Services.

The guidelines, or goals, address the American problem of obesity and the billion dollar industry that caters to its cure. Additionally, the entire structure of the American diet and its devastating effects on health and longevity have been examined. The purpose of the guidelines is to reduce the incidence of chronic, degenerative diseases; i.e., heart disease, hypertension (high blood pressure), cancer, obesity and diabetes mellitus.

DIETARY GUIDELINES FOR AMERICANS
Eat a variety of foods
Maintain healthy weight
Choose a diet with plenty of vegetables, fruits, and grain products
Choose a diet low in fat, saturated fat, and cholesterol
Use sugars only in moderation
Use salt and sodium only in moderation
If you drink alcohol, do so in moderation

These guidelines are suggested for most Americans who are already in generally good health. They suggest a wellness or preventive approach to health. They are not intended for people with diseases or conditions that interfere with normal nutritional needs, or those on a special therapeutic diet. These people may need individual dietary counseling from a registered dietitian, in consultation with their own physician.

GOAL 1 - EAT A VARIETY OF FOODS

Although most foods contain more than a single nutrient, it is the combination of the different food groups that provides adequate nutrition. There are some 52 different nutrients needed to stay healthy.

One way to ensure variety and meet the R.D.A. (Recommended Daily Allowance) for protein, calories, vitamins and minerals is to select a diet based on the five food groups. On the basis of their similar nutrient content, these foods are grouped together. The five food groups are: meat, bread-cereal, fruit-vegetable, milk, and fats and oils. Foods recommended within each group are the best choices for a healthy heart meal plan.

The **MEAT GROUP** includes well-trimmed, lean red meats, skinless poultry, fish and other seafoods as well as some vegetable sources like dried beans, peas and other legumes. Meats in the diet provide protein, iron, thiamin and niacin. Protein is needed for cell growth and repair of muscles, organs, blood, skin and hair. It also helps form substances in the blood called "antibodies" which help the body fight infection. Iron is needed for the blood to carry oxygen and carbon dioxide to and from the cells. It also helps prevent iron-deficiency anemia, and its accompanying fatigue.

The **BREAD-CEREAL GROUP** contains breads, cereals, grains, rice, potatoes and pastas. Whole grain, fortified and enriched products are recommended for their increased nutritional value. These foods are valued for their carbohydrate, thiamin, iron and niacin content. Carbohydrates are the body's most readily available source of fuel or energy. The two B-Vitamins, thiamin and niacin, aid in the utilization of energy, aid in digestion, promote normal appetite and help form a healthy nervous system. Iron, as previously mentioned, plays important functions in our body's system.

The **FRUIT-VEGETABLE GROUP** includes all vegetables and fruits except dried beans and peas, which, because of their high protein content, are placed in the meat group. Best choices include fresh, raw and unprocessed fruits, as well as fresh, cooked or raw vegetables. The fruit-vegetable group provides excellent sources of vitamins, particularly A and C, as well as minerals and fiber in the diet. Dark green leafy vegetables and/or deep orange fruits and vegetables are recommended 3 to 4 times per week for the Vitamin A they provide. Vitamin A helps prevent night blindness, is necessary for growth, for healthy skin and for healthy mucous membranes which line the body cavities and tracts and help resist infection. A serving of citrus fruit is recommended daily to replenish the body's supply of Vitamin C, since this vitamin is water soluble and cannot be stored in the body. Vitamin C is important for maintaining body cell integrity, for healthy gums and for the healing of wounds and broken bones.

The **MILK GROUP** is the fourth group and is relied upon to meet the body's calcium requirements, as well as protein, riboflavin and many other nutrients. Many people are under the misunderstanding that dairy products should be eliminated from a low-fat, low-cholesterol diet. This is not true. Milk and dairy products are the major sources of calcium. Calcium is necessary to form strong bones and teeth, help clotting, help muscles contract and help regulate the use of other minerals by the body. Best choices include skim or 1% low-fat milk, low-fat and cholesterol-free cheeses, part skim cheeses such as mozzarella, farmers, low-fat ricotta and low-fat cottage cheeses. Many companies have replaced the butterfat with polyunsaturated corn oil, and these cheeses too are acceptable choices. Also, consumer demand has resulted in many lowfat and nonfat reduced calorie cheeses which are appearing in grocery stores. Some non-dairy sources of calcium include salmon or sardines (with the bones), tofu processed with calcium sulfate, broccoli, bok choy, collards and other deep green leafy vegetables.

#The Recommended Daily Allowance for calcium varies with age and stage in the life cycle.

CHART I - DAILY CALCIUM

Do you get enough calcium every day?

Every day, depending on your age and stage in the life cycle, the following amounts of calcium are recommended:

MILLIGRAMS DAILY (mg)

Children	800
Teenagers	1200
Adults	800
Pregnant and nursing women	1200
Pregnant and nursing teenagers	1600

#R.D.A. are set by scientists serving on the Food and Nutrition Board of the National Academy of Sciences.

CHART II - CALCIUM AND FAT CONTENT OF SOME SELECTED FOODS

Food	Serving Size	Calcium(mg)	Fat(gr)
Skim milk	1 cup	316	.5
Instant non-fat, dry skim milk powder	¼ cup	220	.2
Lowfat buttermilk	1 cup	296	2.0
1% lowfat cottage cheese	1 cup	131	2.3
Part skim mozzarella	1 ounce	183	4.5
Part skim ricotta cheese	½ cup	337	9.8
Lowfat plain yogurt	1 cup	452	3.5
Salmon, pink, canned	⅖ cup	196	5.9
Sardines, Pacific, canned in brine	3½ ounces	303	12.0
Tofu processed w/calcium sulfate	3½ ounces	128	4.2
Bok choy	½ cup	126	0
Collard greens, from raw	½ cup	179	0
Collard greens, from frozen	½ cup	149	0

References, U.S.D.A. Handbook #456 and U.S.D.A. Handbook 8-1, Food Values of Portions Commonly Used. Pennington and Church, 1985.

FATS AND OILS comprise the fifth group. Fats serve as carriers for the fat-soluble vitamins A, D, E and K. Polyunsaturated fats and oils (safflower, sunflower, canola, corn, etc.) are a source of linoleic acid, an "essential fatty acid." [3]

One teaspoon of a poyunsaturated oil each day would supply sufficient linoleic acid. Olive oil has recently received much attention and is now referred to as a heart-healthy fat. It appears to be able to differentiate, and lower, the undesirable type of LDL cholesterol, while not affecting the good type, HDL. Polyunsaturated fats have long been known to lower cholesterol, but, they lower both LDL and HDL cholesterol. (More of HDL & LDL's later.)

There are no known advantages to consuming excess amounts of any one nutrient. You will rarely need to take vitamin or mineral supplements if you eat a wide variety of foods. Emphasis should be on fresh unprocessed foods. Exceptions to this general rule include: pregnant or breast-feeding women, women in the childbearing years and infants. Detailed advice and counseling should come from physicians and dietitians. Other groups: heavy smokers, heavy drinkers or those who keep stressful, hectic schedules and haphazard eating patterns or those who just don't consume a balanced diet may benefit from a daily multivitamin. If a person chooses to take a multivitamin, it should not exceed 100% of the R.D.A. Chart III lists some of the necessary vitamins and the heart-safe foods which supply them. With a diet of proper foods, vitamin supplements are not needed.

CHART III - VITAMINS IN HEART-SAFE FOODS

VITAMINS   FOOD SOURCES

VITAMINS	FOOD SOURCES
A	Dark green leafy vegetables, yellow and orange fruits and vegetables, tomatoes, fortified skim or lowfat milk
D	Fatty fish, fortified skim or lowfat milk and margarine
E	Vegetable oil, margarine, most nuts, sunflower kernels, wheat germ, green leafy vegetables
K	Green leafy vegetables, broccoli, cauliflower, green beans, peas, cabbage
B-1 (thiamine)	Lean pork, fish and poultry, whole grain and enriched breads, cereals, peanuts, wheat bran, beans, peas, legumes
B-2 (riboflavin)	Enriched breads and cereals, skim and lowfat milk and cheeses, lean meat, green leafy vegetables, wheat bran
B-3 (niacin)	Lean meat, poultry, fish, nuts, fresh ground peanut butter, enriched bread and cereals
B-6 (pyridoxine)	Wheat bran, lean meat, poultry, fish, green leafy vegetables, potatoes, nuts, whole grains
B-12 (cobalamin)	Lean meats, fish, shellfish, skim and lowfat milk and cheeses
C	Citrus fruit, green leafy vegetables, green pepper, strawberries, cauliflower, cantaloupe, broccoli, tomatoes
Folic Acid (folacin)	Fish, green leafy vegetables, nuts, whole grains and cereals, oranges
Biotin	Skim and lowfat milk, nuts, dried beans and peas
Pantothenic acid	Lean meat, poultry and fish, whole grain breads and cereals, legumes

In summary, the greater the variety of food choices, the less likely you are to develop either a deficiency or excess of any nutrient. Variety also reduces your likelihood of being exposed to any possible contaminants from excessive amounts of any single food item.

GOAL 2 - MAINTAIN HEALTHY WEIGHT

Besides cosmetic concerns, obesity is a major risk factor for a number of chronic diseases. Hypertension is twice as common in obese people, and the risk of developing adult onset diabetes (most common type), particularly if there is a family history, is increased. Obesity forces your heart and lungs to work harder and is also associated with increased levels of cholesterol and triglycerides in the blood. Both the above-mentioned conditions are associated with increased incidence of cardiovascular disease, heart attacks and strokes.

So, what should you weigh? How can a person determine his or her desirable weight? Charts are available that give ranges of weight, but, for a general assessment, the following formula works quite well.

CHART IV IDEAL BODY WEIGHT

1. Determine Frame Size*; Place your thumb and middle finger around the wrist of your non-dominant hand. If thumb and middle finger just meet, you have a medium frame. If fingers do not meet, you have a large frame. If fingers overlap, you have a small frame.

*Actual measurements can be taken to more accurately determine frame size, but this will generally apply.

2. **General Weight Formula***

Frame Size	Women	Men
Medium	Allow 100 pounds for 5 feet of height; add 5 pounds for each additional inch	Allow 106 pounds for 5 feet of height; add 6 pounds for each additional inch
Small	Subtract 10%	Subtract 10%
Large	Add 10%	Add 10%

*This general weight formula is only a guide, as are other general weight and height charts.

A person can have a normal or desirable weight, but still have too much body fat. One of the natural courses our body takes as we grow older is to convert lean body mass to fat.

Aerobic exercises, on a regular basis (3 to 4 times a week for 30 minutes), can help slow down or keep fat conversion to a minimum. Exercise both burns calories and increases Basal Metabolic Rate (BMR) during and after the exercise event. BMR refers to the amount of energy needed to maintain normal body functions at rest. The BMR usually remains elevated for 6 to 24 hours after 30 minutes of moderate exercise.[*4]

Caloric needs vary with age, sex, size, activity levels and a person's own body metabolism. As we grow older, our body requires fewer calories to maintain itself. Younger people require more calories due to growth.

People with a weight problem usually have two basic imbalances; 1) They are consuming excessive amounts of calories and 2) They do not exercise enough to compensate or burn up these extra calories. An imbalance in either intake (calories) or output (exercise) will lead to weight gain.

Males have a higher metabolism than females on the basis of general differences in anatomy. A man's physique is higher in lean muscle mass whereby a woman's is higher in adipose or fatty tissue. The higher a person's percentage of lean muscle mass, the more calories this person will burn in normal activities.

A smaller person tends to have a lower BMR than does a larger person. Not only do women have less muscle mass and more fat, but they are generally smaller, requiring fewer calories for metabolic functions.[*5]

Understanding calories and the role of exercise is crucial in weight control. Some basics:

+ 3500 food calories = 1 pound fat

+ 500 calorie deficit a day for seven days would result in a one pound per week weight loss.

+ Gradual weight loss (1 pound per week) would, of course, result in a 52 pound weight loss per year.

+ Best forms of aerobic exercise are those that utilize large muscle groups (walking, jogging, swimming, bicycling and rope jumping).

+ Exercising for 20 to 30 minutes 3 or 4 times a week results in the best form of calorie utilization and cardiovascular fitness.

+ Regular aerobic exercise increases the efficiency of the heart muscle and allows the heart to pump blood more efficiently.

+ Increased physical activity burns calories, lowers heart rate, reduces risk of coronary heart disease and reduces risk of osteoporosis (age-related bone disease).

In summary, a combination of reduced caloric intake and increased caloric expenditure through aerobic exercise is the ideal way to achieve weight loss.

Weight loss through dieting alone is 75 percent fat and almost 25 percent lean body mass. On the other hand, weight loss through a combination of diet and physical activity is about 98 percent body fat.*[6]

Remember, to lose weight and keep it off, it is necessary to permanently modify your eating and exercising habits.

BEHAVIOR MODIFICATION

You must now become familiar with techniques you can use to modify your eating habits. Below are some helpful techniques and suggestions:

1) Keep A Food Diary

As an important step in your weight reduction program, it is suggested for you to keep a 7-day Food Diary which will be used to help you become familiar with your eating patterns. You may want to purchase a small pocket-size notebook to carry with you during the day to record the following information:

1. What time did you start eating?
2. How long did you spend eating?
3. Where were you when you were eating?
4. Who were you with when you were eating?
5. How hungry did you feel?
6. What was your mood# when you were eating?
7. What and how much did you eat?

Be sure to look over your food diary at the end of the day. By following this diary, you will become increasingly aware of your eating habits. It is important to get a clear picture of your eating habits before you actually start trying to change them.

#Mood: Bored, depressed, restless, angry, sociable, lonely, etc.

2) Determine How Important It Is For You To Lose Weight

List on paper all the reasons you want to take off excess pounds, and post it in a visible place like the refrigerator door or the bathroom mirror.

Examples:
I want to look and feel better.
I don't feel good about myself. I feel self-conscious and uncomfortable.
My clothes are too tight.

I want to look good at the upcoming class reunion.

Etc., etc., etc.

3) Describe At Least 5 Ways To Avoid Tempting Contact With Food

Example - In the supermarket:

I will not shop when I am hungry.

I will shop from a prepared list and not depart from it or buy tempting goodies. (See Weekly Meal Planning beginning on page 251.)

I will not purchase high calorie, high fat, snack foods.

4) Practice Eating More Slowly and Enjoy The Taste of the Food

Most overweight people tend to eat faster than persons of normal weight. Consequently, they tend to eat more food over the same period of time. It is important to practice ways to slow down the eating process. Examples:

Putting food on smaller size plate.

Cutting food into smaller pieces.

Putting food or utensils down between bites.

Taking a sip of water after every other bite.

Chewing each bite thoroughly before swallowing.

5) Identify At Least 4 Ways To Reward Yourself For Good Behavior (other than food)

Hint: Rewards can be doing things you enjoy doing or avoiding things you do not like to do. These rewards do not necessarily mean material things.

6) Substitute "Incompatible Behavior" For Eating

List several alternate things that you could do when you have an urge to hit the refrigerator. They are termed "incompatible behavior" because it is impossible to eat and do the behaviors at the same time. Examples:

Do ten jumping jacks and five sit-ups.

Fix a cup of tea, coffee or bouillon.

Find a job to do around the house.

Go weigh yourself, and use your success or failure as a motivator to avoid eating.

Put on your walking shoes and go for a 15-minute walk.

7) Recognize That You Do Have Control Over Your Eating

Overweight people often feel helpless in controlling their eating behavior. It is as if they are convinced that "will-power" is something they lack. By saying NO to a food temptation and then looking back over the day and feeling proud that you did not "give in" is one way of teaching yourself only you have complete control over your destiny in your weight program. By learning to substitute "incompatible behaviors," (refer to item #6) for eating, you realize that you can control your own responses to food.

GOAL 3
CHOOSE A DIET WITH PLENTY OF VEGETABLES, FRUITS AND GRAIN PRODUCTS

The healthy heart plan suggests that the majority of calories in the diet come from starches and complex carbohydrates. Foods like potatoes, pastas, rice, dried beans, peas, whole grain breads and cereals are examples of complex carbohydrate starchy foods. These are mainly carbohydrates with some protein. They are rich in many essential nutrients and fiber, as well as being cholesterol free and low in fat. As can be seen in Chart V, ounce per ounce, carbohydrates and proteins contain about half as many calories as fats.

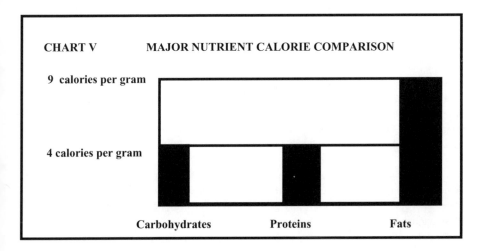

CHART V   MAJOR NUTRIENT CALORIE COMPARISON

9 calories per gram

4 calories per gram

Carbohydrates   Proteins   Fats

Some people still believe breads and potatoes should be eliminated or restricted on a weight reduction diet because they feel these are the "fattening" foods. **NOT TRUE!** As already mentioned, these are the lower calorie foods. It's the margarines, gravies, mayonnaises, creams and sauces you add to them which greatly increase the caloric value and fat levels of these items. In Chart VI note that each portion of complex carbohydrates provides approximately 80 calories, and no more.

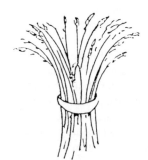

CHART VI - NORMAL SERVINGS OF SELECTED
COMPLEX CARBOHYDRATE FOODS (80 calories each)

1	slice whole grain bread
½ cup	cooked pasta; noodles, macaroni, spaghetti
½ cup	cooked hot cereal; oats, cream of wheat, grits, etc.
¾ cup	dry, unsweetened, unfrosted cereals
½ cup	green peas
½ cup	corn
1 med.	potato, baked
½ cup	cooked lentils

The American Heart Association recommends that carbohydrates be 50 to 55 percent of caloric intake with emphasis on the usage of vegetables, fruits and grains.*[7] One way to work towards this goal is to incorporate meatless meals into the diet once or twice a week. Instead of animal proteins, use combinations of vegetable proteins.

Animal sources of protein (pork, beef, poultry, fish, dairy products and eggs) are known as complete proteins because these foods provide the eight essential amino acids (building blocks of protein) your body needs. They are referred to as "essential amino acids" because your body does not produce these, so they must be derived from the foods we eat. The animal sources provide protein, as well as a lot of cholesterol and saturated fat.

Vegetables or plant sources of protein are considered "incomplete proteins" because they do not contain all of the 8 essential amino acids in the right amounts. There is a great variety of vegetable or plant protein sources: legumes, grains, nuts, and seeds. The following reviews these major classes:

Legumes:
 Bean varieties such as: navy, northern, pinto, black and soy beans
 Pea varieties such as: split, field and cowpeas
 Peanuts
 Lentils

Grains:
 Wheat, rye, oats, buckwheat, bulgur, couscous, barley, rice and corn; flours, breads and cereals, provided they are made from these grains.

Nuts and Seeds:
 Commonly used, unsaturated, heart-healthy selections include almonds, pecans, walnuts, filberts and Brazil nuts. (No cashews or macadamia nuts as these are high in saturated fat.)
 Pumpkin, sunflower and sesame seeds.
 When carefully combined, plant proteins are equivalent to animal proteins providing the 8 essential amino acids. It is important for the vegetable proteins to be present in the digestive system at the same time and be present in the correct proportions for the body to be able to use these as complete proteins. Plant/vegetable protein sources are cholesterol free and, with the exception of the nuts and seeds, contain only trace amounts of fat.

Compare values among the various animal and vegetable protein foods:

+ 1½ cups cooked beans or peas = 20 grams of protein, 1.5 grams of fat, and 0 milligrams of cholesterol.
+ 3 ounces boneless cooked sirloin steak = 20 grams of protein, 27.2 grams of fat and 77 milligrams of cholesterol.
+ 3 ounces cheddar cheese = 20 grams of protein, 27.3 grams of fat and 90 milligrams of cholesterol.#

#Reference: Culinary Hearts Kitchen-American Heart Association, 1985

The use of vegetable proteins and low-fat dairy products are encouraged to make heart-healthy "complete proteins." Chart VII shows the proper way to combine these foods to make "complete proteins."

CHART VII - HEART-HEALTHY COMPLETE PROTEIN COMBINATIONS

COMBINATIONS	EXAMPLES
Legumes and grains	Black beans and rice, recipes on pages 203 and 214
Legumes and nuts	Mixed beans and slivered almonds
Legumes and seeds	Hummus, recipe on page 61
Grains and low-fat dairy products	Brown rice pudding (brown rice, low-fat or skim milk and egg substitutes)
Nuts or seeds and low-fat dairy products	Cottage cheese and chopped walnuts

In summary, it is not necessary to eliminate animal proteins or meats from the diet, but they should be used in moderation. Learning to incorporate vegetable proteins can help lower total cholesterol and fat intake and is one way to work towards reaching the goal of 50 to 55 percent of your calories coming from carbohydrates.

GOAL IV - CHOOSE A DIET LOW IN FAT, SATURATED FAT AND CHOLESTEROL

Scientific studies show that having an elevated blood cholesterol level increases one's chances of developing coronary artery disease. On the other hand, similar studies support the fact that people who take steps to reduce their cholesterol intake also reduce their risk of heart disease. (For proper blood cholesterol ranges and related risks, see page 13.)

Serum total cholesterol should be measured in all people every 5 years, beginning at age 20; this measurement may be made in the non-fasting state. As the charts on page 13 state, anything beyond (240mg/dl) is a value above which risk of coronary heart disease rises steeply, and corresponds with approximately 75 percent of the United States adult population. Patients with high blood cholesterol should undergo a complete lipid profile.*[8]

The American Academy of Pediatrics recommends that cholesterol levels be tested in children over the age of two, especially those who have either a family history of elevated blood-fat levels or early coronary heart disease. For children with confirmed high cholesterol values 176mg/dl or above, repeated testing is necessary. If it remains elevated, individual dietary counseling should be considered.

A complete lipid profile includes total serum (blood) cholesterol, HDL cholesterol and triglycerides. From these values, LDL cholesterol is calculated. High density lipoproteins (HDL's) refer to substances in the blood composed of fats and proteins. HDL's are referred to as the good type, removing excess cholesterol from the body tissues to the liver where it can be excreted. A high level of HDL's correlates with a decreased risk of coronary artery disease. Low density lipoproteins (LDL's) are the main cholesterol carriers in the blood. They are believed to carry cholesterol through the bloodstream, leaving fatty streaks of plaque/cholesterol on the artery walls. High levels of LDL's are undesirable, and are correlated with premature atherosclerosis and coronary disease. Triglycerides are glycerol and fatty acid compounds. They may be of vegetable or animal origin and also can be manufactured by your body from the fats, alcohol and sugar in your diet.

Blood cholesterol levels are affected by diet, lack of exercise, a stressful lifestyle and the body's own mechanism for the production and excretion of cholesterol.

Excess cholesterol and excess saturated fat are food factors that affect blood cholesterol. Fiber also affects cholesterol levels. One of the most encouraging findings about fiber is the ability of certain types of fiber in lowering blood cholesterol levels.*[9] These fibers have an affinity for bile, and when the diet is rich in these fibers, more bile is excreted, and this effectively reduces total body cholesterol.

Beneficial fibrous foods include:

+ Pectins (found in most fruit skins)
+ Guar gums (garbanzos and most legumes)
+ Rolled oats/oat bran

Cholesterol is a waxy alcohol made primarily in the liver and small intestine which is used to make strong cell membranes. It molds sheaths that protect nerves and produces vitamin D and certain hormones, including sex hormones. Even if your diet contained no cholesterol, your body would create it out of the fats and carbohydrates in your diet. In a single day, the body churns out about 1,000 milligrams (mg) of cholesterol to meet its needs. Cholesterol is found only in animal foods; foods derived from plants do not contain cholesterol.

Populations like ours, with diets high in saturated fat and cholesterol, tend to have elevated cholesterol levels and show a greater risk of having heart attacks than people from countries whose diets don't include a large intake of meats, but instead, eat diets low in fat, including lots of grains and vegetable plant proteins.

Let's get to the heart of this! Goal number one is to reduce total consumption of all types of fat to 30 percent of daily caloric intake or less. This fat intake should be more or less equally divided between mono-unsaturated, polyunsaturated and saturated fats.

A review of the types of dietary fat can be seen on Chart VIII. Saturated fats tend to raise serum cholesterol, whereas polyunsaturated fats have a tendency to help lower blood cholesterol.

CHART VIII
THE FOUR MAJOR CLASSIFICATIONS OF FAT

MONO-UNSATURATED FATS
(Mostly From Plants)
Recent studies have shown these
fats appear to lower cholesterol:

Peanut oil
Canola oil (Rape seed)
Olive oil
Most nuts (except walnuts which
are polyunsaturated)

10% or less total calorie intake per day.

POLYUNSATURATED FATS
(Mostly From Plants)
"Good Guys"

Tendency to lower serum cholesterol and decrease tendency
toward blood clots.

MOST POLYUNSATURATED

Safflower oil
Sunflower oil
Corn oil
Walnut oil
Soybean oil
Sesame oil
Cottonseed oil

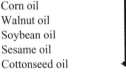

LEAST POLYUNSATURATED

Walnuts

Margarines - Be sure to buy one
with liquid polyunsaturated oil as
the first ingredient. Shop for a
margarine that has twice as much
polyunsaturated fat as saturated
fat. Tub margarines are best.

10% or less total calorie intake per day.

SATURATED FATS
(Mainly Animal Sources, Also
Some Vegetable Sources)
Tendency to raise serum cholesterol.

Used in the commercial production
of cookies, pastries and cream
substitutes.

Visible fat on meat
Lard & Suet
Butterfat
Coconut Oil
Palm Oil
Cocoa Butter
Chocolate
Cashew nuts
Macadamia nuts
       MOST SATURATED
Lamb
Beef
Pork
Chicken
Fish
       LEAST SATURATED

10% or less total calorie intake per day.

HYDROGENATED FATS
(Unsaturated or Polyunsaturated
Fats, Hardened Artificially)
This makes them solid at room
temperature to protect them from
rancidity.

Tendency to raise serum cholesterol.

Found in processed foods and
convenience foods.
Solid shortening found in processed
snack foods like crackers, cookies,
mixes, etc.

In recent studies, olive oil, a source of mono-unsaturated fat, has been shown to be able to differentiate and lower the undesirable LDL cholesterol while not affecting the good HDL cholesterol. Other studies have praised the value of the oils found in fish (omega 3) as a desirable agent in the fight against cholesterol. The fish high in fat content appear to be best. Remember, all fin-fish are acceptable in the healthy-heart diet.

CHART IX - FAT LEVELS IN SOME FISH

Low-Fat, Fine-Texture
American Plaice, butter sole, Dover sole, fluke, flounder, rex sole, sand dab

Low-Fat, Firm-Texture
Catfish, cod, croaker, haddock, hake, halibut, lingcod, orange roughy, perch, pike, pollock, red snapper, scrod, tilefish, turbot, whiting, grouper

Moderate-Fat, Firm-Texture
Buffalofish, chum salmon, corbina, mahi-mahi, pink salmon, pompano, sea bass, striped bass, swordfish, sea trout

High-Fat, Fine-Texture
Bluefish, butterfish, herring, sablefish, sardine, shad

High-Fat, Firm-Texture
Albacore, bluefin tuna, Atlantic salmon, king salmon, Spanish mackerel, king mackerel, silver salmon, sturgeon, whitefish, yellowfin tuna

---

The American Heart Association recommends that dietary cholesterol be limited to 1000 mg. per 1000 kilocalories, not to exceed 300 mg. per day. This allows for differences in caloric intake in various groups.*[10] To put this into perspective, refer to Chart X for cholesterol values of some common foods.

For a food to have cholesterol, it must originate from an animal. Red meats, seafood, fish, poultry, pork, whole milk and all dairy products, and other animal fats like lard, chicken fat and beef suet are food sources containing cholesterol. Foods especially high in cholesterol include eggs and organ meats such as kidney, heart and liver.

CHART X - CHOLESTEROL IN SOME COMMON FOODS

AVERAGE
CHOLESTEROL

PORTION	FOOD	In Milligrams
3 ounces	Beef, lean, cooked, trimmed of separated fat	77
3 ounces	Lamb, lean, cooked	83
3 ounces	Pork, lean, cooked, trimmed	77
3 ounces	Veal, lean, cooked	86
3 ounces	Chicken, dark meat	76
3 ounces	Chicken, light meat	54
3 ounces	Turkey, dark meat, without skin, roasted	86
3 ounces	Turkey, light meat, without skin, roasted	65
3 ounces	Variety meats; liver (beef, calf, lamb) cooked	372
3 ounces	Chicken liver	480
3 ounces	Fish, cooked	60
3 ounces	Crab	85
3 ounces	Clams	55
3½ oz.	Lobster, Maine, raw	100+
3 ounces	Oysters	40
½ cup	Scallops	45
3 ounces	6-7 Medium shrimp	100-150
1	Egg yolk, large	213
1	Egg white, large	0
1 cup	Ice cream	56
1 ounce	American cheese	18
1 ounce	Cheddar cheese	30
4 ounces	Cottage cheese, creamed	17
4 ounces	Cottage cheese, 2% lowfat	10
1 ounce	Part skim mozzarella cheese	16
1 ounce	Swiss cheese	26
1 cup	Whole milk	35
1 cup	Skim milk	5
1 teaspoon	Butter	10
1 teaspoon	Mayonnaise	5
1 teaspoon	Vegetable oil margarine	0
1 cup	Legumes, cooked	0
1 handful	Peanuts	0
1 cup	Fruit	0
1 cup	Vegetables	0
1 cup	Rice, oats, pasta, cooked	0

References: **The Cholesterol Countdown,** The American Dietetic Assoc., Chicago, IL, 1986

Friesen, A., R.D., **Sea Net.** Florida Department of Natural Resources, Bureau of Seafood Marketing, Volume I, Issue I, June 1987.

Pennington, J.A., Church, H.N., **Food Values of Portions Commonly Used,** 14th edition, Harper and Row, Publishers.

CHART XI - SATURATED FAT

Other sources of saturated fats; coconut & palm oils, cocoa butter, lard, butterfat, hydrogenated oils, household shortening.

Food	Saturated Fat
COTTAGE CHEESE	
SHELLFISH	
WHITE FINFISH	
TURKEY, LIGHT	
CHICKEN, LIGHT	
TURKEY, DARK	
SALMON	
TUNA	
CHICKEN, DARK	
1CUP LOWFAT MILK	
CANNED HAM	
ROUND STEAK	
FRESH HAM	
1 CUP WHOLE MILK	
PORK LOIN, LEG OF LAMB	
COLD CUTS	
LAMB SHOULDER	
BEEF BRISKET	
T-BONE STEAK	
BACON	
FULL FAT CHEESES, CHEDDAR, ETC.	

20GM   15GM   10GM   5GM

All meats will have relatively similar amounts of cholesterol; the difference lies in the saturated fat content. In the healthy-heart diet, emphasis is placed on the use of skinless chicken, turkey and fish because of their low saturated fat content. The advantage of poultry, fish and other seafoods can be seen in Chart XI from a 1982 publication of the Sun Valley Health Institute. Note the meats are specified as 3-ounce portions.

GOAL 5 - USE SUGARS ONLY IN MODERATION

All carbohydrates, whether starch or sugar, are a source of calories, contributing 4 calories per gram. (See Chart V) Sugars are classified as simple carbohydrates. They are commonly referred to as "empty calories" foods because they provide calories with very few, if any, nutrients. One teaspoon of sugar has 4 grams of carbohydrates or 16 calories.

The major health hazard from eating too much sugar is tooth decay (cavities). The risk of cavities is increased by the number of times you eat sugary foods. It is best not to eat sugary foods between meals. Reduce the frequency of eating sweets and cut down on "sticky" sweets like dried fruits, caramels and jelly beans that adhere to teeth.

Sugar has a variety of chemical forms. Sucrose, or common table sugar, is refined from sugar cane or sugar beets. Lactose is the naturally occurring sugar in milk. Maltose is the sugar from the malt often used in milkshakes. Fructose is what sweetens fruit and honey. When consumed, the body does not distinguish sources of carbohydrates. It digests and metabolizes "naturally occurring," processed or refined sugars in a similar way.

Sugar is a leading food additive in our food supply. It is estimated that two-thirds of our sugar intake comes from processed foods and one-third from sugar added to foods at home.*[11] Chart XII shows the number of added teaspoons of sugar in some foods.

CHART XII

ADDED TEASPOONS OF SUGAR IN SOME SELECTED FOODS & BEVERAGES

FOOD OR BEVERAGE	TEASPOONS OF ADDED SUGAR
1 cup fruited yogurt	6 teaspoons
1 ounce granola bar	3.3 teaspoons
12 ounces carbonated beverage	10 teaspoons
1 ounce bran cereal	1.3 teaspoons
12 ounces tonic water	8.4 teaspoons
1 slice fruit pie	6 teaspoons
½ cup plain jello	6 teaspoons
½ cup sherbet	6 teaspoons

References: Center for Science in the Public Interest
U.S. Department of Agriculture
American Dental Association

The beverage industry (soft drink, beer and wine producers) is the leading industrial user of refined sugar and high fructose corn syrup.*[12] The following names are examples of the wide variety of sugars and sweeteners found in some common foods:

+ **Sucrose**	+ **Turbinado Sugar**
+ **Lactose**	+ **Levulose**
+ **Maltose**	+ **Sorbitol**
+ **Dextrose**	+ **Xylitol**
+ **Corn Syrup**	+ **Molasses**
+ **Honey**	+ **High Fructose Corn Syrup**
+ **Brown Sugar**	+ **Maple Syrup**

Most commercial desserts like bakery or packaged cookies, pies, pastries or cakes are restricted in the healthy-heart diet mainly because of the shortening, lard or saturated fats used in the product, not because of the sugar.

Homemade desserts made with heart-safe ingredients can be eaten in the healthy-heart diet providing a person is eating a balanced diet (see page 17 in Eat A Variety of Foods) and maintaining a desirable body weight. In many desserts, baked goods and other recipes, the sugar amount can be cut down by ¼ to ⅓ without altering texture and acceptance of a product. The use of sugar substitutes is also an acceptable way to reduce sugar intake.

On the ingredient list of a food label, the ingredient used in the largest amount is listed first, the next largest is listed next, and so on. If a caloric sweetener is listed in the first three ingredients or if an item has multiple sweeteners listed, it may add up to a lot of sugar. If sugar is listed only once on a label or as a minor ingredient (further down on the list), it is probably acceptable to incorporate into the diet.

To meet this goal of avoiding too much sugar, try to reduce intake of all sugars, read labels for clues on sugar content, use sugar substitutes and learn to rely more on fresh fruits or fruits packed in their own juice.

GOAL 6 - USE SALT AND SODIUM ONLY IN MODERATION

The average American consumes 2,300 to 6,900 milligrams (mg) of sodium per day which is the equivalent of about 1 to 3 teaspoons of salt.*[13] The healthy body needs and can only use about 220mg of sodium a day, which is less than the amount in $\frac{1}{10}$ tea-spoon salt. Sodium in excess of needed amount is excreted by the kidneys to maintain the proper water balance in the body.

The American Heart Association believes that the epidemiologic evidence is compelling and that a reduction of sodium intake to 1 gram per 1000 calories, not to exceed 3 grams, is safe, feasible and likely useful in prevention of high blood pressure in many Americans. This represents 2 grams of sodium per day for the average person consuming 2000 calories.*[14]

Twenty to forty percent of the adult population is susceptible to high blood pressure. Unfortunately, it is difficult to determine in advance who will be susceptible to the pressure-raising effects of salt. Certain groups like blacks are twice as likely as whites to develop high blood pressure. Based on the body's minimal need for sodium and its association with the development of high blood pressure, it is safe and reasonable to make efforts to reduce sodium in the diet.

Salt ranks second to sugar as a leading food additive. Sodium is found in varying amounts in foods, but table salt (sodium chloride) is the main source. One teapoon of table salt contains 1,938mg of sodium. Sodium contents of foods are usually expressed in terms of weight measurements. For example:

1 gram (gm) = 1000 milligrams (mg)
1 milli-equivalent (meq) of sodium = 23 milligrams (mg)

Food labels usually list sodium content in milligrams. Chart XIII shows the sodium content of some common foods.

CHART XIII - SODIUM CONTENT OF SOME COMMON FOODS (in milligrams)

DAIRY PRODUCTS
1 ounce bleu cheese = 396
1 ounce regular cheddar = 176
1 ounce feta cheese = 316
1 ounce part skim mozzarella = 132
½ cup part skim ricotta = 155
1 ounce Swiss cheese = 74
1 cup skim milk = 122
1 cup low-fat buttermilk = 310
1 cup low-fat plain yogurt = 159

FRUITS
1 raw apple = 2
1 cup applesauce = 5
1 cup blueberries = 1
½ canteloupe melon = 24
1 raw nectarine = 1
1 cup cooked prunes = 8

LEGUMES AND NUTS
1 cup dry cooked narthern beans = 5
1 cup dry cooked chick peas = 13
1 cup dry cooked black eyed peas = 12
1 cup unsalted peanuts = 8
1 cup dry roasted, salted peanuts = 986

VEGETABLES, VEGETABLE JUICES
Asparagus, fresh, 4 spears = 4
Asparagus, canned, 4 spears = 298
Snap beans, fresh, 1 cup = 5
Snap beans, canned, 1 cup = 326
Celery stalk, one, raw = 25
Carrot, one, raw = 34
Corn, one ear, fresh = 1
Corn, canned, creamed, 1 cup = 671
1 cup tomato juice = 878
1 cup tomato juice, low-sodium = 9

MEATS, SEAFOODS, POULTRY, EGGS
1 whole egg = 59
3 ounces raw snapper = 56
3 ounces cooked pompano = 48
3 ounces smoked herring = 5,234
3 ounces water-packed tuna = 288
3 ounces raw shrimp = 137
3 ounces cooked lean beef = 55
3 ounces cooked fresh lean pork = 59
3 ounces cooked ham = 1,114

CEREALS AND GRAIN PRODUCTS
1 slice whole wheat bread = 132
1 cup cooked spaghetti = 2
1 medium English muffin = 293
1 large shredded wheat biscuit = 3
1 cup Puffed Rice = 1
1 cup Rice Krispies = 240

SOUPS
1 cup cubed beef broth = 1,152
1 cup condensed chicken noodle with water = 1,107
1 cup vegetable beef, condensed, = 957
1 cup vegetable beef, low sodium = 51
1 cup tomato, condensed with water = 872

CONDIMENTS, FATS, OILS, SUGARS, SWEETS
1 teaspoon baking powder = 339
1 tablespoon catsup = 156
1 teaspoon meat tenderizer = 1,750
1 teaspoon salt = 1,938
1 tablespoon soy sauce = 1,029
1 tablespoon A-1 sauce = 275
1 tablespoon mayonnaise = 78
1 tablespoon vegetable oil = 0
1 tablespoon sugar = 4
1 tablespoon jelly = 3

Reference: The Sodium Content of Your Food, USDA Home and Garden Bulletin - No. 233, August, 1980. U.S. Government Printing Office, Washington, D.C. 20402.

In the typical diet, about one-third of the sodium comes from naturally-occurring food sources, one-third from sodium added to foods during processing and one-third from the salt shaker on your table while cooking.

Most of the foods we eat and the water we drink have some sodium in them naturally. Unprocessed foods are generally low in sodium. As a rule, foods served in the natural state have the least amount of sodium. Fresh fruits and vegetables have insignificant amounts of sodium- five to ten milligrams per average serving. Legumes, nuts, seeds and grains are also very low in sodium. Fresh meats like round steak, chicken, fish and fresh pork have an average of 25mg of sodium per ounce. It is the processing and curing of pork that increases the sodium from 59mg per 3-ounce serving of a pork chop to 1,114mg of sodium for an equal 3-ounce serving of ham.

Though milk doesn't taste salty, one cup skim milk contains 122mg of sodium. One egg provides 59mg of sodium. The sodium content of cheeses can range from 74mg per ounce of Swiss to 396mg per ounce of bleu cheese. A slice of whole wheat bread contains 132mg, and a teaspoon of margarine has 50mg. So, it adds up. A varied diet with some meats, lowfat dairy products, limited fats, fruits, grains and vegetables will usually contribute about one-third of your daily sodium intake.

The next third comes from processed foods. The more processed a food is, the higher the sodium content. As can be seen in Chart XIV, processing means sodium, sodium and more sodium.

CHART XIV - SODIUM COMPARISONS NATURAL VS PROCESSED FOODS

3 oz. cooked, lean beef = 55mg	3 oz. cooked, corned beef = 802mg	3 oz. dried chipped beef = 3,657mg
3 oz. fresh cooked, lean pork = 59mg	4 slices bacon (1 oz.) = 548mg	3 oz. cured ham = 1,114mg
1 ear, fresh corn =1mg	1 cup regular whole kernel canned corn = 384 mg	1 cup, creamed style canned corn = 671mg
1 whole fresh cucumber = 4mg	1 whole cucumber with 2 TBS Italian dressing = 236mg	1 dill pickle = 928mg
1 fresh tomato = 14mg	1 cup canned whole tomatoes = 390mg	1 cup canned tomato sauce = 1,498mg
1 medium, baked potato = 5mg	1 cup instant potatoes reconstituted = 485mg	1 cup pkg'd. au gratin potatoes = 1,095mg

Reference: The Sodium Content of Your Food, USDA Home and Garden Bulletin No. 233, August, 1980. U.S. Government Printing Office, Washington, D.C.

The salty taste of many foods, pickles, olives and smoked, cured meats is an obvious clue to the high sodium content. Not so obvious is that 1 teaspoon baking powder has 339mg of sodium, and 1 teaspoon baking soda has 821mg sodium. Other high sodium condiments include garlic, celery and onion salts, soy and teriyaki sauces, Worcestershire sauce, bouillon cubes, catsup and meat tenderizers. Many sodium compounds are added to foods during processing. In reading labels look for these compounds:

+ **Monosodium glutamate (MSG)** + **Sodium nitrate**
+ **Sodium benzoate**   + **Sodium sulfate**
+ **Sodium caseinate**   + **Sodium saccharin**
+ **Sodium nitrate**   + **Brine**
+ **Disodium phosphate**

Salt added at the table or in cooking accounts for the other one-third of the normal sodium intake. Seasoning salts used in cooking contain high amounts of sodium.

Mineral water, softened waters, some dentrifices and some over-the-counter drugs, particularly antacids, contain significant amounts of sodium. Be sure to read labels and discuss the use of these items with your physician.

A gradual reduction in the use of table salt, salty seasonings and condiments and the elimination of high-salt snack items is a suggested way to reduce sodium intake. Using "Lite Salt" (½ sodium chloride and ½ potassium chloride) instead of regular salt, for healthy adults, is one way to reduce added salt by 50 percent. However, salt substitutes are not advisable without your physician's recommendation since most contain large amounts of potassium chloride which may be dangerous to some people due to individual physical or medical problems.

The following are some tips to help you reduce salt in your diet:

+ Creative and increased usage of dried or fresh herbs and spices. (½ teaspoon dried herbs for dish serving four people, use 3 times the quantity if using fresh herbs.) See Chart XV.

+ Add a bay leaf to cooking water for pastas and rice, also great in soups and stews.

+ Experiment with the many available herb and spice blends from your grocery store. (Mrs. Dash, Mr. Pepper, Lawry's Natural Choice, McCormick's Parsley Patch). All of these are potassium and sodium-free — great for anyone to use!

+ Try using fresh lemon and citrus juice to perk up flavors. Grated lemon, lime or orange rind may also be used.

+ Switch to garlic, onion and celery powders instead of salts.
1 teaspoon garlic powder = 1mg sodium
1 teaspoon garlic salt = 1,850mg sodium

+ Drain canned vegetables into a strainer, rinse 1 to 2 minutes in tap water. Heat in fresh tap water. This will reduce sodium substantially.

+ Try using fresh ginger, garlic, green onions and parsley in cooking.

In summary, keep in mind it is not the intent for the population at large to be on a salt-free diet, but that sodium intake should be limited to 1,000 to 3,000 milligrams per day.

CHART XV - HERB AND SPICE SUGGESTIONS TO REPLACE SODIUM

VEGETABLES:
Asparagus: lemon juice, nutmeg, caraway seeds, sesame seeds.
Black Beans: oregano, vinegar, wine, onion, cumin, bay leaf, green pepper.
Broccoli: lemon juice, oregano, tarragon.
Green Beans: marjoram, lemon juice, nutmeg, rosemary, dillweed.
Cabbage: mustard dressing, dill, mace, lemon, vinegar, sugar.
Carrots: parsley, dillweed, nutmeg, lemon juice, chopped chives, mint.
Corn: green pepper, tomatoes, chives, onion, curry, chili powder.
Peas: mushrooms, onions, parsley, pepper, mint, marjoram, savory, thyme, green pepper, dillweed.
Lentils: turmeric, cumin, oregano, garlic, onions, parsley, red pepper flakes.
Potatoes: parsley, ground mace, onion, dillweed, rosemary, green pepper, garlic, black pepper.
Tomatoes: basil, celery, onion, marjoram, tarragon, thyme, pepper, oregano, garlic.
Winter Squash: chopped pecans, ginger, mace, nutmeg, onion, black pepper.

MEATS:
Poultry: paprika, allspice, thyme, cardamom, cumin, curry, sage, basil marjoram, ginger, wine, lemon, parsley, garlic.
Pork: garlic, sage, onion, marjoram, spiced apples, applesauce, thyme.
Fish: bay leaf, dry mustard, paprika, curry, mushrooms, tomatoes, lemon or lime juice, garlic, basil, tarragon, thyme, wine.
Beef: bay leaf, pepper, chives, onion, dry mustard, sage, thyme, tomatoes, marjoram, nutmeg, garlic, allspice, tarragon, curry, vinegar or wine for marinating, mushrooms.
Egg Substitutes or Eggs: chives, curry, dry mustard, tarragon, green pepper, mushrooms, onion, basil, paprika, parsley, wine, tomatoes.

GOAL 7
IF YOU DRINK ALCOHOL, DO SO IN MODERATION

Alcoholic beverages are referred to as calorie dense, meaning they provide calories but only insignificant nutrients. Surveys indicate that alcohol contributes 5 percent of all calories consumed by Americans and approximately 10 percent of all calories when only those who drink are considered. When intake is below 50 milliliters of ethanol a day, no significant ill effects of alcohol consumption on health have been observed in healthy adults.[14]

The ill effects of excessive drinking are well established; increased accidental death, cirrhosis of the liver and certain types of cancer, as well as possible birth defects or other problems when consumed by women during pregnancy. In susceptible individuals, there is some evidence of a link between development of high blood pressure and alcohol. For those who drink more than three or four drinks a day, there is a significant rise in the incidence of high blood pressure.[15]

Moderate alcohol consumption may have some beneficial effects on cardiovascular health. High density lipoproteins (HDL's) tend to be higher, and in some studies, the incidence of coronary heart disease is lower than in those who abstain. However, no studies have demonstrated that increasing alcohol intake will significantly reduce cardiovascular disease in human or animal models.[16]

Personal choice, with moderation as a guide, seems best. One or two standard size drinks daily appear to cause no harm in normal, healthy, nonpregnant adults. Twelve ounces of regular beer, 5 ounces of wine, or 1½ ounces of distilled spirits contain equal amounts of alcohol.[17]

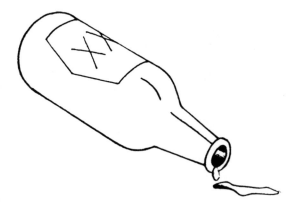

FOOTNOTES

1 Diet in the Healthy Child. American Heart Association Circulation. (67:1411A, 1983)

2 Dietary Guidelines for Americans, Second Edition, 1985, U.S. Department of Agriculture, U.S. Department of Health and Human Services. Home and Garden Bulletin No. 232.

3 R.B. Alfin-Slater and L. Aftergood, "Fat and Other Lipids," *Modern Nutrition in Health and Disease*, 5th Edition, eds. R.S. Goodhart and M.E. Shils (Philadelphia: Lea and Febiger, 1973) pp. 117-141.

4 Holloway, E.C. "Don't Be Afraid of Exer-size." *Life and Health*, pp.7-8, April, 1981.

5 Weight Management: A Summary of Current Theories and Practice, 0070, 1985. National Dairy Council, Rosemont, IL, p. 20.

6 Stuart, R.B. and B. Davis. *Slim Chances in a Fat World*. Champaign, IL: Research Press, 1972.

7 Dietary Guidelines for Healthy American Adults/A Statement for Physicians and Health Professionals by the Nutrition Committee, American Heart Association, Dallas, TX, 1986, p.1.

8 National Cholesterol Education Program. Report of the expert panel on detection, evaluation and treatment of high blood cholesterol in adults. 10/5/87. National Heart, Lung and Blood Institute. Bethesda, MD 20802.

9 Brody, J., *Jane Brody's Nutrition Book*, p. 150, Bantam Books, W.W. Norton and Co., 1982.

10 Dietary Guidelines for Healthy American Adults/A Statement for Physicians and Health Professionals by the Nutrition Committee, American Heart Association, Dallas, TX, 1986, p.1.

11 Templeton, E.; Moody, L.; Funk, P.; E.H.E. *Sugar and Other Sweeteners*, Fact Sheet #653. Florida Cooperative Extension Service Institute of Food and Agricultural Sciences/University of Florida, Gainesville, FL 32611.

12 Lecos, Chris, *"Sugar, How Sweet It Is - And Isn't,"* FDA Consumer, HEW Publication No. 80-2127, February 1980.

13 The Sodium Content of Your Food, USDA Home and Garden Bulletin No. 233, August, 1980, p.3, U.S. Government Printing Office, Washington, DC

14 Ibidem, Number 10.

15 Hennekens, C.H. *"Alcohol,"* Prevention of Coronary Heart Disease, editors Kaplan, N.M. and Stamler, J., Philadelphia, W.B. Saunders Co., 1983, pp. 130-138.

16 Dietary Guidelines for Healthy Americans. A Statement for Physicians and Health Professionals by the Nutrition Committee, American Heart Association, 1986, p. 4.

17 Dietary Guidelines for Healthy Americans. Second Edition, 1985, U.S. Department of Agriculture, U.S. Department of Health and Human Services, p. 23

ODDS
AND ENDS

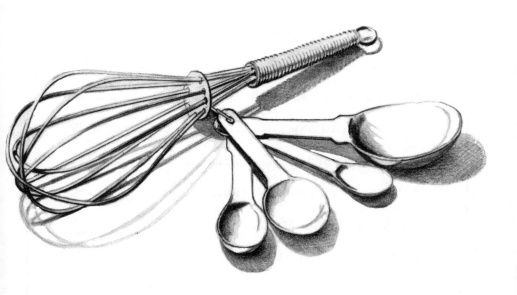

ODDS AND ENDS

This book is not unlike an insurance policy on your heart and health. Beginning with this chapter, we will deal with products and recipes designed and created for a healthier you.

In Odds and Ends, we have gathered many "little tidbits" of information to make your life in the kitchen a much easier and more pleasant experience.

COMMON FOOD EQUIVALENTS

FOOD	UNIT	APPROXIMATE MEASURE
Apples	1 pound	3 medium (3 cups sliced)
Bananas, mashed	1 pound	3 medium (about 2 cups)
Bananas, sliced	1 pound	3 medium (2½ cups)
Beans, dried	1 pound (2½ cups)	6 cups cooked
Bread	1 slice	¼ cup dry crumbs
Cabbage	1 pound	4½ to 5 cups shredded
Celery	2 stalks	1 cup sliced
Cheese, grated	2 ounces, weight	½ cup
Chicken	3½ pounds	3 cups cooked, diced
Broiler chicken	2½ pounds	About 1 pound meat
Egg, large, white only	1	About 2 tablespoons
Egg, large, yolk only	1	About 1 tablespoon
Fish	1 pound	1¾ cups cooked, flaked
Flour, sifted	1 pound	4 to 4½ cups
Cake flour, sifted	1 pound	4¾ to 5 cups
Whole wheat, unsifted	1 pound	3½ cups
Oat flour	1¼ cups, rolled	1 cup, floured
Gelatin	1 envelope	1 tablespoon
Graham crackers	14 squares	1 cup fine crumbs
Ham	1 pound	3 cups, cubed
Lemon, medium, juice	1	2 to 3 tablespoons
Lemon, rind, grated	1	1½ to 2 teaspoons
Nuts, almonds	1 pound	3½ cups, shelled
pecans	1 pound	4 cups, shelled
peanuts	1 pound	3 cups, shelled
walnuts	1 pound	4 cups, shelled
Onion	1 medium	¾ cup, chopped
Orange, medium juice	1	⅓ to ½ cup
Orange rind, grated	1	1 to 2 tablespoons
Pasta, elbow macaroni	8 ounce pkg.	2 to 2¼ cups, cooked
noodles	8 ounce pkg.	3 to 3½ cups, cooked
spaghetti	1 pound pkg.	About 4 cups, cooked
Peas, dried	2 cups (1 pound)	5 cups cooked
Peaches, peeled, sliced	1 pound (3 to 4)	2 to 2½ cups
Potatoes	1 pound	2 to 2½ cups cooked
Raisins	1 pound	2½ cups
Rice, uncooked	1 pound	2¼ to 2⅓ cups
Rice, uncooked	4 ounces, weight	1 cup
Strawberries, hulled	1 pint	About 1½ cups
Sugar, granulated	1 pound	2 cups
brown	1 pound	2¼ cups
confectioners	1 pound	3½ cups, sifted
powdered	1 pound	2⅓ cups
Tuna or salmon	6 ½ ounce can	¾ cup, flaked
Yeast, active dry	1 envelope	2½ teaspoon

TO COOK PASTA

DRY Weight	PASTA Measure	POT Size	Water	SALT (opt.)	COOKED Pasta
2 oz.	¼ pkg.	2 qt.	1 qt.	½ teaspoon	1 to 1¼ cup
4 oz.	½ pkg.	3 qt.	2 qt.	1 teaspoon	2 to 2½ cup
8 oz.	1 pkg.	4 qt.	3 qt.	2 teaspoons	5 cups

RECOMMENDED SUBSTITUTIONS
FROM THE HEALTHY HEART GOURMET

Unless otherwise instructed, the recipes in this book use the following food products:

> Salt - Lite salt or Salt Sense
> Milk - Skim milk
> Cottage Cheese - 1% fat
> Mozzarella - Part skim milk or fat-free cheese
> Other cheeses - Lowfat or fat-free, when available
> Sugar substitute - Equal or Sweet 'N Low
> Butter or margarine substitute - Butter Buds, liquid form only
> Egg substitute - Fleischmann's Egg Beaters
> Bacon and salt pork substitute - BAC*OS (bacon flavored bits)
> Capers - Crosse & Blackwell
> White cooking wine - Sauterne or sherry
> Red cooking wine - Burgundy
> Preferred thickening agent - Cornstarch
> Mayonnaise - Cholesterol free or fat and cholesterol free
> Margarines - Tub margarine - Promise Extra Light
> Stick margarine - Fleischmann's light corn oil spread

SUGGESTIONS AND HELPFUL HINTS

1. A little oil added to the water when boiling pasta will help prevent the pasta from sticking together and help keep the water from boiling over.

2. When preparing fish for cooking, soak the fish for ½ hour to remove any strong, unwanted tastes or odors. Use a liquid which will compliment the flavor of your planned recipe. 1) milk; 2) Lemon juice and water; 3) Lime juice and water.

3. If you do not own a whisk, buy one! Better yet, buy three or four whisks of varying sizes. Whisking sauces will produce smoother sauces, with less effort and fewer

spills. Remember to take your time when making a sauce. A good sauce may seem to take forever, but the final results are well worth it.

4. You should have a rotary beater, either manually or electrically operated. The preparation of some desserts, breads and some vegetables are greatly simplified with such a tool.

5. Medallions are cross grain cuts of meat or, in our case, turkey breast. They are cut about ½ inch thick and are beaten slightly between two pieces of waxed paper, until about ¼ inch thick.

6. Whenever you are cooking vegetables, use a small amount of unsalted water. Save flavors created by mixing several different vegetable juices are wonderful, as well as nutritious. Use juices in soups, stews and recipes calling for vegetable bouillon. If you don't need the juice right away, freeze the liquid until needed.

7. Parsley - When you buy a bunch of parsley, chop it all at once, preferably in a small food processor. If you wash first, pat dry before processing. Then pack into plastic containers, freeze and use as needed.

8. Tahini - is made by hulling and grinding sesame seeds. It has the texture of peanut butter. It can be found in most health food stores and has many uses in near east recipes or can be eaten like peanut butter. Don't overuse this product, it contains high levels of mono-unsaturated fat.

9. Capers - are the flower buds of a Mediterranean shrub preserved in brine. They usually come in a 3½ ounce jar and after opening should be refrigerated. Capers are especially good with fish and poultry.

10. Chutney - (see page 52) is a pungent sauce or relish of East Indian origin made of ingredients which may be combinations of sweet, sour and spicy hot. It should be refrigerated after opening.

11. Shallot - is a plant of the lily family whose bulb forms bulblets which have a flavor somewhere between onion and garlic. Usually found in the produce section of your market these delightful flavor enhancers can be chopped and frozen, to be used when needed or when they are out of season and expensive. A simple sauce of Butter Buds, shallots and white wine has a heavenly aroma and can be used with many foods from vegetables to seafood. Add some crushed capers, and it gets even better.

LIQUID BUTTER BUDS

Yield: 1 cup

Butter Buds come in a shaker or packaged in a yellow box. We are only concerned with those in the box. Prepare as follows: Purchase a glass or plastic cruet for ease of shaking and pouring. Pour 6 ounces very hot tap water into a measuring cup; stir in a double packet of the Butter Buds powder. Mix thoroughly. When dissolved, add enough canola oil to fill to one cup; mix well. Pour into cruet, and store in the refrigerator. Butter Buds pour best at room temperature. Shake well before using.

Per ½ cup: Calories - 224; Total Fat - 20.8g; Saturated Fat - 1.6g; Cholesterol - 0

Per tablespoon: Calories - 28; Total Fat - 2.6g; Saturated Fat - .2g; Cholesterol - 0

IF YOU LIVE IN AN AREA WHERE BUTTER BUDS IN THE YELLOW BOX IS NOT READILY AVAILABLE, YOU MAY SUBSTITUTE AN EXTRA LIGHT MARGARINE. HOWEVER, PLEASE BE REMINDED THAT THE FOOD ANALYSIS WILL BE ALTERED. FATS AND CALORIES WILL BE ELEVATED!

HOW TO BOIL SHRIMP

If you are fortunate enough to live in an area where you can buy fresh, heads-on shrimp, you are blessed. There is nothing quite like fresh shrimp.

Remove the heads with a twisting motion and clean shrimp bodies. If frozen, thaw and clean. Place about 1 pound shrimp in a large saucepan or kettle; add 12 ounces room temperature beer and let the shrimp soak for about ½ hour. Cover; bring to a boil; cook, covered, for 1 minute, or until shrimp are pink. Drain shrimp and run cold water over them to stop the cooking process.

Shrimp are now ready for a great cocktail sauce, see page 228; for use in salads, or any recipes calling for cooked shrimp. **ENJOY!**

HOW TO TOAST ALMONDS

Yield: 3 tablespoons

1 tablespoon liquid Butter Buds, see page 48
2 tablespoons slivered almonds

In a small skillet, over medium heat, warm the Butter Buds; add the almonds; stir to coat, then, stirring frequently, heat over medium low until almonds are nicely browned.

Great in salads, with chicken, or over fish in an almandine sauce.

Calories - 110; Total Fat - 9.8g;
Saturated Fat - .9g; Cholesterol - 0

GARLIC CROUTONS

Yield: 2 servings

4 slices, fairly thick Italian bread   **Garlic powder, to taste**
Vegetable oil spray   **Salt (opt.) to taste**

Remove crust from bread and cube slices.

Spray a cookie sheet with the oil. Add bread cubes; spray with more oil, and sprinkle with garlic powder and salt. Bake in a 400F oven for 10 to 12 minutes, or until lightly browned. Use in salads, or to enhance soups.

Per serving: *Calories - 165; Total Fat - 1.3g;*
                    Saturated Fat - Tr; Cholesterol - 0

OK REFRIED BEANS

Yield: 2 cups

1 16-ounce can red kidney beans, rinsed and drained	1 tablespoon canola oil
	½ teaspoon chili powder
½ cup finely chopped onion	⅛ teaspoon cayenne pepper

In a medium, non-stick skillet, saute the onion in the canola oil. Slightly mash the beans with a fork and add to the skillet. Mix the remaining ingredients together, and stir into the bean mixture. Fry until lightly browned. Serve with your favorite Mexican dish.

Per ¼ cup: Calories - 69; Total Fat - 2.1g;
*   Saturated Fat - Tr; Cholesterol - 0*

HOMEMADE PEANUT BUTTER

Yield: ½ cup

Many markets will coarse-grind fresh peanuts for you. Take home 1 cup of these fresh- ground peanuts and place contents in a food processor. While processing, add small amounts of salt and sugar, to taste. Process until creamy smooth. Place peanut butter in a jar with a tight-fitting screw-on top and store in a cabinet away from heat. Do not refrigerate. By adding your own seasonings you can be sure of the amounts added.

Some commercially prepared peanut butters have large amounts of salt and sugar plus some hydrogenated oils to prevent separation.

MOCK SOUR CREAM
Yield: 1¼ cups

1 cup 1% fat cottage cheese   **½ teaspoon lemon juice**
¼ cup low-fat plain yogurt

In a small food processor combine all the ingredients. Blend into a smooth consistency. Place in a plastic or glass container, seal and refrigerate.

Keeps for about 1 week.

Use in place of real sour cream or as a substitute for heavy cream in sauces. At only 14% fat from calories this is a must for healthy meal preparation.

Per ¼ cup: *Calories - 39; Total Fat - .6g;*
                    Saturated Fat - Tr; Cholesterol - 2.7mg

SALT PORK SUBSTITUTE
Yield: About 2 tablespoons

For any recipe which begins with "fry a little salt pork", or "add some bacon fat", try the following: In a saucepan, heat 2 tablespoons canola oil over low heat. Add 1 tablespoon of BAC*OS and cook until they are just beginning to brown. Discard the bits or reserve them for use in your recipe.

You will have a little more than 1 tablespoon of bacon flavored cooking oil. This works well with chowders and soups. Great with "southern style" greens, see page 206.

Per teaspoon: *Calories - 52; Total Fat - 5g;*
                    Saturated Fat - .3g; Cholesterol - 0

MANGO CHUTNEY

Yield: About 5 cups

3 ripe mangoes, peeled and
  coarsely chopped
3 golden delicious apples, peeled,
  cored and coarsely chopped
½ cup white sugar
½ cup brown sugar
¾ cup golden raisins

1 large onion, coarsely chopped
2 garlic cloves, pressed
2 to 3 tablespoons freshly-grated
  ginger root
1 teaspoon cinnamon
1 teaspoon crushed red pepper
½ teaspoon ground allspice

In a large bowl, mix all ingredients together. Cover and let sit on counter for 24 hours, stirring occasionally.

Place mix in Dutch oven, cover, and bring to a boil; then simmer for 2 hours. Run mix through food processor until it reaches desired consistency. Divide mixture into jars, cover tightly and refrigerate.

Appears to keep indefinitely if refrigerated.

Per ½ cup: *Calories - 183; Total Fat - .4g;*
              Saturated Fat - Tr; Cholesterol - 0

HOW TO MAKE YOGURT CHEESE

Yield: About ¾ cup

You can purchase a yogurt funnel, use several layers of cheesecloth, or you can even use a coffee strainer. No matter which you prefer, the method is still the same.

If you use non-fat plain yogurt be sure to buy yogurt without gelatin added.

In the refrigerator, strain 1 cup of yogurt through whichever vehicle you have chosen to use. This process will take from 12 to 24 hours. When most of the liquid has drained from the yogurt you will have what is called yogurt cheese.

Its uses are similar to those for cream cheese and cottage cheese. It makes a great low-fat cheesecake. Try using it as the basis for sauces, dressings and mayonnaise.

SPICY HOT MUSTARD
Yield: About 1 cup

1 cup cider vinegar	2 bay leaves
4 whole cloves	1/4 teaspoon salt
8 green peppercorns, softened	1 cup dry Coleman's mustard
in hot water, drained	¼ cup sugar

Place first 5 ingredients in a small saucepan; bring to a boil, and simmer for 5 minutes. Strain into a small bowl.

Mix the mustard and sugar together. Slowly add the vinegar mixture, whisking until smooth. Refrigerate overnight. Divide into small glass jars with tightly-fitting lids. Keep refrigerated. Makes great neighborhood gifts at holiday times. Keeps for months.

Per teaspoon: Calories - 17; Total Fat - .5g;
Saturated Fat - Tr; Cholesterol - 0

TOMATO BUTTER
Yield: About 3½ quarts

7½ pounds ripe tomatoes,	2 cups cider vinegar
skinned and coarsely chopped	1½ tablespoons cinnamon
4 pounds sugar	1 teaspoon ground cloves

Place all ingredients in a large kettle; bring to a boil. Simmer for 3 to 4 hours, or until butter is the thickness of marmalade. BURNS EASILY, so stir frequently.

Seal in canning jars and store in a cool dry place. Keeps indefinitely.

Use over meats and as a replacemant for chutney.

Great for neighborhood gifts at the holidays!

Per tablespoon: Calories - 30; Total Fat - Tr;
Saturated Fat - Tr; Cholesterol - 0

MY STORY

I always assumed that I ate well and kept myself in fairly good condition. Yet here I was, mowing the lawn, and with each trip across the yard, the chest pains were getting worse. Surely, it was indigestion, or just gas. Me with heart trouble - - - **NEVER!**

After a brief stopover at a cardiologist's office, I found myself spending Thanksgiving Day in the hospital awaiting the balloon procedure called Angioplasty. Guess what? It failed! One minute I was being prepped for the angioplasty, and the next (two days later) I was counting staples down the middle of my chest - staples concealing triple bypass surgery.

Worse yet, my cardiologist and my dietitian announced my new diet - a diet necessary to keep me healthy and out of the operating room in the future - a diet consisting of what I thought were bland, uninteresting foods. I thought to myself, *"Why bother?"*

For years my wife and I had been developing a cookbook, a gourmet cookbook filled with great tasting rich foods. Now all those dreams were gone - *or were they?*

The first light at the end of the tunnel, and the birth of this book, came in a local supermarket where we met an old teaching colleague who also had bypass surgery. He introduced us to Butter Buds. At first we used this product as suggested by its manufacturer, Cumberland Packing Co. - good but not good enough. We tried some experimenting. **EUREKA!** Mixed with another ingredient, we found it was possible to duplicate the main essentials of gourmet cooking: **RICH-TASTING SAUCES.** Butter Buds, egg substitute, BAC*OS, mock sour cream, sugar substitute, cheese alternatives and other products low in fat, cholesterol and calories gave us the tools to rebuild our cookbook.

Next came the problem of high-fat meats. The solution: **TURKEY!** Seasoned properly, you can make turkey taste like many things it was never meant to be. Barbecued Pork , Near East Lamb Kabobs, Hungarian Goulash, Veal Oscar and many other great meals are possible, and with far fewer harmful *"side effects."*

In deciding to go ahead with this cookbook, my wife, Arlene, and I are offering a chance for those of you who really enjoy rich-tasting foods to continue experiencing those foods without the horrors of the final chapter - *heart disease.* **THIS BOOK WORKS!** The recipes not only satisfy my own gourmet taste buds, but I have lost 30 pounds in the process, my blood analysis is normal, and I feel better than I have in 15 years.

Tom Mills
Heart Patient

APPETIZERS

APPETIZERS

For most people appetizers are not considered necessities in daily meal planning. However, there are times when they are a nice added treat and will most likely be expected at any dinner party.

Most of the appetizers contained in this book are "make-ahead" dishes. All are heart-safe, even the deviled eggs. Some, like the Bacon - Cheese - Relish Dip and Simulated Guacamole have important places in other meals.

BACON-CHEESE-RELISH DIP

Yield: 3½ cups
Serves 18 as appetizer, 6 as lunch

⅓ cup BAC*OS (bacon
  flavored bits)
2 cups 1% fat cottage cheese
½ cup relish, well drained

¼ teaspoon paprika
⅓ cup onion, finely chopped
⅓ cup fat and cholesterol-free
  mayonnaise

Combine all ingredients, mixing well. Chill. Serve with crackers or small pieces of pita bread or Pita Toasts, see page 111.

Per tablespoon, without cracker: Calories - 15; Total Fat - Tr;
Saturated Fat - Tr; Cholesterol - Tr;

May be served as a lunch in pita bread halves, at only 9% fat.

Per pita half: Calories - 164; Total Fat - 1.6g;
Saturated Fat - Tr; Cholesterol - 2mg

CEREAL MUNCHIES

Yield: 8 cups

8 cups corn/rice cereal pieces
⅓ cup light corn oil spread
1 teaspoon onion powder

4 teaspoons worcestershire sauce
½ teaspoon garlic powder

Measure cereal into a 13x9x2-inch baking pan.

Melt the spread in a small saucepan. Add the remaining ingredients; mix well.

Pour hot mixture over the cereal, turning with a large spoon until cereal is well coated.

Bake in a 250F oven for 1 hour, stirring every 10 minutes.

Store in a cookie tin with a tight-fitting lid.

Per ¼ cup serving: Calories - 69; Total Fat - 1.3g;
Saturated Fat - Tr; Cholesterol - 0

CHICKEN AND SWEET PICKLE CANAPES

Yield: 36 servings

2 large chicken breasts, cooked, skinned and finely chopped
Salt (opt.) and pepper, to taste
½ cup shredded mozzarella cheese alternative
½ cup-finely chopped sweet pickles
½ cup fat and cholesterol-free mayonnaise
½ teaspoon worcestershire-wine sauce
6 drops Tabasco sauce
1 loaf party rye bread, or 8 slices rye bread, quartered

Combine all ingredients, except the bread. Spread the chicken mixture on the bread slices. Arrange the slices on a sprayed cookie sheet.

Bake in a 425F oven for 10 minutes, or until the cheese is melted.

Per serving: *Calories - 42; Total Fat - 1.1g;*
Saturated Fat - Tr; Cholesterol - 4.6mg

BAKED STUFFED CLAMS

Yield: 15 servings

15 large hard shelled clams (quahogs)
1½ cups seasoned bread crumbs
½ teaspoon salt (opt.)
⅓ cup freshly-grated parmesan cheese
¼ teaspoon pepper
½ teaspoon parlsey
½ teaspoon garlic powder
1 large onion, finely chopped
1 tablespoon sugar
4 ounces Italian sausage, see page 87
¼ teaspoon red pepper flakes
Paprika to taste

In a large kettle, steam the clams open in 1 cup water. Coarsely chop the clam meat, reserving the cooking liquid. Combine the remaining ingredients, except paprika; mix with the clam meat, adding enough reserved liquid to make the mixture moist and able to hold itself together.

Spray 15 half shells, and mound each with the stuffing mixture. Sprinkle with paprika and bake in a 350F oven for 30 to 35 minutes.

Per half shell: *Calories - 102; Total Fat - 2.5g;*
Saturated Fat - 1.2g; Cholesterol - 19.3mg

CRAB MEATBALLS
Yield: About 30 meatballs

3 tablespoons liquid Butter Buds,
   see page 48
1 tablespoon finely-minced onion
3 tablespoons finely-chopped celery
1 cup imitation crabmeat, minced
⅓ cup seasoned bread crumbs
1 tablespoon finely-chopped parsley
¼ teaspoon Dijon mustard

¼ cup egg substitute
⅛ teaspoon paprika
1 teaspoon lemon juice
2 tablespoons grated Swiss
   cheese alternative
Salt (opt.) and pepper, to taste
6 drops Tabasco sauce
Dash of worcestershire sauce

In a covered saucepan, simmer the onion and celery in the Butter Buds for 3 minutes. Remove from heat; add remaining ingredients; mix well. Don't worry about the moistness. Dust hand with flour or additional bread crumbs.

On wax paper-lined cookie sheet, form mixture into little balls about 1 inch in diameter. Freeze. When frozen, place in plastic bags; store in freezer until needed.

To cook, place crab balls on sprayed cookie sheet and broil 5 inches from heat for 8 to 10 minutes, or until slightly browned.

Per meatball: *Calories - 18; Total Fat - .5g;*
   Saturated Fat - Tr; Cholesterol - 1.4mg

APPLE DIP
Yield: About 2 cups

½ cup dried apples, finely chopped
1 cup 1% fat cottage cheese, whipped
   in blender or food processor

3 tablespoons frozen apple juice
   concentrate, thawed
5 tablespoons honey
¼ cup pecans, finely chopped

Mix all ingredients in a food processor, in the order of ingredients.

Serve with cinnamon graham crackers. This dip also works well as a light dessert.

Per ½ tablespoon, without cracker: Calories - 25; Total Fat - .6g;
   Saturated Fat - Tr; Cholesterol - Tr

HARMLESS DEVILED EGGS

Yield: 16 halves

8 large eggs
1 cup egg substitute
1¾ teaspoons Dijon mustard
1½ teaspoons sugar

4 tablespoons fat and cholesterol-free
   mayonnaise
½ teaspoon salt (opt.)
⅛ teaspoon pepper
Paprika to dust eggs

Hard boil the eggs. Cool, peel, cut in half lengthwise and discard yolks. Meanwhile, pour egg substitute into a heavy 8-inch non-stick skillet, and cover with a tight-fitting lid. Cook over very low heat for 10 minutes, or until well set. Remove from heat and allow to stand, covered, for 10 minutes more. Place egg substitute in a bowl, and mash with a fork.

Add remaining ingredients, except paprika, and mix well. Place mixture in a small food processor and process until light and fluffy. Fill the egg halves; dust with paprika and chill overnight.

Per half stuffed egg: *Calories - 22; Total Fat - Tr;*
                            Saturated Fat - 0; Cholesterol - 0

VEGETABLE "CAVIAR"

Yield: 2 cups

1 medium eggplant, about 1 pound
1 medium tomato, peeled and diced
1 tablespoon chopped onion
1 jalapeño pepper, finely chopped,
   wear rubber gloves

½ cup chopped parsley
Salt, to taste (opt.)
⅛ teaspoon pepper
2 tablespoons lemon juice
½ tablespoon olive oil

Pierce eggplant with fork; place in baking dish, and bake in 375F oven for 40 to 45 minutes, or until tender. When cool, peel and scoop out pulp; chop in a blender or food processor. Drain off excess liquid.

In a large bowl, mix next 6 ingredients until smooth. Add eggplant, lemon juice and oil; mix well. Turn into serving bowl; cover and refrigerate for 2 hours. Serve with crackers, or Pita Toasts - see page 111.

Per ½ tablespoon serving, with cracker: *Calories - 15; Total Fat - .5g;*
                                              Saturated Fat - Tr; Cholesterol - 0

SIMULATED GUACAMOLE

Yield: 1¼ cups

1 10-ounce package frozen broccoli
¼ cup mock sour cream, see page 51
2 tablespoons chopped onions
1 small chili pepper, chopped, wear
  rubber gloves
1 small bell pepper, chopped

1 tablespoon fat and cholesterol-
  free mayonnaise
2 teaspoons lemon juice
¼ teaspoon chili powder
⅛ teaspoon curry powder

Cook broccoli as directed. Drain well; cut into chunks.

Combine all ingredients in a blender or food processor. Puree, stopping several times to scrape down the sides of the container. Place in serving bowl, and refrigerate over night.

Serve with corn chips or use as a condiment with Mexican meals.

Per tablespoon, without corn chips: *Calories - 7; Total Fat - Tr;*
                                          Saturated Fat - Tr; Cholesterol - Tr;

HUMMUS

Yield: 100 ½ tablespoon servings

1 1-pound, 3-ounce can chick peas,
  drained, liquid reserved
2 garlic cloves, pressed
1 tablespoon minced onion
2 tablespoons Tahini, see page 47

¼ teaspoon black pepper
1 tablespoon lime juice
Pita bread (pocket bread)
½ cup finely-chopped onions
2 tablespoons finely-chopped parsley

In a blender or food processor, mash the chick peas. Add the next 5 ingredients mixed with enough bean liquid to make ½ cup total. Process until smooth. Refrigerate for a few hours.

Tear the pita bread into pieces about the size of a small cracker. Serve the Hummus, at room temperature, with the bread pieces, plain crackers or Pita Toasts - see page 111. Garnish with the chopped onions and parsley.

Per serving without the bread: *Calories - 9; Total Fat - Tr;*
                                     Saturated Fat - Tr; Cholesterol - 0

BROILED OYSTERS

Yield: 12 servings

12 oysters on the half shell, (use
western oysters, if available)
Tabasco sauce
BAC*OS (bacon flavored bits)
Worcestershire sauce

Lemon juice
½ cup seasoned bread crumbs
2 tablespoons liquid Butter Buds,
see page 48

Use sprayed custard dishes if you have no shells. Sprinkle each oyster with the next 4 ingredients. Cover each oyster with seasoned bread crumbs; top with a drizzle of Butter Buds.

Broil 6 to 8 inches from the heat for 10 to 12 minutes, or until the bread crumbs begin to turn brown and the edges of the oysters begin to curl.

Per oyster: *Calories - 62; Total Fat - 1.8g;*
                   Saturated Fat - Tr; Cholesterol - 29mg

COLD CRABMEAT DIP

Yield: About 2½ cups

1 cup 1% fat cottage cheese, whipped
in blender until smooth
1 cup imitation crabmeat, coarsely
chopped
⅓ cup fat and cholesterol-free
mayonnaise
¼ teaspoon sugar

⅛ teaspoon garlic powder
½ teaspoon seasoned salt
1 to 1½ tablespoons cream style
horseradish
2 tablespoons finely-chopped onion
2 tablespoons finely-chopped
parsley

Combine all ingredients well, and refrigerate until serving time. Best when refrigerated overnight.

Serve with crackers or raw vegetables.

Per ½ tablespoon: *Calories - 6; Total Fat - Tr;*
                        Saturated Fat - Tr; Cholesterol - .6mg

SAUSAGE STUFFED MUSHROOMS
Yield: 10 to 12 servings

2 pounds medium mushrooms (40)
8 ounces Italian turkey sausage,
 finely chopped, see page 87
1 teaspoon red pepper flakes
1 onion, finely minced
1 clove garlic, minced

Vegetable oil spray
Salt (opt.) and pepper, to taste
½ cup grated mozzarella
 cheese alternative
½ cup seasoned bread crumbs

Remove stems from mushrooms; set caps aside. Finely chop stems; set aside. In a non-stick skillet, cook the chopped sausage mixed with the red pepper flakes. Remove sausage to a medium-size mixing bowl.

Spray same skillet with vegetable oil; cook the garlic and onion, covered, until softened. Add the stems; cover and cook until stems are tender, stirring occasionally. Place in bowl; mix well with the sausage. Add salt, pepper and cheese; mix well. Add the bread crumbs and mix well. Add crumbs only until mixture is stiff.

Fill mushroom caps with the mixture; place on sprayed cookie sheet. Bake in a 450F oven for 15 minutes, or until mushrooms are tender and cheese is melted.

Per mushroom: Calories - 20; Total Fat - .5g;
Saturated Fat - Tr; Cholesterol - 4mg

NORTH STREET DIP
Yield: About 2⅓ cups

1 cup 1% fat cottage cheese,
 whipped in blender
3 tablespoons white wine vinegar

3 tablespoons sugar
¾ cup finely-chopped green pepper
¾ cup finely-chopped onion

In a medium mixing bowl mix first 3 ingredients together until smooth. Add the chopped pepper and onion; mix well.

Make dip one day ahead and refrigerate until served. Serve with crackers or raw vegetables.

Per ½ tablespoon: Calories - 5; Total Fat - Tr;
Saturated Fat - Tr; Cholesterol - Tr

HOT SAUSAGE IN SOUR CREAM
Yield: 36 sausage balls

¾ pound Italian turkey sausage, see
   page 87
2 teaspoons Italian seasoning
¼ cup flour (oat flour)
Vegetable oil spray

¼ cup mango chutney, see page 52,
   or use commercially bottled
¼ cup sherry
¼ cup mock sour cream, page 51
⅛ teaspoon cayenne pepper

In a bowl, mix the Italian seasoning and the flour with the sausage. Make bite-size balls with the mixture.

Coat large non-stick skillet with the vegetable oil spray, and cook the balls until they are cooked through; turning frequently. Remove balls to a chafing dish.

In the same skillet, combine the remaining ingredients; mix well; heat thoroughly. Pour over and coat the sausage balls. Keep warm until served.

Per meatball: Calories - 22; Total Fat - Tr;
*   Saturated Fat - Tr; Cholesterol - 6.7mg*

HOT SPINACH BALLS
Yield: 50 spinach balls

1 10-ounce package chopped spinach,
   cooked and well drained
1 cup seasoned bread crumbs
2 tablespoons finely-chopped onion
½ teaspoon garlic powder
¼ cup freshly-grated parmesan
   cheese

¼ cup grated mozzarella cheese
   alternative
¾ cup egg substitute
4 tablespoons liquid Butter Buds,
   see page 48
¼ teaspoon salt (opt.)
¼ teaspoon pepper

Combine all ingredients; mix well. Roll into 1-inch diameter balls. Place on a cookie sheet covered with wax paper and freeze. The balls may then be stored in plastic bags, in freezer, until needed.

To serve, bake the frozen balls for 10 to 15 minutes at 350F.

Per spinach ball: Calories - 17; Total Fat - Tr;
*   Saturated Fat - Tr; Cholesterol - Tr*

SWEDISH MEATBALLS

Yield: 50 meatballs

Vegetable oil spray
⅓ cup minced onion
¼ cup egg substitute
½ cup skim milk
½ to ¾ cup fresh bread crumbs
   (2 to 3 slices)
1 teaspoon salt (opt.)
1 packet sugar substitute, or
   2 teaspoons sugar
½ teaspoon allspice

¼ teaspoon nutmeg
¾ pound freshly-ground turkey
½ pound ground round beef
2 tablespoons light corn oil spread
½ cup flour
1 teaspoon sugar
1 teaspoon salt (opt.)
⅛ teaspoon pepper
1 cup water
1½ cups skim milk

Spray a small non-stick skillet, and cook the onion, covered, until softened. In a large mixing bowl, combine the egg substitute, milk and crumbs; let stand for 5 minutes. Add the spices, meats and onion; mix well. Chill for 1 hour. Shape into 1-inch balls. Spray a large skillet with vegetable oil, and brown the meatballs over medium heat; remove from skillet and set aside.

Reduce heat to low; add corn oil spread to skillet. In a bowl combine flour, sugar, salt, pepper and water; pour into skillet and stir constantly. As the gravy begins to smooth out, add the milk and simmer, stirring until thickened.

Return meatballs to gravy, and simmer, covered, for 10 minutes, stirring occasionally. Gravy is great over mashed potatoes.

Meatballs will have more flavor if prepared one day ahead. Reheat slowly over low heat, or in the top of a double boiler.

Per meatball: *Calories - 43; Total Fat - 1.8g;*
                     Saturated Fat - .6g; Cholesterol - 9.8mg

BROCCOLI PARTY SNACKS

Yield: 32 servings

2 to 2½ cups finely-chopped broccoli, stalks and flowerettes, about 12 oz.
½ cup finely-chopped onion
½ cup finely-chopped red pepper
½ teaspoon dried basil
½ teaspoon dried thyme
¼ teaspoon fresh ground black pepper
⅛ teaspoon garlic powder

3 tablespoons liquid Butter Buds, see page 48
½ cup grated fat-free mozzarella cheese alternative
½ cup freshly-grated Parmesan cheese
32 slices party pumpernickel bread, or 8 slices pumpernickel bread

If you have a food processor, chop broccoli stalks; set aside. Then chop the flowerettes.

In a covered skillet saute the broccoli and the next 6 ingredients in the Butter Buds, until the broccoli is crisp tender, or place in a 2 quart microwave dish; cover and cook on HIGH for 5 to 7 minutes, stirring once. Remove from heat; cool slightly; add cheeses; mix well.

Line a large cookie sheet with sprayed foil; spread bread slices with broccoli mixture.

Bake in a 425F oven for 5 minutes, then broil 3 inches from heat for 1 to 2 minutes, or until cheese is melted. If using regular pumpernickel bread slice into quarters.

Per serving: *Calories - 32; Total Fat - .8g;*
                   Saturated Fat - Tr; Cholesterol - 1mg;

Placed on 8 regular slices of uncut pumpernickel bread, this recipe becomes open faced sandwiches serving 4 for lunch.

Per slice: *Calories - 130; Total Fat - 3.2g;*
                 Saturated Fat - 1g; Cholesterol - 4mg

BEAN PATE

Yield: About 2 cups

1 16-ounce can chick peas -
  SAVE BEAN LIQUID
4 teaspoons bottled teriyaki marinade
½ tablespoon olive oil

1 tablespoon sesame seeds, toasted in
  small skillet until golden
½ teaspoon garlic powder
¼ teaspoon ground cumin

Drain the beans, reserving liquid. In a food processor or blender, add 2 tablespoons of the reserved liquid to the remaining ingredients, and blend until seeds are broken down.

With the motor running, gradually add the beans; blend until smooth. Add more bean liquid, if needed. Chill; serve with crackers, or Pita Toasts - see page 111.

Per teaspoon serving: *Calories - 7; Total Fat - Tr;*
                           Saturated Fat - Tr; Cholesterol - 0

HOT CRABMEAT DIP

Yield: About 1¼ cups

¾ cup 1% fat cottage cheese,
  whipped in blender
1 cup imitation crabmeat, finely
  chopped
2 tablespoons minced onion
1 tablespoon skim milk

½ tablespoon cream style
  horseradish
¼ teaspoon sugar
Dash of pepper
¼ teaspoon salt (opt.)
¼ cup sliced, blanched almonds
  (opt.)

In a medium mixing bowl, mix the first 8 ingredients together. Pile into an 8-inch pie plate; sprinkle with almonds.

Bake in a 375F oven for 15 to 20 minutes. Serve with crackers.

Per ½ tablespoon: *Calories - 8; Total Fat - Tr;*
                       Saturated Fat - Tr; Cholesterol - 1.2mg

BRUNCHES
AND LUNCHES

BRUNCHES AND LUNCHES

We especially love this section. What a variety! There are basic, but heart safe breakfasts, plus a few very romantic brunches such as Eggs and Champagne. There are meals which satisfy light eaters and those which pack enough oomph to be a main course at dinner.

Even if you have to "brown-bag-it" you are way ahead of the game. There are many healthy recipes which are easily carried off to work. Compare that to fast food emporiums where the high fat and cholesterol food is almost a guaranteed one-way-ticket to health problems.

BLT'S

Yield: 1 sandwich

If you really like bacon, lettuce and tomato sandwiches, as we do, but realize that bacon and real mayonnaise are "no-nos," try the following:

Toast two slices of your choice of bread. Spread one slice with fat and cholesterol free mayonnaise; sprinkle with BAC*OS (bacon flavored bits). Add tomato slices, lettuce, salt and pepper. Top with the other piece of toast. Result - flavor without the problem of high fat and cholesterol, and isn't that what it's all about.

Per sandwich: Calories - 198; Total Fat - 3.1g;
*   Saturated Fat - .6g; Cholesterol - 0*

BROCCOLI-MUSHROOM QUICHE

Yield: 4 servings

½ cup plus 2 tablespoons grated
  Swiss cheese alternative
½ cup grated cheddar cheese
  alternative
1 cup egg substitute
1½ cups skim milk
1 10-ounce package frozen chopped
  broccoli, cooked and well drained

1 cup sliced mushrooms
2 tablespoons grated onion
1 9-inch pie crust, chilled, page 246
Dash nutmeg
1 teaspoon salt (opt.)
¼ teaspoon pepper
1 tablespoon BAC*OS (bacon
  flavored bits)

In a bowl mix cheeses; set aside one-half mixture for top.

In another bowl, combine egg substitute, ½ cheese mixture and milk. Add broccoli, mushrooms and onion. Mix well.

Pour mixture into unbaked pie crust. Sprinkle with nutmeg, salt, pepper, BAC*OS and top with remaining cheese mixture.

Bake at 425F for 15 minutes. Reduce heat to 325F; bake 40 minutes more, or until a knife inserted into center of quiche comes out clean.

Per serving: Calories - 322; Total Fat - 13.7g;
*   Saturated Fat - 3.2g; Cholesterol - 0*

BAKED BURGERS

Yield: 4 servings

1 pound freshly ground turkey
½ cup sliced mushrooms
1¼ cups cream of mushroom
 soup, see page 118

⅓ cup white wine
¼ teaspoon black pepper
1 teaspoon worcestershire-wine sauce
2 English muffins, split and toasted

Make 4 patties with the turkey; place in a casserole dish just large enough to hold them. Sprinkle mushrooms over and around.

In a mixing bowl combine the soup, wine, pepper and worcestershire-wine sauce. Pour over burgers; cover and bake at 350F for 30 to 35 minutes, or until they are done. Spoon sauce over burgers, and let sit, covered, for 5 minutes. Serve on English muffin halves.

Per serving: *Calories - 295; Total Fat - 6.5g;*
                   Saturated Fat - 2g; Cholesterol - 85.5mg

CHEESE PUFF

Yield: 4 servings

6 slices stale sandwich bread,
 crusts removed
¾ cup grated cheddar cheese
 alternative
1 small onion, finely chopped
1 tablespoon liquid Butter Buds,
 see page 48

½ cup egg substitute
1 cup skim milk
½ teaspoon Dijon mustard
½ teaspoon worcestershire-wine
 sauce
1 tablespoon chopped parsley
Dash of pepper

Arrange 3 slices of bread, cut into thirds, in the bottom of a well-sprayed 1½-quart baking dish. Sprinkle with the cheese; add the other 3 slices of bread.

In a small covered non-stick skillet, saute the onion in the Butter Buds until softened. Meanwhile, in a medium-size bowl, whisk the remaining ingredients together; mix in the onions, and pour over the bread. Chill the puff, covered, for at least 1 hour. Bake, uncovered, in a 325F oven for 60 minutes or until golden.

Per serving: *Calories - 201; Total Fat - 6.1g;*
                   Saturated Fat - 1.7g; Cholesterol - 1mg

ITALIAN BROILED CHEESE SANDWICHES
Yield: 4 servings

4 1-inch thick slices Italian bread
4 tablespoons marinara sauce
4 slices turkey salami

2 slices mozzarella cheese
   alternative
Crushed oregano

Place on each slice of bread: One tablespoon marinara sauce, spread evenly; one slice turkey salami; cheese to cover; sprinkle of oregano.

Place sandwiches on a foil-lined, sprayed cookie sheet and broil until cheese melts and begins to brown.

Per serving: *Calories - 214; Total Fat 7.9g;*
                  Saturated Fat - 2.9g; Cholesterol - 27.5mg

COOL SUMMER SALAD
Yield: 4 servings

1 cup chick peas (garbanzo beans),
   well drained
2 green onions, sliced
½ cup celery, chopped
1 small red or green pepper, chopped
¼ cup pineapple tidbits, well-drained
1 small zucchini, coarsely chopped

¼ cup sliced ripe olives
½ cup feta cheese, crumbled
⅓ cup oil-free Italian salad
   dressing
4 6-inch whole wheat pita breads
Lettuce leaves

Combine first 8 salad ingredients well. Mix in salad dressing. Cover and chill for 2 hours.

Cut pita breads in half, line with lettuce leaves; fill with salad mixture.

Per pita half: *Calories - 174; Total Fat - 4.8g;*
                    Saturated Fat - 2.3g; Cholesterol - 12.5mg

SPECIAL CHICKEN SALAD

Yield: 4 servings

2 chicken breasts, skinned	1 small onion, quartered
6 to 8 celery leaves	¼ teaspoon whole peppercorns
½ teaspoon salt (opt.)	1 small carrot, coarsely chopped

Put chicken into a small Dutch oven. Cover with water; add remaining ingredients and bring to a boil. Simmer for 30 minutes, or until juices run clear when chicken is pricked with a fork. Cool breasts in broth; remove meat from bones, and chop coarsely.

Strain liquid, and refrigerate overnight; skim fat from top and freeze broth for later use.

SALAD

¼ cup sliced ripe olives, drained	1 tablespoon juice from mandarin
¼ cup toasted slivered almonds,	oranges
see page 49 (opt.)	1 teaspoon lemon juice
¼ cup chopped green onion	½ teaspoon hot curry powder
4 tablespoons fat and cholesterol-	½ (11-ounce) can mandarin
free mayonnaise	oranges, reserve liquid

In a large bowl combine the first 3 ingredients; mix in the chicken pieces. In a separate bowl, mix the next 4 ingredients together. Combine with the chicken mixture and refrigerate for several hours.

At serving time make a bed of lettuce on salad plates. Spoon salad onto lettuce; top each with 2 tablespoons of well-drained mandarin orange sections.

Per serving: *Calories - 166; Total Fat - 5.7g;*
Saturated Fat - 1g; Cholesterol - 36.5mg

CRAB AND RICE SALAD

Yield: 4 servings

½ pound imitation crabmeat,
  chopped
1 cup frozen peas, blanched for 1
  minute, drained
1 cup cooked long grain rice
½ cup diced celery
2 green onions, chopped

1 teaspoon hot curry powder
¼ teaspoon sugar
¼ teaspoon black pepper
¼ teaspoon lemon juice
⅓ cup fat and cholesterol-
  free mayonnaise
2 teaspoons capers, drained

Combine all ingredients; chill for several hours or overnight.

Serve on a bed of lettuce.

Per serving: *Calories - 148; Total Fat - Tr;*
                  Saturated Fat - Tr; Cholesterol - 5mg

HOT CRAB SALAD

Yield: 4 servings

½ pound imitation crabmeat,
  chopped into small pieces
½ cup chopped green pepper
¼ cup chopped onion
½ cup diced celery
¼ cup toasted slivered almonds,
  see page 49 (opt.)
½ teaspoon worcestershire-
  wine sauce

½ cup fat and cholesterol free
  mayonnaise
¼ teaspoon salt (opt.)
Dash pepper
8 drops Tabasco sauce
½ cup bread crumbs
2 tablespoons liquid Butter Buds,
  see page 48

Combine all ingredients except the bread crumbs. Fill 4 sprayed ramekins with the mixture; top with the bread crumbs; drizzle with Butter Buds.

Bake at 350F for 30 minutes.

Per serving: *Calories - 169; Total Fat - 2.1g;*
                  Saturated Fat - Tr; Cholesterol - 10.6mg

EGGPLANT SUBMARINE SANDWICHES

Yield: 2 servings

1 eggplant, ½ to ¾ pounds, peeled
  and sliced ¼-inch thick
¼ cup flour for dredging, seasoned
  with salt, pepper & garlic powder
¼ cup egg substitute
2 tablespoons water

½ cup seasoned bread crumbs
Vegetable oil spray
2 small submarine or hoagie rolls
½ cup marinara sauce
4 tablespoons grated mozzarella
  cheese alternative

Place eggplant slices on a large plate; salt them and cover with paper towel. Weight down with another plate, and let set for 30 minutes. Pat the eggplant dry with a paper towel. Dip slices in seasoned flour, then into a mixture of egg substitute and water; finally into the bread crumbs. Place slices on cookie sheet sprayed with vegetable oil, and bake at 375F for 10 to 15 minutes or until golden.

Slice the rolls nearly through; open rolls. Place 3 tablespoons marinara sauce in each roll. Line roll with eggplant slices; drizzle 2 tablespoons sauce over, and top with the cheese. Bake rolls in 375F oven until hot and bubbly.

Per sandwich: *Calories - 466; Total Fat - 11.1g;*
                     Saturated Fat - 4g; Cholesterol - 6.8mg

EGGS AND CHAMPAGNE

Yield: 2 servings

2 shallots, finely chopped
½ red bell pepper, finely chopped
3 tablespoons liquid Butter Buds,
  see page 48
1 tablespoon chopped parsley

1 tablespoon champagne or
  sherry
¼ pound imitation crabmeat,
  finely chopped
¾ cup egg substitute

In a covered, non-stick, medium skillet, saute the shallots and pepper in the Butter Buds, over low heat, until softened. Add the parsley and wine. Add crabmeat; heat thoroughly. Add the egg substitute and scramble the mixture. When eggs are firm, serve over toast points with a glass of champagne - by the fireplace.

Per serving, without the toast: *Calories - 150; Total Fat - 4g;*
                                       Saturated Fat - .6g; Cholesterol - 10mg

EGG SALAD

Yield: 2 salads or 4 sandwiches

1 cup egg substitute
2 whole eggs, hard boiled,
  yolks discarded
¼ teaspoon salt (opt.)
Dash white pepper

1 teaspoon sugar
1 teaspoon Dijon mustard
2 tablespoons 1% fat cottage cheese
3 tablespoons fat and cholesterol-
  free mayonnaise

Pour egg substitute into a heavy, non-stick, 8-inch skillet. Cover and cook over very low heat for 10 minutes. Remove from heat and allow to stand, covered, for 10 minutes more. Chop egg whites and cooked egg substitute in a small mixing bowl. Add remaining ingredients; mix well. Chill several hours or overnight.

Serve on a bed of lettuce as a salad for 2 people or make into 4 sandwiches.

Per salad serving: *Calories - 117; Total Fat - Tr;*
                        Saturated Fat - Tr; Cholesterol - 1.2mg;

Per sandwich: *Calories - 198; Total Fat - .7g;*
                        Saturated Fat - Tr; Cholesterol - .6mg

POACHED EGGS WITH BEARNAISE SAUCE

Yield: 2 servings

2 large eggs
3 cups water
¼ cup vinegar
Pepper, to taste
1 teaspoon low-sodium dry beef bouillon

2 English muffins, halved and
  toasted
½ cup Bearnaise Sauce, see
  page 224

Crack eggs into 2 shallow dishes; let stand for 15 minutes. Combine the water, vinegar, pepper and bouillon in a large saucepan. Bring to boil; gently slide eggs into water; be careful to keep them separated. Bring back to boil; turn burner off; cover and cook until eggs reach the desired doneness. Lift out with a slotted spoon; place each on a toasted English muffin half; pour heated Bearnaise Sauce over. Butter other half English muffin; serve on the side with jam.

Per serving: *Calories - 286; Total Fat - 10.9g;*
                  Saturated Fat - 2.4g; Cholesterol - 213mg

FRENCH TOAST

Yield: 4 servings

1 cup egg substitute
⅓ cup skim milk
¼ teaspoon sugar
⅛ teaspoon nutmeg

Dash of salt (opt.)
8 slices bread, preferably Italian
Vegetable oil spray

Combine first 5 ingredients in a shallow dish; mix well. Dip bread into egg mixture, and coat well on both sides. Spray skillet; fry bread until golden on each side. Serve with syrup, honey, jelly, etc.

Per serving without topping: *Calories - 166; Total Fat - 2.1g; Saturated Fat - .7g; Cholesterol - Tr*

KLYDE'S HOT DOGS

Yield: 6 servings

6 95% fat-free beef hot dogs
6 hot dog rolls
Vegetable oil spray

½ cup chopped onion
2 tablespoons sweet relish
3 slices Swiss cheese alternative

In a skillet or in the microwave oven cook the hot dogs until just warmed through. Spray the inside of each roll; divide the onion and relish among the rolls. Add a hot dog, and top with strips of cheese.

Place the filled rolls in a shallow baking dish; bake in 350F oven until the cheese melts and rolls are golden, or microwave on HIGH until cheese melts.

Per serving: *Calories - 235; Total Fat - 9.7g; Saturated Fat - 4.3g; Cholesterol - 20mg*

ITALIAN SUBMARINE SANDWICHES
Yield: 2 servings

2 medium sub rolls
Olive oil
Salt (opt.) and pepper, to taste
Garlic powder
3 slices turkey salami
2 slices Swiss cheese alternative

½ onion, thinly sliced
½ tomato, thinly sliced
¼ green bell pepper, cut into strips
2 pepperoncini, cut into strips
4 lettuce leaves, shredded

Split rolls lengthwise; do not cut through. Sprinkle inside with olive oil and dust with garlic, salt and pepper. Lay on the salami, cheese, onions and tomatoes. Add peppers and lettuce.

Hint: For an added treat, place sandwiches in a brown bag; seal top and heat in a 350F oven for about 5 minutes or until cheese melts.

Per sandwich: *Calories - 308; Total Fat - 11.8g;*
Saturated Fat - 3g; Cholesterol - 30mg

LUNCHEON JELLO SALAD
Yield: 4 servings

1 3-ounce pkg. sugar-free lemon jello
½ teaspoon salt (opt.)
1 cup boiling water
¾ cup cold water
2 tablespoons cider vinegar
⅓ cup mock sour cream, see page 51
⅓ cup fat and cholesterol free-
  mayonnaise
½ teaspoon worcestershire-wine sauce

1 teaspoon grated onion
Dash of cayenne pepper
⅓ cup chopped celery
⅓ cup chopped sweet pickle
1 cup blanched green peas, drained
1 2-ounce jar diced pimento,
  drained
1 6½-ounce can tuna, packed in
  water, drained

In a large mixing bowl, dissolve jello and salt in boiling water. Add the cold water and vinegar; chill until very thick. Fold in remaining ingredients; pour into a sprayed 1½-quart mold. Chill until firm. Unmold and serve on a bed of lettuce.

Per serving: *Calories - 135; Total Fat - 1.7g;*
Saturated Fat - .7g; Cholesterol - 30mg

MACARONI-VEGETABLE-HAM SALAD
Yield: 4 servings

¾ cup corkscrew macaroni,
  cooked per package instructions
½ cup blanched frozen peas, drained
1 cup cooked very lean ham chunks

¼ cup chopped green pepper
2 finely-chopped green onions
1 medium tomato, chopped
¼ cup black olives, chopped

Mix all ingredients together in a 2-quart bowl. Cover and refrigerate for 2 hours, or overnight. Serve on a bed of lettuce.

Suggested salad dressings - Greek style salad dressing, ranch, creamy Italian, or any other low-fat, or fat-free dressing of your choice.

Per serving without salad dressing: Calories - 199; Total Fat - 6.3g;
Saturated Fat - 1.8g; Cholesterol - 22mg

MAN-SIZE OPEN-FACE SANDWICHES
Yield: 2 servings

2 1-inch thick slices of Italian or
  sourdough bread
3 slices low-fat muenster cheese
2 tablespoons BAC*OS (bacon
  flavored bits)
4 thin slices smoked turkey
6 slices tomato

2 green onions, sliced lengthwise
  and cut into 2-inch pieces
4 mushrooms, thinly sliced
⅓ cup alfalfa sprouts
2 tablespoons oil-free Italian
  dressing
Salt and pepper, to taste

On each slice of bread, place 1½ slices cheese, and bake at 425F for 4 to 5 minutes, or until cheese melts. Remove to a plate; add remaining ingredients in order, topped with 1 tablespoon Italian dressing, salt and pepper. Serve with a fork and a sharp knife.

Per sandwich: Calories - 380; Total Fat - 11.2g;
Saturated Fat - 1.7g; Cholesterol - 23mg

NO PROBLEM PANCAKES

Yield: 4 servings

1½ cups white flour
½ cup oat flour, or whole
  wheat flour
1 tablespoon baking powder
½ cup egg substitute

2 teaspoons sugar or 1 packet
  sugar substitute
1¾ to 2 cups skim milk, or until
  desired consistency is reached
3 tablespoons canola oil

In a medium bowl, whisk all ingredients together until they are smooth. Spray a griddle, or heavy skillet with vegetable oil spray; heat griddle and ladle on 4 small pancakes. Cook until golden brown on both sides. Serve with your favorite topping.

Keeps for days refrigerated in a tightly sealed container.

Per serving without topping: *Calories - 365; Total Fat - 5.8g;*
Saturated Fat - .9g; Cholesterol - 2mg

PASTA CASSEROLE

Yield: 6 servings

8-ounce package eggless noodles
½ cup slivered almonds
½ cup 1% fat cottage cheese
½ cup mock sour cream, see page 51
¼ teaspoon garlic powder
2 tablespoons white wine

1¼ cups homemade cream of
  mushroom soup, see page 118
½ cup fresh bread crumbs
3 tablespoons liquid Butter Buds,
  see page 48

Cook noodles as directed. Put half into a sprayed 2-quart casserole. In a medium bowl blend the next 6 ingredients together. Spread the mixture over the noodles. Add the remaining noodles; sprinkle with bread crumbs and drizzle with the Butter Buds. Bake at 350F for 25 to 30 minutes.

Per serving: *Calories 329; Total Fat - 10.3g;*
Saturated Fat - 1.1g; Cholesterol - 4mg

CONFETTI POCKET BREAD SANDWICHES

Yield: 4 servings

1 packet sugar substitute
1½ cups 1% fat cottage cheese
2 green onions, sliced
1 2-ounce jar diced pimentos, well
   drained
¼ cup sliced black olives
¼ teaspoon salt (opt.)

¾ cup each, uncooked zucchini
   and yellow squash, finely
   chopped and well drained
⅛ teaspoon black pepper
2 tablespoons oil-free Italian
   salad dressing
4 4-inch whole wheat pita breads

Drain any excess liquid from the cottage cheese. Combine all ingredients in a serving bowl. Chill at least one hour. Cut pita breads in half, and fill each half with the mixture.

Per serving: *Calories - 276; Total Fat - 4.8g;*
                    Saturated Fat - .9g; Cholesterol - 3.8mg

PROSNA (SERBIAN DISH)

Yield: 4 servings

1 pound 1% fat cottage cheese
¼ teaspoon pepper
¼ teaspoon salt (opt.)
1 egg, slightly beaten
½ cup egg substitute
6 slices lite yellow American cheese,
   shredded

2 tablespoons liquid Butter Buds,
   see page 48
3 tablespoons flour
1 small onion, finely chopped
1 10-ounce package broccoli or
   spinach, thawed, well drained

Blend all ingredients in a large mixing bowl; pour into a sprayed 2-quart baking dish.

Bake at 350F for 1 hour or until set and golden brown on top.

Per serving: *Calories - 201; Total Fat - 8.4g;*
                    Saturated Fat - 2.4g; Cholesterol - 55.8mg

SHRIMP PASTA SALAD

Yield: 4 servings

12 ounces cooked shrimp, halved
4 ounces linguini, cooked as directed
2 ounces snow peas, blanched one
   minute, drained
2 green onions, chopped

1 medium tomato, peeled, chopped
   and drained
1 stalk celery, coarsely chopped
2 tablespoons green bell pepper,
   coarsely chopped

Combine shrimp, linguini and vegetables; mix well.

DRESSING

2 tablespoons olive oil
2 tablespoons chopped parsley
¼ cup white wine vinegar
⅛ teaspoon Tabasco sauce

⅛ teaspoon garlic powder
¼ teaspoon dried oregano
½ teaspoon dried basil
Salt (opt.) and pepper to taste

Combine salad dressing ingredients; toss lightly with the pasta mixture. Chill for several hours or overnight.

Per serving: Calories - 274; Total Fat - 9.2g;
Saturated Fat - 1.3g; Cholesterol - 110mg

TACO SALAD

Yield: 2 servings

½ pound freshly-ground turkey
1 tablespoon liquid Butter Buds,
  see page 48
¼ cup chopped onion
1 teaspoon chili powder
¼ teaspoon ground cumin
¼ teaspoon dried oregano

Dash of garlic powder
¼ teaspoon salt (opt.)
1 can (16-ounce) kidney beans,
  drained and rinsed
1 tablespoon House Dressing, see
  page 223
2 cups shredded lettuce

Cook turkey meat in Butter Buds with the next 6 ingredients. Stir in the beans and the House Dressing.

Place a bed of shredded lettuce on each plate; add meat and bean mixture; finish with your choice of the following toppings:

Chopped tomato
Coarsely-chopped onion
Crushed tortilla chips

Shredded cheddar cheese alternative
Salsa, see page 233
Mock sour cream, see page 51

Per serving, without toppings: *Calories - 480; Total Fat - 13.7g;*
Saturated Fat - 3.5g; Cholesterol - 98mg

TUNA MELTS

Yield: 4 servings

1 6½-ounce can tuna, packed in
  water, drained
4 slices Swiss cheese alternative,
  grated
2 tablespoons onion, finely chopped

½ cup sweet pickle relish
½ cup fat and cholesterol-free
  mayonnaise
Dash of salt and pepper
4 hamburger buns

Combine first 6 ingredients; spread on hamburger bun halves. Broil 3 to 5 minutes or until hot and bubbly.

Per serving: *Calories - 314; Total Fat - 7.1g;*
Saturated Fat - 2g; Cholesterol - 26mg

VEGETABLE-PASTA SALAD

Yield: 4 servings

1 cup tri-colored macaroni,
cooked and drained
2 small carrots, diced, parboiled
and drained
½ cup frozen peas, parboiled
and drained
2 green onions, chopped

1 2-ounce jar diced pimento,
drained
1 can (16-ounce) kidney beans,
drained and rinsed
½ cup celery, diced
2 tablespoons chopped parsley

Combine the above salad ingredients in a 2-quart bowl.

DRESSING

¼ cup oil-free Italian salad
dressing
2 tablespoons fat and cholesterol
free mayonnaise

⅛ teaspoon dried marjoram
⅛ teaspoon black pepper
Cayenne pepper, to taste

Mix the dressing ingredients together and pour over the salad. Mix gently but thoroughly. Refrigerate, covered, overnight.

Serve on a bed of lettuce; garnish with tomato wedges.

Per serving: *Calories - 242; Total Fat - 1.2g;*
Saturated Fat - Tr; Cholesterol - 0

WEEK-END WAFFLES

Yield: 6 7-inch waffles

1 cup all-purpose flour	¼ teaspoon salt (opt.)
1 cup whole wheat flour	⅓ cup light corn oil spread
2 teaspoons baking powder	1½ cups skim milk
2 teaspoons sugar	¼ cup egg substitute
½ teaspoon baking soda	1 tablespoon canola oil

In a large bowl, mix the dry ingredients together; cut in spread with a pastry blender, or two forks, until mix is crumbly. Add the milk, egg substitute and canola oil. Beat with an electric beater until smooth. Batter will be thick. Best when made up the night before.

Preheat waffle iron following manufacturer's directions. Pour about ⅔ cup batter onto grid. Close and bake until done to your choosing.

Serve with your favorite topping.

Per waffle, without topping:　　　*Calories - 230; Total Fat - 8.3g;*
　　　　　　　　　　　　　　　　Saturated Fat - 1.4g; Cholesterol - .9mg

PASTA SALAD WITH ARTICHOKES

Yield: 6 servings

6 ounces uncooked spaghetti
1 6-ounce jar marinated artichokes,
   drained, reserving liquid
¾ cup sliced fresh zucchini
⅔ cup shredded carrots
2 slices turkey salami, cut into strips
¼ cup freshly-grated parmesan cheese

2 tablespoons Balsamic vinegar
1 teaspoon dry mustard
½ teaspoon dried oregano
½ teaspoon dried basil
Garlic powder to taste
Pepper to taste

Break spaghetti in half and cook following package instructions (no salt); drain and cool.

Chop artichokes and combine, in a large bowl with the spaghetti, zucchini, carrots, salami and parmesan cheese. In a glass jar combine the artichoke liquid and the remaining 6 ingredients. Cover jar and shake to blend. Pour over salad and toss gently to coat. Cover and refrigerate for at least 2 hours.

Per Serving: *Calories - 180; Total Fat - 4.9g;*
              Saturated Fat - 2.2g; Cholesterol - 14mg

SHRIMP, CRAB AND ANGEL'S HAIR PASTA SALAD

Yield: 2 servings ·

3 ounces angel's hair pasta
4 ounces cooked shrimp, coarsely
  chopped
4 ounces imitation crab meat,
  coarsely chopped

½ green bell pepper, chopped
2 small stalks celery, chopped
2 green onions, chopped
1 tablespoon regular onion, chopped
1 teaspoon capers, drained

Cook pasta in lightly salted boiling water for 5 minutes; drain and chop pasta into bite-size lengths. Mix vegetables and capers with the seafood.

DRESSING

2 tablespoons cholesterol-free
  mayonnaise
3 to 4 tablespoons reduced calorie, or
  fat-free French dressing

¼ teaspoon lemon juice
Dash of pepper
Dash of garlic powder

Whisk dressing ingredients together in a small bowl. Stir into salad, mixing well; chill several hours or overnight.

Per Serving: *Calories - 362; Total Fat - 9g;*
                    Saturated Fat - 1.6g; Cholesterol - 83mg

ITALIAN SAUSAGE

Yield: 20 patties

3 pounds freshly-ground turkey
  (preferably ground fine)
1 tablespoon salt
1 tablespoon fennel seed, crushed

1½ tablespoons paprika
½ teaspoon black pepper
½ teaspoon garlic powder
1 teaspoon red pepper flakes

In a large bowl combine all ingredients; mix well. Form the mix into patties. Package separately and freeze until needed.

To cook, spray a non-stick skillet. Over medium heat add thawed sausage patties and cook slowly until cooked through, turning once or twice.

Per patty: *Calories 119; Total Fat 3.6g;*
                  Saturated Fat - 1.2g; Cholesterol - 52.4mg

MAIN DISH TUNA/LIMA BEAN SALAD

Yield: 4 servings

1 garlic clove
1 9-ounce package frozen baby
  Lima beans
½ cup diced carrots, steamed until
  crisp tender
2 hard boiled eggs, yolks discarded,
  whites coasely-chopped
1 tablespoon capers, drained

2 tablespoons chopped green onion
1 6½-ounce can tuna packed in
  water, drained and flaked
½ teaspoon salt (opt.)
Dash of pepper
½ cup fat and cholesterol-free
  mayonnaise
2 cups shredded lettuce

Make a couple of slashes in the garlic, and cook with the Lima beans in a little water for 12 minutes; add the chopped carrots, and continue cooking for 3 minutes more; drain and discard garlic.

Meanwhile, combine the remaining ingredients in a large mixing bowl; add the beans and carrots; mix well and refrigerate, covered, for several hours.

Per Serving: *Calories - 184; Total Fat - 1.5g;*
         Saturated Fat - Tr; Cholesterol - 27mg

TABBOULEH IN POCKET BREAD

Yield: 4 servings

½ cup uncooked bulgur wheat
1¼ cups boiling water
¾ cup cucumber, seeded and
  chopped
1 medium tomato, chopped
½ cup chopped parsley
2 green onions, chopped
1 pepperoncini pepper, drained
  and chopped
4 to 6 slices cucumber pickles, chopped
8 fresh mint leaves, chopped

¼ teaspoon freshly-ground pepper
¼ teaspoon dried oregano
Dash garlic powder
Dash cayenne pepper
2 tablespoons lemon juice
2 tablespoons olive oil
8 teaspoons fat and cholesterol-
  free mayonnaise
2 slices cholesterol-free Swiss
  cheese alternative
Lettuce leaves to line bread
4 6-inch pita breads

In a small bowl stir the boiling water into the bulgur; let stand, covered for 1 hour. Drain any excess water. If you prefer softer bulgur, cook, covered, on high in the microwave for 2 minutes after the 1-hour sitting time. Again, drain any excess liquid.

In a bowl combine the next 13 ingredients. Add the bulgur and mix well. Refrigerate overnight.

Cut pita breads in half; spread inside of each half with 1 teaspoon mayonnaise; add ½ piece cheese and some lettuce; add a generous helping of the tabbouleh. Enjoy!

Per ½ pita half: Calories - 153; Total Fat - 4.2g;
Saturated Fat - .6g; Cholesterol - 0

LENTIL BURRITOS

Yield: 4 servings

1½ cups dried lentil beans
1½ to 2½ cups water
2 cups low-sodium beef bouillon
1 bay leaf
¼ cup chopped onion
1 garlic clove, pressed
1 teaspoon chili powder
½ teaspoon salt (opt.)
¼ teaspoon dried oregano
¼ teaspoon cumin

¼ teaspoon dried thyme
8 burrito or taco shells
1½ cups shredded lettuce
½ cup green onion, chopped
½ cup grated cheddar cheese
  alternative
1 tomato, coarsely chopped
1 cup dark kidney beans, rinsed and
  drained
¼ cup salsa, see page 233, or bottled

Wash and pick over the lentil beans. In a Dutch oven place the beans in water with the next 9 ingredients, and bring to a boil. Cover, reduce heat and simmer 1½ hours; add additional water if necessary. Discard bay leaf.

Warm burritos; spoon lentils onto each burrito; top with lettuce, onion, cheese, tomato, beans and salsa. Roll up burrito.

Note: Freeze remaining bean mixture in 8-ounce containers for future use.

Per burrito: *Calories - 179; Total Fat - 4.5g;*
          Saturated Fat - .9g; Cholesterol - Tr

CHEESE PIZZA

Yield: 8 slices

Vegetable oil spray
½ recipe pizza dough, see page 100
1 cup pizza sauce, see page 233

1½ cups grated mozzarella
  cheese alternative

Lightly spray a 12-inch pizza pan, and shape dough in bottom. Make raised edges to hold sauce. Cover evenly with the pizza sauce; top with the cheese.

Spray lightly with vegetable oil spray, and bake at 450F for 25 to 30 minutes, or until browned.

Per slice: *Calories - 162; Total Fat - 4.9g;*
         Saturated Fat - 1.3g; Cholesterol - 0

BREADS

BREADS

Although many of the store-bought breads are now being made with more awareness toward the wholesome and natural, it's still very comforting to know-for-sure that only heart-safe ingredients have been used. For this reason we suggest you bake more breads at home. The aroma of baking bread permeating the whole house is wonderful and definitely nostalgic.

The Beer Bread recipe is especially nice with shellfish, and the Jamaican Corn or Zucchini Muffins compliment meatless entrees, as well as luncheon salads and soups. Of course nothing can beat Old-Fashioned Loaf Bread.

BANANA BREAD

Yield: 16 slices

1¾ cups sifted flour
2 teaspoons baking powder
¼ teaspoon baking soda
½ teaspoon salt
⅔ cup sugar

½ cup egg substitute
⅓ cup canola oil
1 cup mashed bananas (about
   3 bananas)

In a large mixing bowl, sift dry ingredients together. In a smaller bowl combine egg substitute, oil and bananas; add to dry ingredients. Beat until smooth. Pour into sprayed 8½x4½x2½-inch loaf pan. Bake at 350F for 1 hour.

Per slice: *Calories - 139; Total Fat - 4.9g;*
                 Saturated Fat - Tr; Cholesterol - 0

BEER BREAD

Yield: 16 slices

3 cups self-rising flour
3 tablespoons sugar
1 12-ounce can light beer
   (at room temperature)

3 tablespoons liquid Butter Buds,
   see page 48

In a large bowl, combine the flour and sugar; mix well. Gradually add the beer, stirring just until combined. Pour into a sprayed and floured 9x5x3-inch pan, and bake at 350F for 55 to 60 minutes, or until done.

Brush the top with the Butter Buds; cool loaf for 10 minutes; remove from pan to a wire rack to finish cooling.

Per slice: *Calories - 99; Total Fat - .7g;*
                 Saturated Fat - Tr; Cholesterol - 0

CARROT BREAD

Yield: 16 slices

1½ cups flour
1 teaspoon baking powder
1 teaspoon baking soda
1 teaspoon cinnamon
¼ teaspoon allspice
¼ teaspoon ground cloves
¼ teaspoon ground nutmeg

½ teaspoon salt
6 tablespoons canola oil
1 cup sugar
½ cup egg substitute
1 cup grated carrots
½ cup chopped pecans (opt.)

In a large mixing bowl, sift the first 8 ingredients together. Combine the oil and sugar in another bowl, and beat in the egg substitute. Add the dry mix; beat until smooth. Stir in the carrots and nuts. Pour into a sprayed and floured 9x5x3-inch loaf pan; bake at 350F for 55 to 60 minutes.

Per slice: *Calories - 139; Total Fat - 5.4g;*
                 Saturated Fat - Tr; Cholesterol - 0

CASSEROLE BREAD

Yield: 12 slices

1 envelope active dry yeast
1 cup water (105F to 115F)
3 cups all-purpose flour
1 cup oat or whole wheat flour

2 packets sugar substitute
2 teaspoons salt
3 tablespoons liquid Butter Buds,
    see page 48

Dissolve yeast in the water. Combine the flours, sugar substitute and salt in a large mixing bowl; add the yeast and its water; mix well. Gradually add more water to make a soft dough; mix well. Cover and allow to rise until double in size. A closed oven with its light on works well. This takes about 1½ to 1¾ hours.

Flour hands and beat down the dough. Knead dough a few times; divide into thirds. Place in 3 sprayed 20-ounce round casserole dishes. Cover; let rise again until double in size. This takes about 60 minutes.

Bake in 400F oven 20 to 25 minutes. Remove breads from baking dishes; brush with Butter Buds; let cool on racks.

Per slice: *Calories - 148; Total Fat - 1.2g;*
                 Saturated Fat - Tr; Cholesterol - 0

CRANBERRY BREAD

Yield: 16 slices

2 cups all-purpose flour
½ teaspoon salt
1½ teaspoons baking powder
½ teaspoon baking soda
1 cup sugar

Juice and rind of one orange
2 tablespoons canola oil
¼ cup egg substitute
½ cup chopped pecans
1½ cups chopped cranberries

In a large mixing bowl, sift the first 5 ingredients together. In a measuring cup, combine the orange juice, grated rind, oil and enough boiling water to measure ¾ cup.

Add the egg substitute and the liquid mixture to the dry mix; stir gently.

Fold in the nuts and cranberries. Spoon into a sprayed and floured 8½ x 4½ x 2½-inch loaf pan, pushing up the edges. Bake one hour at 325F.

Per slice: *Calories - 171; Total Fat - 6.5g;*
                  Saturated Fat - .5g; Cholesterol - 0

SOFT DINNER ROLLS

Yield: 2 dozen

1 cup scalded skim milk
4 tablespoons light corn oil spread
2 hefty tablespoons sugar
1 teaspoon salt
1 envelope active dry yeast

2 tablespoon hot water (105F-115F)
¼ cup egg substitute
3 cups all-purpose flour
¼ cup liquid Butter Buds, see
    page 48

In a large bowl, combine the first 4 ingredients. Dissolve the yeast in the hot water and add to the bowl. Add the egg substitute; mix well. Gradually add the flour; beat until smooth; cover; let rise, in oven with the light on, until doubled in size, about 1½ hours.

Stir down dough, and put 2 spoonsful in each greased section of a muffin pan. Cover and let rise for about 40 minutes, or until double in size. Bake in a 350F oven for about 12 minutes, or until rolls are brown on top. Brush tops with Butter Buds; cool and serve.

Per roll: *Calories - 80; Total Fat - 1.9g;*
                 Saturated Fat - Tr; Cholesterol - Tr

JAMAICAN CORN MUFFINS

Yield: 12 muffins

1 cup all-purpose flour, sifted
¾ cup yellow corn meal
½ teaspoon salt
2½ teaspoons baking powder
½ cup sugar

¼ teaspoon cinnamon
¼ cup egg substitute
1 cup skim milk
½ teaspoon vanilla
¼ cup canola oil

In a large bowl, sift the first 6 ingredients together. Add remaining ingredients, stirring rapidly until batter is well mixed.

Fill sprayed muffin tins ⅔ full.

Bake at 425F for 20 minutes or until golden brown.

Per muffin: Calories - 124; Total Fat - 4.8g;
Saturated Fat - Tr; Cholesterol - Tr

KATHRYN'S BREAD

Yield: 3 loaves (48 slices)

2 cups boiling water
1 cup oatmeal, uncooked
⅓ cup bran
⅓ cup wheat germ
2 teaspoons salt
3 tablespoons liquid Butter Buds,
  see page 48

1 cup scalded skim milk
½ cup light molasses
¼ cup honey
2 packages active dry yeast,
  dissolved in ¾ cup 110F water
2½ cups whole wheat flour
5 to 6 cups all-purpose flour

Mix first 6 ingredients together in a large bowl; let cool. Add milk, molasses, honey and yeast. Slowly stir in the whole wheat flour. Add enough all-purpose flour to make dough elastic and "kneadable." Place in a clean, sprayed bowl, cover with a tea towel and let rise in a warm place until double in size.

Punch down; put dough into 3 sprayed 8½x 4½x 2½-inch bread pans. Again let rise, covered, until double in size. Bake at 375F for 35 to 40 minutes.

Per slice: Calories - 104; Total Fat - .6g;
Saturated Fat - Tr; Cholesterol - Tr

MAYONNAISE MUFFINS

Yield: 6 muffins

1½ cups self-rising flour   3 tablespoons fat and cholesterol-
¾ cup skim milk   free mayonnaise

In a large bowl, combine all ingredients; stir until smooth. Fill each cup of a sprayed six-cup muffin pan ⅔ full. Bake at 425F for 10 to 12 minutes.

Per muffin: *Calories - 125; Total Fat - .5g;*
                        Saturated Fat - Tr; Cholesterol - .5mg

BUD'S MASHED POTATO BREAD

Yield: 2 loaves (32 slices)

3 servings Instant Mashed Potatoes,   1 tablespoon salt
  prepared with no butter or seasonings   7½ to 8 cups unbleached flour
2 packages active dry yeast   ½ cup liquid Butter Buds, see
2 cups warm water (110F)   page 48
¼ cup sugar

In a large bowl ,mix the first 5 ingredients together. Add the flour slowly, mixing well. Place in a sprayed bowl, cover with a tea towel; put in oven with light on. Let rise until double in size, about 1½ hours.

Punch down and divide between 2 sprayed 8½x 4½x 2½-inch loaf pans. Bake for 40 minutes in a 350F oven. Remove from oven and pour Butter Buds over.

Per slice: *Calories - 129; Total Fat - 1.3g;*
                      Saturated Fat - Tr; Cholesterol - 0

ZUCCHINI MUFFINS

Yield: 12 large muffins

2 cups all-purpose flour
3 tablespoons sugar
1 tablespoon baking powder
1 teaspoon cinnamon
½ teaspoon salt
¼ cup egg substitute

1 cup skim milk
¼ cup canola oil
½ cup shredded zucchini, well
  drained
¼ cup finely-chopped pecans (opt.)

In a large mixing bowl, sift the first 5 ingredients together. In a smaller bowl combine the egg substitute, milk and oil. Stir egg mixture into the bowl with the dry ingredients; add zucchini and pecans. Mix well.

Pour into sprayed muffin pans. Bake at 400F for 20 minutes or until lightly browned.

Per muffin: *Calories - 133; Total Fat - 4.9g;*
                  Saturated Fat - Tr; Cholesterol - Tr

SOFT PRETZELS

Yield: 20 pretzels

4 cups all-purpose flour
1 teaspoon salt
1 tablespoon sugar
2 packages active dry yeast

1½ cups warm water (110F)
¼ cup egg substitute
Kosher salt, to taste

In a large mixing bowl, combine the first 3 ingredients. Dissolve the yeast in the warm water; add to the dry ingredients. Knead dough until smooth, adding more flour as needed.

Pinch off small pieces of dough; roll into 6-inch long cylinders; shape into pretzel shapes (or any shape you desire.) Place on sprayed cookie sheets; paint with egg substitute. Sprinkle with desired amount of kosher salt, and bake in a 425F oven for 10 minutes. Cool on wire racks.

Per pretzel: *Calories - 90; Total Fat - Tr;*
                   Saturated Fat - Tr; Cholesterol - 0

OLD-FASHIONED LOAF BREAD

Yield: 2 loaves

5 or more cups all-purpose flour	**½ cup water**
4 tablespoons sugar	**3 tablespoons liquid Butter Buds,**
2 teaspoons salt	**see page 48**
1 package active dry yeast	**2 tablespoons liquid Butter Buds,**
1½ cups skim milk	**see page 48**

In a large bowl, combine 2 cups of flour with the next 3 ingredients, and mix well. In saucepan combine the next 3 ingredients, and heat until the liquid reaches 110F.

Gradually add the liquid to the flour mix, beating well. Add the remaining flour and enough additional flour to make a soft dough.

Roll out onto a well floured surface and knead, adding flour, if needed, for 7 to 8 minutes, or until dough is elastic. Shape into a ball, and place into a well-sprayed bowl, turning dough to coat on all sides.

Cover with a tea towel and let rise in a warm place. Put in oven with light on. Let rise until double in size, about 1 hour. Punch down the dough, and turn out onto a lightly floured surface; knead for 1 minute.

Divide the dough in half; roll each half into a 14x7-inch rectangle; roll up in a jelly roll fashion. Press to eliminate any air pockets. Pinch ends to seal. Place, seam side down, in well-sprayed 9x5x3-inch loaf pans. Cover and let rise again for 1 hour, or until double in size.

Bake at 375F for 35 minutes, or until the loaves sound hollow when tapped. Remove from the pans immediately; brush with the remaining Butter Buds, and cool on wire racks.

Per slice: *Calories - 80; Total Fat - .6g;*
            Saturated Fat - Tr; Cholesterol - Tr

PIZZA DOUGH

Yield: 2 12-inch pizza shells

¼ cup warm water
¼ teaspoon sugar
1 envelope active dry yeast
3 cups all-purpose flour

½ teaspoon salt
2 teaspoons olive oil
¾ cup warm water

In an 8-ounce measuring cup, mix well the ¼ cup water with the sugar and the yeast. Place in oven with light on for 10 to 12 minutes, or until yeast becomes bubbly.

In a large bowl, mix the flour and salt. Make a well in the center; add the yeast mixture, the olive oil and the remaining water. Stir to blend. Finish mixing with your hands until dough forms a ball. Place on a lightly-floured surface, and knead for 5 to 8 minutes, or until dough becomes smooth and elastic.

Place the dough in a large sprayed bowl. Cover with a tea towel. Place bowl in the oven with the light on for 1½ to 2 hours, or until doubled in size.

At this time punch down, and knead dough in the bowl for 1 minute. Divide in half. If only one pizza is to be made, the remaining dough may be frozen at this time.

Analysis per pizza: *Calories - 684; Total Fat - 6.3g;*
Saturated Fat - 1.9g; Cholesterol - 0

SOUPS

SOUPS

Soups, wonderful, heart-safe, versatile soups. Low sodium, low fat, low cholesterol, low calorie, low sugar, soups.

Some of the following soups, such as Broccoli or Shrimp Bisque, lend themselves as willing partners with sandwiches. Others can be used as satisfying main dish meals. Black Bean Soup, Lentil Bean Soup or Hearty Turkey-Barley Soup need only a crisp loaf of homemade bread and a salad to make a hearty eater happy. For special occasions, French Onion Soup, Vichyssoise or Creamy Zucchini Soup will never let you down.

If you find yourself in a pinch, Microwave Corn Chowder will rescue you. It's a cinch to make.

CREAM OF ASPARAGUS SOUP

Yield: 2 servings

½ cup cooked asparagus, mashed   Salt and white pepper, to taste
2 cups Bechamel Sauce, see page 225   Dash of nutmeg
Reserved asparagus cooking liquid

Mix mashed asparagus with the Bechamel Sauce. Add the reserved vegetable liquid to obtain the desired consistency. Season with the salt and pepper; top each serving with a dash of nutmeg.

Per serving: *Calories - 227; Total Fat - 5.9g;*
             Saturated Fat - .8g; Cholesterol - 4mg

BLACK BEAN SOUP

Yield: 8 servings

2 cups dried black beans   2 tablespoons olive oil
¼ cup BAC*OS (bacon   2 teaspoons dried basil
    flavored bits)   1 teaspoon dried mustard
2 onions, diced   1 teaspoon salt (opt.)
2 carrots, diced   Dash of cayenne
2 stalks celery, sliced   ¼ cup red wine

Wash the beans, and soak them overnight in a 6-quart kettle with enough water to cover beans by 1-inch. Drain beans, reserving the liquid; add enough water to make 2 quarts. Return beans to the liquid.

In a 10-inch saucepan, saute the onions, carrots, celery and BAC*OS in the olive oil until soft. Add the vegetables to the beans along with the remaining ingredients, except for the wine. Cover and simmer for 2½ to 3 hours. Add boiling water if necessary.

Run the soup through a blender. It should be the consistency of heavy cream. When ready to serve, heat the soup and add the red wine.

Garnish with chopped mild white onion, such as a Vidalia or Texas Sweet.

Per serving: *Calories - 129; Total Fat - 4.4g;*
             Saturated Fat - .6g; Cholesterol - 0

BORSCH/BORSCHT

Yield: 4 servings

5 beets, trimmed, scrubbed
2 carrots, sliced
1 small head cabbage, chopped
1 large onion, chopped
3 stalks celery, chopped
3 tablespoons liquid Butter Buds,
   see page 48

2 to 3 cups low-sodium beef broth
¼ cup red wine
4 tablespoons cream-style
   horseradish
1 tablespoon lemon juice
Salt (opt.) and pepper, to taste
4 tablespoons mock sour cream,
   see page 51

In a saucepan, boil the beets, in enough water to cover, until they are soft. Saving cooking water, remove beets from pan with a slotted spoon, cool, peel and slice.

In the beet water, boil the carrots until soft. Remove with a slotted spoon, and set aside. In same water, boil cabbage until soft. Remove with a slotted spoon, and set aside.

Meanwhile, in a covered, non-stick skillet, over low heat, saute the onion and celery in the Butter Buds until soft.

Place all vegetables in a kettle; add the vegetable broth plus enough beef broth to make 1 quart. Add the red wine, horseradish, lemon juice, salt and pepper. Simmer for 30 minutes; cool. Run through blender until smooth.

Return soup to kettle; simmer for 30 minutes more; cool. Refrigerate for 24 hours. Serve either hot or cold with a dollop of mock sour cream on each serving.

Per serving: *Calories - 129; Total Fat - 2.8g;*
                 Saturated Fat - .6g; Cholesterol - 1.8mg

BROCCOLI BISQUE

Yield: 4 servings

1 10-ounce package frozen
  chopped broccoli
1 small onion, sliced
2 cups chicken broth
1 whole clove
⅛ teaspoon pepper

1 tablespoons chopped parsley
2 or 3 celery leaves
¼ teaspoon dried thyme
1 cup skim milk
1 tablespoon white wine

Place first 8 ingredients in a medium-size saucepan; cover and cook until broccoli is soft. In a blender, process soup until smooth.

Pour soup back into saucepan; stir in milk and heat thoroughly. Stir in the wine; serve at once.

Per serving: *Calories - 62; Total Fat - .9g;*
                   Saturated Fat - Tr; Cholesterol - 1.5mg

CREAM OF BRUSSELS SPROUTS SOUP

Yield: 4 servings

3 cups Brussels sprouts, about 1
  pound, trimmed and washed
½ cup finely chopped onion
3 tablespoons liquid Butter Buds,
  see page 48

Salt and pepper, to taste
2 cups skim milk
¼ cup mock sour cream,
  see page 51
Croutons for garnish

Cook the Brussels sprouts in 2 cups water. Reserve one cup of the cooking liquid. Chop the sprouts, coarsely.

In a covered saucepan, over low heat, saute the onion in the Butter Buds until soft; add the Brussels sprouts and the salt and pepper. Cook mixture for about 5 minutes. Stir in the milk and the 1 cup reserved cooking liquid; bring to a boil. Reduce heat; simmer for 10 minutes.

In a blender, puree the soup; pour back into saucepan. Reheat over low heat. Stir in mock sour cream and adjust seasonings. Serve with croutons.

Per serving, without croutons: *Calories - 109; Total Fat - 2.7g;*
                                     Saturated Fat - .6g; Cholesterol - 3.8mg

CARROT SOUP

Yield: 4 servings

1 garlic clove, pressed
2 shallots, minced
1 tablespoon fresh gingerroot,
 minced
2 tablespoons liquid Butter Buds,
 see page 48
2 cups low-sodium chicken bouillon

3 tablespoons white wine
½ pound carrots, washed, unpeeled,
 sliced into ½-inch pieces
Cayenne pepper, ground nutmeg and
 black pepper, to taste
1¼ cups skim milk

In a covered saucepan, over low heat, saute the garlic, shallots and gingerroot in the Butter Buds until softened. Add remaining ingredients, except for milk. Cook mixture slowly for ½ hour, or until carrots are tender. Run mixture through a blender; stir in milk and refrigerate overnight. Serve cold with chopped chives.

Per serving: *Calories - 70; Total Fat - 2g;*
Saturated Fat - Tr; Cholesterol - 1.8mg

ISLAND CLAM CHOWDER

Yield: 5 or more servings

1 tablespoon BAC*OS (bacon
   flavored bits)
1 tablespoon canola oil
3 onions, coarsely chopped
½ cup liquid Butter Buds,
   see page 48

5 potatoes, cut into ½-inch cubes,
   boiled until just crisp tender
15 hard-shelled clams (quahogs)
Tabasco sauce, to taste
Pepper, to taste
¾ cup skim milk

Scrub clams. In a large kettle steam clams open in 1 cup water; reserve liquid.

Rinse out kettle and, in it saute BAC*OS in oil until they begin to brown. Add the onions and ½ the Butter Buds; cover and cook until the onions are soft. Add the boiled potatoes, clams, coarsely chopped, clam juice and a little extra water. Heat thoroughly; add the remaining Butter Buds, about 6 drops Tabasco sauce and pepper. Simmer for ½ hour.

Let chowder stand overnight. Reheat slowly; add milk. If not thick enough, add corn starch mixed with a little of the chowder liquid. Return to pan, and stir until it thickens.

Per serving: *Calories - 286; Total Fat - 8.1g;*
                     Saturated Fat - .7g; Cholesterol - 23.8mg

CORN CHOWDER

Yield: 2 to 3 servings

1 tablespoon BAC*OS (bacon
flavored bits)
1 tablespoon canola oil
¼ cup chopped onion
1 Jalapeno, seeded and minced
(use rubber gloves)
½ cup chopped celery
1 bay leaf
Pinch of sage
1 tablespoon chopped parsley
1 teaspoon salt (opt.)

White pepper, to taste
1 medium potato, ½ inch dice
1½ cups hot water
3 to 4 tablespoons flour
1 12-ounce can whole kernel corn or
1½ cups fresh kernels
1 cup warmed skim milk
2 tablespoons liquid Butter Buds,
see page 48
¼ cup egg substitute
Paprika

In a large saucepan, cook the BAC*OS in the oil until they begin to brown. Add the onion, Jalapeno and celery; saute 3 to 4 minutes. Add next 7 ingredients; cook until potato is crisp tender.

Thicken mixture with flour mixed with warm water to make a paste. Stir constantly until thickened.

Mix corn with the scalded milk and stir into the potato mixture. Bring to a boil, cover and remove from heat. When pan has cooled, refrigerate overnight. To serve, reheat and stir in the Butter Buds. Remove from heat; stir in the egg substitute. Sprinkle each bowlful with paprika.

Per serving for 3:   *Calories - 270; Total Fat - 8g;*
                           Saturated Fat - .7g; Cholesterol - 1.3mg

MICROWAVE CORN CHOWDER

Yield: 4 servings

2 tablespoons liquid Butter Buds,
  see page 48
1 medium onion, finely chopped
1 16-ounce can whole kernel
  yellow corn, no-salt added
1 can cream of potato soup

½ cup skim milk
⅛ teaspoon white pepper
6 dashes Tabasco sauce
2 tablespoons chopped chives
  for garnish
Paprika to top

Place Butter Buds and onion in a 2-quart glass casserole and microwave, covered, on HIGH for 5 minutes, stirring once.

Drain ¼ cup liquid from corn; add corn and remaining liquid to casserole along with the potato soup, milk, pepper and Tabasco sauce. Mix well; microwave on HIGH, uncovered, for 8 minutes, stirring occasionally. Garnish with chives and top with a sprinkle of paprika.

Per serving: *Calories - 162; Total Fat - 5.6g;*
Saturated Fat - 1.5g; Cholesterol - 2mg

GASPACHO

Yield: 4 to 6 servings

1 garlic clove, peeled and halved
32-ounces tomato juice
1 2¼-ounce can sliced ripe olives,
  drained
1 medium cucumber, ½-inch dice
1 bell pepper, ½-inch pieces
5 radishes, sliced
½ cup green onions, sliced
  into ½-inch pieces
1 tablespoon sugar
1 tablespoon chopped parsley

1 tablespoon fresh chopped tarragon,
  or 1 teaspoon dried
1 tablespoon fresh chopped basil,
  or 1 teaspoon dried
2 tablespoons white wine vinegar
2 tablespoons lemon juice
2 teaspoons paprika
6 drops Tabasco sauce
1 tablespoon worcestershire sauce
Salt (opt.) and pepper to taste

Wipe a 2-quart bowl with the garlic. Add remaining ingredients. Mix, cover, and refrigerate for at least 24 hours. Serve cold.

Per serving: *Calories - 76; Total Fat - 2.3g;*
Saturated Fat - Tr; Cholesterol - 0

HAM SOUP

Yield: 4 servings

1 pound cabbage, cut in
  julienne strips
1 garlic clove, pressed
1 tablespoon liquid Butter Buds,
  see page 48
1¼ cups cream of celery soup,
  see page 117
¼ cup white wine

2 tablespoons cream style
  horseradish
½ cup skim milk
2 tablespoons fresh dill, chopped,
  or 2 teaspoons dried
Squirt of lemon juice
White pepper, to taste
1 cup cooked lean ham, diced
1 8-oz. can English peas, with juice

Soften cabbage by immersing in ½-inch boiling water 3 to 5 minutes. Drain the cabbage, reserving the liquid.

In a covered saucepan over low heat, saute the garlic in the Butter Buds until softened. Add the cream of celery soup and the next 6 ingredients; heat until mixture bubbles.

Add cabbage and reserved liquid; cook over low heat for 5 minutes. Add ham, and cook for 5 minutes more.

Finally, add peas with their juice; simmer for ½ hour.

Serve with soft dinner rolls, see page 95.

Per serving: *Calories - 170; Total Fat - 5.6g;*
            Saturated Fat - 1.9g; Cholesterol - 22.5mg

LENTIL SOUP

Yield: 8 servings

4 large onions, chopped
2 carrots, chopped
3 tablespoons olive oil
1 teaspoon dried thyme
1 teaspoon dried marjoram
1 tablespoon worcestershire-wine
  sauce
½ cup white wine
6 cups low-sodium beef broth

2 cups dried lentil beans, washed
½ cup chopped parsley
1 1-pound 12-ounce can, plus
  1 16-ounce can, tomatoes,
  chopped
2½ tablespoons sugar, or 4
  packets sugar substitute
Salt (opt.), to taste
Grated Swiss cheese alternative

In a large kettle, saute the onions and carrots in the olive oil for 10 to 12 minutes. Add the remaining ingredients, except cheese, and cook, covered, over low heat for 2 hours, or until beans are tender.

Let soup stand overnight.

To serve, reheat soup. Place a small amount of grated cheese in the bottom of each serving bowl. Spoon soup over. Serve with Pita Toasts - see below.

Per serving: *Calories 166; Total Fat - 6.2g;*
               Saturated Fat - 1g; Cholesterol - 0

PITA TOASTS

Yield: 32 wedges

¼ cup liquid Butter Buds,
  see page 48
1 tablespoon chopped parsley
1 teaspoon lemon juice

1 large garlic clove, pressed
Freshly ground pepper, to taste
2 6-inch pita breads, halved
  horizontally

In a small bowl, combine the first 5 ingredients; let stand, covered, at room temperature for 1 hour. Spread mixture over bread halves, and bake on a non-stick cookie sheet at 450F for 5 minutes, or until toasts are lightly browned and crisp. Cut each half into 8ths.

Per wedge: *Calories - 14; Total Fat - Tr;*
             Saturated Fat - Tr; Cholesterol - 0

MINESTRONE
(This is a Sicilian Staple)

Yield: 6 servings

6 cups boiling water
½ pound dried navy beans
¼ cup BAC*OS (bacon
 flavored bits)
1 large onion, chopped
2 garlic cloves, finely chopped
2 tablespoons olive oil
2 stalks celery, sliced into
 ½-inch pieces
2 carrots, washed, cut into
 ½-inch slices

1 medium potato, diced
¼ head cabbage, shredded
1 tablespoon chopped parlsey
½ teaspoon salt (opt.)
½ teaspoon black pepper
1 quart hot water
¼ cup precooked rice
½ cup fresh or frozen English peas
½ cup no-salt added tomato paste
Freshly-grated parmesan cheese

Gradually add the beans to the boiling water. After boiling for 5 minutes, remove pan from heat, cover, and let stand for 1½ hours. Add the BAC*OS.

In a skillet, heat the onion and garlic in the olive oil until lightly browned.

Add the mixture to the beans with the celery, carrots, potato, cabbage, parsley, salt and pepper. Pour in the hot water; simmer for 1 hour, or until beans are soft.

Add the rice, peas and tomato paste. Stir well and simmer for 10 minutes more. Let stand until cool, and refrigerate for 24 hours. Reheat and serve with the grated cheese.

Per serving, without cheese: *Calories - 180; Total Fat - 5.7g;*
                                    Saturated Fat - .7g; Cholesterol - 0

CREAM OF ONION SOUP

Yield: 4 servings

1¼ pounds white onions,
  peeled and quartered
4 tablespoon liquid Butter Buds,
  see page 48
1 medium carrot, scrubbed and
  sliced

1 stalk celery, sliced
2 cups chicken broth
1 cup reserved liquid from cooking
  onions
Black pepper to taste
¾ cup evaporated skim milk

Put onions in a 2-quart saucepan; cover with water; bring to a boil and cook for 2 minutes. Drain, saving 1 cup cooking liquid.

In a medium covered saucepan, saute the carrots, celery and onions in the Butter Buds for about 12 minutes or until the vegetables begin to soften. Add the broth and the reserved cooking liquid. Simmer for about 30 minutes or until vegetables are done; add pepper. While adding milk, puree soup in a blender.

May be served hot or cold. When reheating soup - be careful not to boil.

Garnish with strips of steamed carrots and celery.

Per serving: *Calories - 131; Total Fat - 5g;*
                   Saturated Fat - 1.2g; Cholesterol - .5mg

FRENCH ONION SOUP

Yield: 6 servings

3 large white onions, halved
  and sliced
2 tablespoons sugar or 3 packets
  sugar substitute
2 tablespoons worcestershire sauce
6 tablespoons liquid Butter Buds,
  see page 48

6 cups low-sodium beef broth,
  (if canned, strain the fat)
⅓ cup red wine
6 thick slices French bread
4 tablespoons freshly-grated
  parmesan cheese

In a large covered saucepan, saute the onions, sugar and 1 tablespoon worcestershire sauce in the Butter Buds over low heat. When the onions are softened and golden, add the beef broth, wine and remaining worcestershire. Bring to a boil; simmer for 20 to 30 minutes. Refrigerate overnight.

To serve, reheat the soup. Spoon soup into 6 small pyrex bowls or flame-proofed soup dishes. Float a slice of bread on each; sprinkle with parmesan cheese. Broil until the cheese begins to brown.

Per serving: *Calories - 222; Total Fat - 7g;*
           Saturated Fat - 2.5g; Cholesterol - 7.3mg

POTATO SOUP (VICHYSSOISE)

Yield: 4 servings

4 medium potatoes, peeled
  and diced
2 medium onions, chopped
2 shallots, chopped
2 cups reserved vegetable juices
  or vegetable bouillon
1 cup low-sodium chicken broth

½ cup white wine
1 teaspoon salt (opt.)
2 cups skim milk
6 drops Tabasco sauce
White pepper, to taste
Chives to garnish, chopped

Place the first 7 ingredients in a large saucepan or kettle, and cook the mixture 45 to 50 minutes, or until vegetables are tender.

In a blender, puree the mixture until smooth. Transfer to a large bowl; add milk, Tabasco and pepper. Serve cold with fresh chopped chives.

Per serving: *Calories - 212; Total Fat - .8g;*
           Saturated Fat - Tr; Cholesterol - 2.3mg

SHRIMP BISQUE

Yield: 4 to 6 servings

¼ cup carrot, finely chopped
¼ cup onion, finely chopped
¼ cup mushrooms, finely chopped
⅓ cup liquid Butter Buds, see
  page 48
1 pound raw shrimp, peeled
¼ cup cornstarch

3 cups skim milk, warmed
½ teaspoon paprika
¼ - ½ teaspoon Tabasco sauce
1 tablespoon lemon juice
1 tablespoon white wine
Salt, to taste (opt.)
Chopped parsley, to garnish

In a large covered saucepan, saute the three vegetables in the Butter Buds until the onion is transparent. While vegetables are cooking, clean and coarsely chop the shrimp. Add the shrimp, and cook for 5 minutes more, or until they turn pink. Stir frequently.

Dissolve the cornstarch in the milk. Gradually add the milk to the soup, stirring constantly, until thickened. Add the paprika, Tabasco sauce, lemon juice, wine and salt. Bring to a boil; reduce heat, and simmer for 5 to 6 minutes.

Serve immediately, garnishing with the parsley.

Per serving: *Calories - 173; Total Fat - 4g;*
                 Saturated Fat - .6g; Cholesterol - 99.8mg

HEARTY TURKEY-BARLEY SOUP

Yield: 10 servings

1 pound freshly-ground turkey
3 tablespoons liquid Butter Buds,
  see page 48
1 quart low-sodium beef broth
2 cups water
2 tablespoons white wine
2 teaspoons worcestershire-wine sauce
1 packet sugar substitute
⅓ cup quick pearl barley
2 stalks celery, cut into 2-inch lengths

1 bay leaf
½ teaspoon dried thyme
4 medium carrots, scrubbed and cut
  into strips 2 inches long
2 medium turnips, cut like carrots
3 medium onions, peeled, quartered
1 9-ounce package frozen cut green
  beans, or 9 ounces of fresh beans
2 tomatoes, peeled and chopped
Salt (opt.) and pepper, taste

In a large Dutch oven, cook the turkey in the Butter Buds until the meat is no longer pink. Remove from kettle and reserve.

In the same kettle, bring the beef broth and the next 3 ingredients to a boil. Add the next 5 ingredients, and cook over low heat for 30 minutes.

Return turkey to kettle along with the remaining ingredients; bring to a boil. Reduce heat and simmer, covered, 45 to 60 minutes, or until vegetables are tender.

This soup freezes well.

Per serving: *Calories 150; Total Fat - 3.6g;*
                   Saturated Fat - 1g; Cholesterol - 34.9mg

CREAMY ZUCCHINI SOUP

Yield: 4 servings

3 medium zucchini, sliced
2 cups low-sodium chicken broth
1 teaspoon salt (opt.)
Dash white pepper
Pinch of celery seed
½ teaspoon dried basil

1 garlic clove, minced
2 medium onions, chopped
6 ounces evaporated skim milk
¼ cup chopped chives
4 tablespoons mock sour cream,
  see page 51

Place first 8 ingredients in a 3-quart saucepan, and cook until the vegetables are tender. Puree in a blender, adding the evaporated milk as you puree.

Serve hot with a dollop of sour cream and a few chopped chives sprinkled on top.

Per serving: *Calories - 94; Total Fat - 2.6g;*
                   Saturated Fat - 1.2g; Cholesterol - 2.3mg

CREAM OF CELERY SOUP

Yield: 6 servings

2 cups white sauce, see page 235
2 cups finely chopped celery
1 cup finely chopped onion
2 cups chicken broth
1 tablespoon chopped parsley

White pepper, to taste
2 tablespoons liquid Butter Buds,
  see page 48
1½ tablespoons cornstarch

Make white sauce; set aside. In a large kettle cook the celery, onion and parsley in chicken broth. When softened, add the white sauce and pepper. Simmer for 5 minutes. Add the Butter Buds; mix well.

To thicken soup, add the cornstarch mixed with a little water. Stir until thickened. To freeze for use in other recipes, puree in a blender or food processor. Package in 8-ounce containers for freezing.

Per serving: *Calories - 107; Total Fat - 3.6g;*
                   Saturated Fat - .7g; Cholesterol - 2.3mg

CREAM OF MUSHROOM SOUP

Yield: 4 servings

½ pound mushrooms, cleaned
  and sliced
4 tablespoons liquid Butter Buds,
  see page 48
2 tablespoons onion, finely chopped
1 cup hot tap water

2 low-sodium beef bouillon cubes
2 tablespoons flour
¼ teaspoon ground pepper
Dash of mace
2 cups skim milk
½ cup egg substitute

In a covered, non-stick skillet over low heat, simmer the mushrooms and onions in the Butter Buds until softened.

In a blender, mix the next 5 ingredients together; add the mushroom mixture and blend briefly, leaving the mushrooms in small chunks.

Place the mushroom mixture in a medium saucepan; add the milk and bring to a boil. Reduce heat to simmer.

Place the egg substitute in the blender; add 2 tablespoons of the hot soup and mix well; add 2 more tablespoons of soup; mix again. Return egg mixture to the pan and cook over low heat for 3 to 4 minutes, stirring constantly.

If soup is not thick enough add 1 tablespoon cornstarch mixed with enough water to make a thick paste. Cook, stirring constantly, until thickened.

Consider freezing some in 8-ounce containers for use in other recipes.

Per serving: *Calories - 117; Total Fat - 3.3g;*
                   Saturated Fat - .6g; Cholesterol - 2.5mg

SALADS

SALADS

Since the amount of meat you will be consuming should be considerably less than before, salads will now take on new dimensions.

Traditionally, tossed salad with low-calorie dressing has merit, but it really is more exciting to branch out and try new salads, and to experiment on your own. If you are out of fresh vegetables, a package of frozen French-style green beans will solve your problem in French Green Bean Salad P.124. Keep no-salt canned white and yellow corn on hand for Country Corn Salad P.122. Tangy dressings take over for the lack of high cholesterol bacon and eggs in the spinach salads found on pages 127 and 128.

Salads are healthy, fiber-filled dishes suited as an accompaniment to dinner or a complete meal for lunch. Enjoy them in good health.

SWEET/SOUR CABBAGE SALAD
Yield: 8 servings

1 cabbage, 1¼ to 1½ pounds	1 mild - sweet onion
1 large bell pepper	

Sliver cabbage by hand or put it through the slicing disc of a food processor. Cut pepper in half and then slice. Finely chop the onion. Layer the cabbage, pepper and onion in a serving dish.

DRESSING

½ cup white wine vinegar, or	½ teaspoon celery seed
½ cup balsamic vinegar	1 teaspoon salt (opt.)
3 tablespoons canola oil	12 packets sugar substitute
½ teaspoon dry mustard	

Combine first 5 ingredients of dressing in a saucepan; bring to a boil. Remove from heat and add the sugar substitute; mix well. Pour over cabbage mixture. Refrigerate, tightly covered, overnight. Toss before serving. Serve with a slotted spoon, draining each spoonful well.

Per serving, drained: *Calories - 74; Total Fat - 2.7g;*
                            Saturated Fat - Tr; Cholesterol - 0

COUNTRY CORN SALAD

Yield: 4 to 6 servings

1 12-ounce can yellow corn, drained
1 12-ounce can white corn, drained
½ cup celery, finely chopped
½ cup green pepper, finely chopped
½ cup onion, finely chopped

1 2-ounce jar diced pimento,
  well drained
½ cup white wine vinegar
⅛ teaspoon garlic powder
12 packets sugar substitute

Combine the first 6 ingredients in a 2-quart serving dish.

In a saucepan, combine the vinegar and garlic powder. Bring to a boil; remove from heat and add sugar substitute. Stir until well mixed. Pour over vegetables and mix well. Chill several hours or overnight.

Per serving for four: *Calories - 151; Total Fat - 1.4g;*
                            Saturated Fat - Tr; Cholesterol - 0

CUCUMBER SALAD

Yield: 4 servings

¾ teaspoon salt
2 large cucumbers, peeled and
  thinly sliced
1 garlic clove, cut in half
1 tablespoon olive oil
¼ cup white wine vinegar

1 tablespoon water
2 teaspoons sugar or 1 packet
  sugar substitute
¼ teaspoon paprika
Dash of white pepper

In a shallow bowl, salt the cucumbers and garlic; let stand for 1 hour, stirring once or twice. Drain; remove garlic.

In a large bowl, whisk the oil, vinegar, water and sugar, mixing well. Add the drained cucumbers; sprinkle with the paprika and pepper. Chill overnight.

Per serving: *Calories - 49; Total Fat - 1.8g;*
                   Saturated Fat - Tr; Cholesterol - 0

SWEET AND SOUR MARINATED CUCUMBERS

Yield: 6 servings

1 cup cider vinegar
½ cup sugar
1 tablespoon celery seed
1 teaspoon salt (opt.)
12 packets sugar substitute

4 cucumbers, unpeeled, sliced in
   a food processor
1 medium Vidalia, or other mild
   onion, thinly sliced

Combine the first 4 ingredients in a 1-quart saucepan; bring to boil. Remove from heat and stir in sugar substitute. Place cucumbers and onions in a 3-quart casserole dish. Strain the hot dressing over them. Refrigerate overnight. More cucumbers and onions may be added until the dressing loses its pungency.

Per serving: *Calories - 93; Total Fat - Tr;*
                     Saturated Fat - Tr; Cholesterol - 0

GREEN AND ORANGE SUPPER SALAD

Yield: 4 servings

6 to 8 romaine lettuce leaves,
   torn into bite-size pieces
6 to 8 iceberg lettuce leaves,
   torn into bite-size pieces
1 small onion, thinly sliced
1 small zucchini, thinly sliced
1½ cups orange sections, or
   1 can mandarin oranges, drained
3 tablespoons orange juice

2 tablespoons red wine vinegar
2 tablespoons canola oil
3 packets sugar substitute
¼ teaspoon salt (opt.)
Dash of Tabasco sauce
Dash of pepper
¼ cup toasted slivered almonds,
   see page 49 (opt.)

In a large bowl, combine the first 5 ingredients. In a small bowl combine the orange juice and vinegar; add canola oil, beating constantly with a wire whisk. Whisk in next 4 ingredients; set aside at room temperature.

Add dressing just before serving; sprinkle with toasted almonds, if desired. Serve with a slotted spoon. Drain well.

Per serving: *Calories - 118; Total Fat - 7g;*
                     Saturated Fat - .5g; Cholesterol - 0

FRENCH GREEN BEAN SALAD

Yield: 2 servings

1 package frozen French-style green
  beans, cooked and drained
2 tablespoons mock sour cream, see
  page 51
1 tablespoon fat and cholesterol
  free mayonnaise

1 packet sugar substitute
2 teaspoons white wine vinegar
¼ teaspoon salt (opt.)
2 green onions, finely chopped
2 teaspoons parsley, finely-chopped

While beans are cooking, combine all the other ingredients in a large mixing bowl. Add the beans and toss gently. Cool at room temperature, then refrigerate overnight. Keeps well for several days.

Per serving: *Calories - 53; Total Fat - Tr;*
Saturated Fat - Tr; Cholesterol - 1.8mg

LIMA BEAN SALAD

Yield: 4 servings

2 cups frozen baby Lima beans
1 garlic clove, halved
½ cup frozen English peas
2 teaspoons Dijon mustard
1 tablespoon lemon juice

Salt (opt.) and pepper, to taste
2 tablespoons canola oil
¼ cup minced onion
1 teaspoon dried tarragon
Lettuce leaves for garnish

In a 2-quart saucepan, bring ¾ cup of lightly salted water to a boil. Add the Lima beans and garlic, bring to a boil, and cook for 10 minutes, covered. Add the peas; cook for 3 minutes, or until they are tender. Drain; set aside; discard garlic.

Meanwhile, in a large bowl, whisk the mustard, lemon juice, salt and pepper together; add the oil in a stream and whisk until the dressing is emulsified.

Add the vegetables to the dressing, along with the onion and tarragon; toss gently.

Divide the salad among 4 chilled plates; garnish with lettuce, or serve warm as a vegetable side dish.

Per serving, drained: *Calories - 183; Total Fat - 7.6g;*
Saturated Fat - .6g; Cholesterol - 0

LIME JELLO SALAD

Yield: 8 servings

1 3-ounce package sugar-free
  lime jello
½ cup boiling water
3 ounces lite cream cheese,
  softened

1½ cups sugar-free ginger ale
1 8-ounce can crushed pineapple,
  in its own juice, well drained
½ cup finely-chopped pecans, (opt.)

In a large bowl, dissolve jello in boiling water; add cream cheese and melt. Add, in order, ginger ale (slowly), pineapple and pecans. Place mixture in a 1-quart mold or baking dish and refrigerate until set.

Per serving: *Calories - 65; Total Fat - 2.6g;*
              Saturated Fat - 1.6g; Cholesterol - 9.4mg

MACARONI SALAD

Yield: 6 servings

1½ cups macaroni, cooked as
  directed
1 carrot, finely grated
1 small green pepper, finely chopped
¼ cup finely chopped onion
1 tablespoon Salad Supreme

1 teaspoon sugar
½ teaspoon salt (opt.)
¼ teaspoon black pepper
½ cup fat and cholesterol-
  free mayonnaise
Lettuce leaves

In a large bowl, mix all ingredients together. Refrigerate overnight. Serve on a bed of lettuce leaves.

Per serving: *Calories - 141; Total Fat - .6g;*
              Saturated Fat - Tr; Cholesterol - 0

PINEAPPLE CHEESE MOLD

Yield: 4 servings

1 3-ounce package sugar-free
 lime jello
1 cup boiling water
1 8-ounce can crushed pineapple,
 in its own juices, undrained

1 tablespoon cream-style horseradish
⅓ cup evaporated skimmed milk
½ cup fat and cholesterol-free
 mayonnaise
1 cup 1% fat cottage cheese

In a large bowl, dissolve jello in boiling water; cool. Add pineapple, horseradish, milk and mayonnaise.

Chill until slightly thickened. Fold in cottage cheese. Turn into a 1-quart sprayed mold. Chill until firm.

Per serving: *Calories - 136; Total Fat - 1.1g;*
Saturated Fat - .6g; Cholesterol - 2.5mg

COLE SLAW

Yield: 4 servings

2 medium carrots
½ medium mild onion
1½ pounds cabbage, cored
 and quartered
¼ teaspoon salt (opt.)

½ cup fat and cholesterol-free
 mayonnaise
2 tablespoons vinegar
2 tablespoons sugar
⅛ teaspoon pepper

In a large mixing bowl, coarsely grate the carrots and finely grate the onion.

Finely slice the cabbage quarters by hand, or use the slicing blade of a food processor. Add the cabbage to the carrot/onion mixture. Add remaining ingredients and mix well. Adjust seasonings to taste. Transfer to a 2½ or 3-quart serving dish.

Chill several hours or, better yet, overnight.

Per serving: *Calories - 111; Total Fat - Tr;*
Saturated Fat - Tr; Cholesterol - 0

POTATO SALAD

Yield: 4 servings

**4 medium potatoes, peeled and
  cut into quarters**
¼ cup chopped green pepper
¼ cup chopped onion
¼ cup chopped celery

**½ cup fat and cholesterol-free
  mayonnaise**
1 teaspoon Dijon mustard
Salt (opt.) and pepper, to taste

In a medium saucepan, cook potatoes, covered, in a small amount of lightly -salted water; cool, and cut into ½-inch cubes. Place drained potatoes in a large bowl. Add chopped vegetables.

Combine mayonnaise with mustard and fold into the salad. Add salt and pepper; mix well. Cover and refrigerate overnight.

Per serving: *Calories - 163; Total Fat - Tr;
                     Saturated - Tr; Cholesterol - 0*

SWEET/SOUR SPINACH SALAD

Yield: 6 servings

DRESSING

5 packets sugar substitute
1 teaspoon canola oil
**4 tablespoons balsamic vinegar,
  or cider vinegar**
½ teaspoon celery seeds

½ teaspoon paprika
¼ teaspoon salt (opt.)
1 green onion, minced
Dash of garlic powder

Combine all ingredients in jar 1 hour before needed. Cover tightly, and shake vigorously. Leave dressing sitting at room temperature.

**5 ounces fresh spinach, torn into bite-
  sized pieces, stalks removed**
6 medium-sized mushrooms, sliced

**1 medium Vidalia onion, or other
  mild, sweet onion, thinly sliced**
1 handful alfalfa sprouts, separated

Mix salad ingredients in a 2-quart salad bowl. Pour dressing over and toss gently.

Per serving: *Calories - 26; Total Fat - .8g;
                     Saturated Fat - Tr; Cholesterol - 0*

ARLENE'S SPINACH SALAD

Yield: 6 servings

SPECIAL DRESSING

1 tablespoon canola oil
6 tablespoons red wine vinegar
4½ packets sugar substitute
9 drops Tabasco sauce

1½ teaspoons chopped parsley
¼ teaspoon salt (opt.)
¼ teaspoon pepper

Combine above ingredients in a jar. Cover tightly and shake well. Make 1 hour before needed; let sit at room temperature.

5 ounces fresh spinach torn into bite-sized pieces, stalks removed
½ cup diagonally-sliced celery
1 medium white onion, sliced into rings

1 11-ounce can mandarin oranges, drained
6 to 8 mushrooms, sliced
¼ cup slivered toasted almonds, see page 49

Combine the above salad ingredients in a large bowl; serve with Special Dressing.

Per serving: *Calories - 61; Total fat - 2.6g;*
                  Saturated Fat - Tr; Cholesterol - 0

LUNCHEON FRUIT SALAD

Yield: 2 servings

Lettuce leaves
1 large apple, unpeeled and diced
1 11-ounce can mandarin oranges drained

1 large banana, sliced
1 cup 1% fat cottage cheese
2 tablespoons finely-chopped pecans

Arrange lettuce leaves on two 8-inch salad plates, leaving the center of the plate open. Divide the fruit evenly in circles on top of the lettuce. Place cottage cheese in center.

1 tablespoon fat and cholesterol-free mayonnaise

4 teaspoons honey

Whisk the above ingredients together; pour over salad. Garnish with pecans.

Per serving: *Calories - 335; Total Fat - 6.3g;*
                  Saturated Fat - 1.3g; Cholesterol - 5mg

MEATS

MEATS

Meats should be eaten in much lower quantities than society demands. It is suggested that, for better health, you should limit yourself to 3 or 4 ounces of red meat in a meal no more than 3 times weekly. The "loss" of substance in the meal can easily be replaced with vegetables and complex carbohydrates (pasta, potatoes, rice, etc.)

Only the leanest cuts of meat should be utilized. In beef, choose filet mignon, London broil or flank steak. In pork and lamb, stay away from the fattier ribs and shoulder cuts. When purchasing a ham, buy lean hams with reduced sodium content. On all cuts of meat - **REMOVE ALL VISIBLE FAT BEFORE COOKING.**

In this section we have put a warning on those recipes with higher fat levels. We suggest that you add a complex carbohydrate to complete those meals. This will help the total fat amount average less than 30%, which is the suggested level for good health.

FILET MIGNON WITH JALAPENO BUTTER SAUCE#

Yield: 2 servings

2 filet mignon steaks, 1 to 1½ inches thick, about 4 ounces each

Steaks should be at room temperature. Grill on medium, turning every minute for even cooking. For rare steaks, grill for 8 to 9 minutes.

Serve with Jalapeno Butter Sauce, see page 230.

Per steak, without sauce: Calories - 203; Total Fat - 8.9g;
Saturated Fat - 3.6g; Cholesterol - 84mg

#THE MEAT IN THIS RECIPE CONTAINS A HIGHER CALORIE TO FAT PERCENT-AGE THAN IS RECOMMENDED. PLEASE INCORPORATE A COMPLEX CARBO-HYDRATE AS A SIDE DISH TO LOWER THE RATIO OF CALORIES FROM FAT TO SAFE LEVELS.

ORIENTAL FLANK STEAK

Yield: 4 servings

¾ pound flank steak	**1 teaspoon garlic powder**
4 green onions, chopped	**1 teaspoon fresh grated ginger**
1 tablespoon canola oil	**2 tablespoons honey**
¼ cup lite soy sauce	**1½ tablespoons vinegar**

Score steak on both sides, and place in a shallow dish just large enough to hold it. Combine the remaining ingredients. Mix well and pour over steak. Cover and refrigerate for 24 hours, turning occasionally.

Drain steak, reserving the marinade. Grill on medium for 9 minutes total, basting and turning every minute for even grilling.

Slice steak across grain into thin slices; serve over rice.

Per serving, with rice: Calories - 474; Total Fat - 16.4g;
Saturated Fat - 6.1g; Cholesterol - 60mg

BROILED HAM HOAGIE

Yield: 4 servings

2 hoagie rolls, split lengthwise
¼ cup liquid Butter Buds, see
  page 48
1 cup finely chopped lean ham
3 tablespoons fat and cholesterol-
  free mayonnaise
¼ cup mock sour cream, see page 51

2 tablespoons finely chopped onion
2 tablespoons finely chopped parsley
⅛ teaspoon garlic powder
¼ cup grated cheddar cheese
  alternative
¼ cup sliced black olives (opt.)
6 slices green bell pepper

Drizzle Butter Buds on the split bread. Mix remaining ingredients together except for the cheese, olives and pepper slices; mound mixture on the bread. Sprinkle on the cheese and top with the olives and pepper slices.

Broil until the cheese is melted.

Per serving: *Calories - 350; Total Fat - 10.6g;*
                   Saturated Fat - 2.5g; Cholesterol - 27.8mg

GRILLED HAM STEAK

Yield: 4 servings

2 tablespoons liquid Butter Buds,
  see page 48
½ cup white wine
1 teaspoon powdered cloves
2 tablespoons Dijon mustard

¼ cup brown sugar
1 teaspoon paprika
2 garlic cloves, pressed
12 ounces ham steak, trimmed
  of all fat

Combine the first 7 ingredients in a bowl. Place ham steak in dish; pour sauce over. Cover, and refrigerate for 24 hours, turning occasionally. Reserve marinade and pat steak dry.

Broil for 10 minutes, 6 inches from heat, turning and basting frequently. If grilling, place steak on sheet of heavy duty aluminum foil, and cook for 15 minutes over low heat. Turn and baste every few minutes. Remove from foil and grill 1 minute more on each side, directly on grill.

Per serving: *Calories - 204; Total Fat - 5.5g;*
                   Saturated - 1.3g; Cholesterol - 39mg

GRILLED LOIN LAMB CHOPS

Yield: 4 servings

¼ cup brown sugar, packed
1 tablespoon cornstarch
1 teaspoon dried basil
½ cup lite soy sauce

½ cup white wine
4 thick loin lamb chops,
   trimmed of all fat, about
   4 ounces each

Combine the first 5 ingredients in a small saucepan, and cook until the mixture thickens and boils, stirring constantly. Cool.

Place the chops in a glass dish that just holds them, and pour the marinade over. Cover and marinate for 3 to 4 hours, turning once.

Place chops on foil-lined grill at medium for 5 minutes. Turn chops; baste and grill for another 5 minutes. Remove foil; baste and grill for 5 minutes. Turn chops; baste and grill 5 minutes more.

Per serving: *Calories - 317; Total Fat - 8.3g;*
                     Saturated Fat - 3.5g; Cholesterol - 105.3mg

GREEK MEATBALLS IN AVGOLEMONO SAUCE#

Yield: 6 servings

2 slices white bread, torn into
  small pieces
¼ cup skim milk
⅓ cup finely-chopped onion
1 large shallot, finely minced
1 garlic clove, pressed
¼ teaspoon allspice
⅛ teaspoon cinnamon
¼ cup chopped parsley
2 tablespoons lemon juice

1 teaspoon Kosher salt
½ teaspoon black pepper
½ pound lean, cooked ham,
  finely chopped
½ pound freshly-ground turkey
½ pound lean ground beef
½ cup bread crumbs
½ cup egg substitute
2 tablespoons light corn oil spread

Soak the bread in milk for a few minutes. Combine the bread, milk and the remaining ingredients, except spread; mix well. Shape into small meatballs. If mixture is too wet, add more crumbs. Place 1 tablespoon spread in a non-stick skillet and gently cook ½ the meatballs. Remove from pan. Add the remaining spread and cook the remaining meatballs.

SAUCE

3 tablespoons liquid Butter Buds,
  see page 48
3 tablespoons cornstarch
½ cup hot low-sodium chicken
  broth plus 1 bouillon cube

1 cup skim milk
1 egg yolk, slightly beaten
¼ cup lemon juice
Salt (opt.) and pepper, to taste

In a saucepan large enough to hold the meatballs, heat the Butter Buds over medium heat. Add cornstarch; mix well. Slowly add the bouillon, whisking constantly until it thickens. Remove from heat; cool slightly.

Combine the milk and egg. Stir into the sauce along with the lemon juice, salt and pepper. Add meatballs to the sauce; simmer until heated through. Do not boil!

Per serving: *Calories - 377; Total Fat - 16.5g;*
                    Saturated Fat - 5.3g; Cholesterol - 127.8mg

#SOME OF THE MEAT IN THIS RECIPE CONTAINS A HIGHER CALORIE TO FAT PERCENTAGE THAN IS RECOMMENDED. PLEASE INCORPORATE A COMPLEX CARBOHYDRATE AS A SIDE DISH TO LOWER THE RATIO OF CALORIES FROM FAT TO SAFE LEVELS.

MEXICAN STEAK SANDWICHES
(FAJITAS)

Yield: 8 fajitas

12 ounces flank steak	½ cup lite soy sauce
3 garlic cloves, pressed	½ cup brown sugar
1 tablespoon olive oil	1 teaspoon black pepper
½ cup tomato juice	8 flour tortillas
½ cup lime juice	

Score steak on each side; place in a shallow bowl and cover with the remaining ingredients, well mixed.

Refrigerate, covered, for 48 hours, turning occasionally.

Drain steak, and cook marinade in a small saucepan until it boils. Grill steak for 9 minutes total, turning and basting with the cooked marinade, every minute for even cooking.

When steak is done, slice thinly, cutting diagonally across the grain.

Fill the burritos with the steak slices and any or all of the following:

Salsa, see page 233	Coarsely-chopped tomatoes
Mock Sour Cream, see page 51	Coarsely-chopped onion
Grated cheddar cheese alternative	Refried Beans, see page 50
Torn or chopped lettuce	Guacamole, see page 61

Per fajita, without toppings: *Calories - 295; Total Fat - 10.8g;*
Saturated Fat - 3.4g; Cholesterol - 30mg

TERIYAKI STEAK AND RICE

Yield: 4 servings

¾ pound London Broil steak,
  trimmed of all fat
½ cup lite soy sauce
6 packets sugar substitute, or
  4 tablespoons sugar

1 tablespoon canola oil
1 garlic clove, pressed
1 green onion, minced

Slice steak into ¼-inch thick pieces; place in bottom of shallow, flat-bottomed glass dish. Combine the remaining ingredients; pour over steak and refrigerate, covered, for 24 hours.

RICE

3 tablespoons liquid Butter Buds,
  see page 48
3 onions, chopped
½ cup mushrooms, sliced
1 cup long grain rice
2½ cups water

1 low-sodium beef bouillon cube
Salt (opt.) and pepper, to taste
1 tablespoon sesame seeds, toasted
  in a heavy skillet until golden
2 medium tomatoes, thinly sliced
2 sprigs parsley, chopped

In a covered skillet, saute the onions in the Butter Buds over low heat until softened. Add mushrooms and cook for 4 minutes more.

Cook the rice in the water and bouillon, adding salt and pepper to taste. When cooked, add the onion and mushroom mixture and enough strained marinade from the drained beef to create a mixture suiting your taste. Mix well and place on a platter.

Place steak pieces in a fish holder. Grill on a gas grill over medium heat for 2 minutes on one side; turn and grill for 1 minute on the other side. Don't overcook! They will become tough!

Arrange steak pieces on the rice mixture; sprinkle with sesame seeds and garnish with the tomato and parsley.

Per serving: *Calories - 476; Total Fat - 14g;*
                Saturated Fat - 4.4g; Cholesterol - 70.3mg

VEAL AND SHRIMP EXTRAORDINARY

Yield: 4 servings

4 veal medallions, 3 to 4 ounces
  each (or turkey breast meat)
¼ cup flour with added salt (opt.)
  and pepper, to taste
⅓ cup egg substitute
2 garlic cloves, pressed
¼ cup liquid Butter Buds, page 48

8 large shrimp, peeled, last segment
  of tail left intact
½ pound mushrooms, sliced
¼ cup Brown Sauce, page 226
½ cup white wine
½ cup Bearnaise Sauce, page 224

Slightly flatten the medallions between two sheets of waxed paper until about ⅛ inch thick.

In a large, non-stick, covered skillet, over low heat, saute the garlic for 2 minutes in the Butter Buds. Add the shrimp and continue cooking 3 to 4 minutes or until shrimp are pink. Remove with a slotted spoon, and keep warm.

Place flour with salt and pepper in a plastic bag; dredge the veal in the flour mixture. Shake off excess flour. Put egg substitute in a shallow dish and dip veal medallions to coat.

Increase heat to medium high; add veal to the skillet; saute for 1 to 2 minutes on each side. Do not overcook. Remove from skillet and keep warm.

Add the wine and deglaze the pan. Add the mushrooms and warmed Brown Sauce. Cook for 2 minutes.

Place the shrimp on top of the veal; spoon mushroom mixture over them. Serve with warmed Bearnaise Sauce.

Per serving: *Calories - 360; Total Fat - 15.5g;*
                   Saturated Fat - 4.6g; Cholesterol - 164mg

If using turkey breasts, cover when cooking. Cook over medium heat until just cooked through.

The analysis using turkey breast in place of the veal is as follows:

Per serving: *Calories - 279; Total Fat - 6.2g;*
                   Saturated Fat - 1.2g; Cholesterol - 114mg

VEAL BIRDS#

Yield: 4 servings

2 garlic cloves, minced
1 tablespoon freshly-grated
  parmesan cheese
2 teaspoons chopped parsley
¼ teaspoon salt (opt.)
¼ teaspoon black pepper
¾ pound veal rump, sliced thin and
  slightly flattened+

3 slices deli turkey ham, cut in half
6 thin slices part skim, or no-fat
  mozzarella cheese
Vegetable oil spray
¼ cup liquid Butter Buds, see
  page 48
¼ cup water

+ About six "birds". Turkey breast may be substituted for the veal.

Combine the garlic, parmesan, parsley, salt and pepper. Set out the veal birds and place a piece of ham on each, followed by 1 teaspoon of the garlic mixture. Top each with a slice of mozzarella. Roll the birds up and secure with toothpicks.

In a skillet, brown the meat on all sides in the vegetable spray. Place browned meat in a casserole. Mix the Butter Buds and water together and pour over the birds.

Cover and cook in a 300F oven for about an hour, or until meat is tender when pierced with a fork.

Per serving: Calories - 304; Total Fat - 15.7g;
Saturated Fat - 5.8g; Cholesterol - 137mg

#SOME OF THE MEAT IN THIS RECIPE CONTAINS A HIGHER CALORIE TO FAT PERCENTAGE THAN IS RECOMMENDED. PLEASE INCORPORATE A COMPLEX CARBOHYDRATE AS A SIDE DISH TO LOWER THE RATIO OF CALORIES FROM FAT TO SAFER LEVELS. SUBSTITUTING TURKEY FOR THE VEAL WILL ALSO ACHIEVE LOWER FAT LEVELS.

Per serving with turkey: Calories - 237; Total Fat - 6.5g;
Saturated Fat - 1.8g; Cholesterol - 89.8mg

WALPOLE VEAL

Yield: 4 servings

1 tablespoon BAC*OS (bacon
  flavored bits)
1 tablespoon canola oil
1 green bell pepper, sliced
1 onion, sliced
1 garlic clove, pressed
¾ pound cubed veal or turkey breast
¼ cup flour, mixed with; salt,
  pepper and paprika, to coat meat

1 16-ounce can tomatoes
1 tablespoon fresh basil, or
  1 teaspoon dried
1½ teaspoons fresh chopped
  oregano, or ½ teaspoon dried
2 teaspoons sugar, or one packet
  sugar substitute
¼ cup sauterne
½ cup mushrooms, sliced

In a medium saucepan, heat the BAC*OS in the oil until they begin to brown. Remove them with a slotted spoon and discard. In same pan, saute the pepper, onion and garlic until they are softened. Remove to a bowl and keep warm.

After dredging the meat in the flour mixture, brown in saucepan. Add more vegetable oil if needed. Add remaining ingredients, and return the vegetables to the pan. Simmer, covered, 20 to 25 minutes, or until meat is cooked through.

Per serving with veal: *Calories - 313; Total Fat - 13.7g;*
                                      Saturated Fat - 4.4g; Cholesterol - 109mg

Per serving with turkey: *Calories - 260; Total Fat - 7g;*
                                      Saturated Fat - 1.2g; Cholesterol - 59mg

CHINESE PORK TENDERLOIN

Yield: 4 servings

¾ pound pork tenderloin,
  trimmed of all fat
2 tablespoons sugar

2 tablespoons lite soy sauce
1 tablespoon white wine
½ teaspoon cinnamon

Cut the tenderloin into equal quarters, lengthwise; place in bottom of shallow dish.

Mix remaining ingredients well and pour over the meat; be sure to cover all surfaces of the meat. Cover and refrigerate for 24 hours, turning once or twice.

Place drained meat on heavy-duty foil on a gas grill over medium heat for 5 minutes; remove foil and brown briefly; about 2 minutes on each side. Serve with spicy mustard, see page 53.

Per serving: *Calories - 174; Total Fat - 4.1g;*
             Saturated Fat - 1.4g; Cholesterol - 79mg

BEEF STIR-FRY

Yield: 2 servings

6 ounces lean beef, cut into thin
  strips, across the grain
1 tablespoon lite soy sauce
1 tablespoon white wine
½ teaspoon sugar
1 large turnip, cut into strips
½ red bell pepper, cut into strips
4 green onions, coarsely chopped
4 mushrooms, sliced

4 ounces pea pods (snow peas)
1 garlic clove, halved
2 thin slices fresh ginger root
1 teaspoon peanut oil
½ teaspoon sesame oil
¼ teaspoon hot chili oil (opt.)
3 tablespoons oyster sauce
½ cup long grain rice, cooked per
  package instructions

In a flat dish, marinate the beef in the next 3 ingredients, mixed well.

In a steel wok, or heavy skillet, heat 1 teaspoon of the peanut oil over high heat; add 1 piece each of garlic and ginger root. Remove before they burn, and discard. Add the turnip; cook, stirring constantly, for 2 minutes. Add pepper; cook and stir for 2 more minutes. Remove vegetables to a bowl and keep warm. Add a teaspoon of peanut oil and the remaining garlic and ginger root; remove before burning. Add remaining vegetables; cook stirring constantly for 2 minutes. Remove vegetables to the warming bowl.

Add beef to the wok and cook for 1 minute, or until done to your liking. Lower heat; add vegetables, oils and oyster sauce; mix well and serve over the rice.

Per serving: *Calories - 485; Total Fat - 14.5g;*
                 Saturated Fat - 3.7g; Cholesterol - 70mg

HAM AND CHEESE LOAF

Yield: 4 servings

1 loaf French bread
1 cup finely-chopped, lean ham
¾ cup grated Swiss cheese
  alternative
¼ cup liquid Butter Buds,
  see page 48

1 garlic clove, pressed
1 small onion, chopped
¼ cup sweet pickle relish
¼ teaspoon black pepper
1 tablespoon white wine

Slice off the top third of the bread, lengthwise. Scoop out the soft center and run through a blender to make bread crumbs. Save ½ cup crumbs for this recipe, freeze remainder for another use. Combine the ½ cup crumbs with the remaining ingredients; mix well. Heat the mixture in the top of a double boiler. Place the warm mix in the hollowed-out bread. Replace top, wrap in foil, and bake in 350F oven for 15 minutes, or until heated through.

If you would like your bread soft, leave wrapped in the foil; set aside to rest for 5 minutes.

Per serving: *Calories - 465; Total Fat 12.8g;*
             Saturated Fat - 3g; Cholesterol - 26mg

MEAT SUBSTITUTES

MEAT SUBSTITUTES

Perhaps we should call this section "imposter foods." Most of these meals are adaptations of world classic recipes. All have been "saved" from their original high fat and cholesterol by judicious alterations.

Turkey, especially the white meat, is an amazing food product. It acts like a sponge when touched by marinades, sauces and spices. Thus turkey can be, flavorwise, many things it was never intended to be - pork, beef, lamb, etc., and it will be "low in fat." This is our favorite section of the book. Learn our secrets and try them on your favorite recipes. It's easy to create great tasting foods that are also healthy.

BRUNSWICK STEW

Yield: 6 servings

1 broiler chicken, skinned and boned,
  cut into serving pieces
⅓ cup flour, well seasoned with
  salt, pepper and paprika
2 tablespoons canola oil
3 onions, thinly sliced
1½ cups boiling water
3 tomatoes, peeled and sliced
2 red bell peppers, coarsely chopped

½ teaspoon dried thyme
¼ cup sauterne
½ pound Lima beans
½ pound okra, stems removed,
  pods cut into 1-inch pieces
1 cup whole kernel corn
1 tablespoon chopped parsley
1 tablespoon worcestershire-wine
  sauce
1 tablespoon cornstarch

Dredge chicken pieces in seasoned flour and brown in the oil with the onions in a large, non-stick skillet. Transfer meat and onions to a large Dutch oven; add boiling water, tomatoes, peppers, thyme and wine. Cover and simmer for 1 hour.

Add Lima beans and the next 4 ingredients; cover and simmer until meat and vegetables are tender.

If desired, thicken the sauce with a paste made from cornstarch and water.

Per serving: *Calories - 328; Total Fat - 11.5g;*
                   Saturated Fat - 2.3g; Cholesterol - 64mg

CABBAGE ROLLS IN SWEET/SOUR SAUCE

Yield: 4 servings

1 medium head cabbage
1 pound freshly-ground turkey
1 onion, finely chopped
½ teaspoon ground ginger
1 teaspoon sugar
½ cup long grain rice, uncooked
1 teaspoon salt (opt.)
Dash of pepper

½ cup water
¼ cup lite soy sauce
1 cup low-sodium beef broth
2 tablespoons white wine
2 tablespoons lite soy sauce
1 tablespoon sweet/sour sauce,
   or Chinese duck sauce

Core the cabbage, and place in a kettle with about 2 inches of water. Bring to a boil. After a few minutes, turn cabbage; keep turning every few minutes. As leaves become soft, remove with tongs and set aside. Cut core down further as it becomes visible. Keep water simmering; continue to pull the loose leaves free until you have 16 or 17; drain leaves in a colander. If stalks are thick, trim them back.

Combine meat and the next 8 ingredients in a large bowl. Shape mix into 16 logs, about 3 inches long. Place each meat log on a cabbage leaf; roll up leaf from core end; hold together with toothpicks.

Place cabbage rolls in a 13x9x2-inch baking dish.

In a small bowl, combine the remaining ingredients. Pour over cabbage rolls.

Cover dish with foil and bake at 350F for 1½ hours. Serve with additional sweet/sour sauce.

Per serving (4 rolls):   *Calories - 349; Total Fat - 6.2g;*
                             Saturated Fat - 2.1g; Cholesterol - 87.3mg

CARIBBEAN RUM STEW

Yield: 4 servings

¼ cup all-purpose flour
¼ teaspoon salt (opt.)
½ teaspoon pepper
¾ pound turkey thigh meat, cut
   into large bite-size pieces
1 tablespoon canola oil
Vegetable oil spray
2 onions, chopped
1 large bell pepper, coarsely chopped
1 garlic clove, pressed

1 tablespoon catsup
½ packet sugar substitute, or
   1 teaspoon sugar
1 bay leaf
1 teaspoon Tabasco sauce
4 pimento-stuffed olives
2 medium tomatoes, peeled and
   cut into wedges
2 tablespoons dark rum

In a plastic bag, combine the flour, salt and pepper; toss turkey pieces in bag until well coated. In a large, non-stick skillet over medium heat, heat the turkey in the canola oil for about 4 minutes, cooking on all sides. Remove meat and keep warm.

Spray skillet; add onions and pepper, cover, and saute for 5 minutes, or until softened. Add garlic; cook for 1 minute more. Stir in catsup, sugar substitute, bay leaf, Tabasco and ½ cup water. Bring to a boil; simmer for 15 minutes, stirring occasionally. Add the turkey; simmer for 6 minutes, or until turkey is tender. Add olives, tomatoes and rum. Heat for 3 minutes more.

Per serving: *Calories - 297; Total Fat - 10.8g;*
                          Saturated Fat - 2.4g; Cholesterol - 72mg

CHICKEN MOUSSELINE AND "VEAL" MEDALLIONS
Yield: 6 servings

2 to 3 ounces chicken breast meat,
  chopped
¼ cup egg substitute
1 teaspoon finely-chopped carrots
1 teaspoon finely-chopped green
  onions

1 teaspoon finely-chopped celery
1 teaspoon finely-chopped parsley
1 teaspoon white wine
½ teaspoon ground sage
½ cup fresh bread crumbs
Salt (opt.) and pepper, to taste

In a food processor, process the chicken with the next 9 ingredients. Add more bread crumbs, if needed, to make the mixture firm but pliable. Refrigerate for 1 hour.

6 turkey medallions, about ¾ pound
Vegetable oil spray
2 shallots, finely chopped
1 tablespoon canola oil

¼ cup red wine
½ cup chicken broth
⅓ cup liquid Butter Buds,
  see page 48

Gently flatten the turkey medallions between 2 sheets of wax paper. Place 1 tablespoon of chicken mixture on each medallion; roll up and secure with a toothpick. In a skillet, "brown" the medallions in the vegetable oil spray; place in a sprayed baking dish, and bake at 400F for 12 minutes, or until done. Remove from oven; keep warm.

In a small pan, brown the shallots in the canola oil; add the wine and chicken broth. Reduce over high heat by half. Add the Butter Buds; strain, and pour over the medallions.

NOTE: Turkey will not brown like veal or other fatty meats. Cook only until the pink color has disappeared.

Per serving: *Calories - 201; Total Fat - 7.4g;*
                Saturated Fat - 1.2g; Cholesterol - 49mg

EGGPLANT LASAGNA

Yield: 4 servings

1 medium eggplant, peeled and
cut into ¼ inch slices
Salt and pepper, to taste
¼ cup egg substitute
2 tablespoons water
½ cup seasoned bread crumbs
Vegetable oil spray
1 garlic clove, pressed

½ pound Italian turkey sausage,
see page 87
½ cup sliced mushrooms
1 16-ounce jar spaghetti sauce or
homemade sauce, see page 234
8 ounces shredded mozzarella
cheese alternative, or non-fat
mozzarella cheese

Place eggplant slices on a cookie sheet. Sprinkle with salt; cover with paper towels. Weight down with plates; let sit for 30 minutes. Rinse slices and pat dry with paper towel. Dip slices in egg substitute mixed with the water; then dip in bread crumbs. Place eggplant slices on sprayed non-stick cookie sheet. Spray eggplant slices. Broil for 3 to 5 minutes about 4 inches from heat; turn, spray and broil for 2 to 3 minutes longer.

Spray a non-stick skillet, and saute the garlic. Add sausage; separate sausage and cook until color is gone. Add the mushrooms and cook for 2 minutes.

Spread a layer of sauce into an 8x8x2-inch baking dish. Follow with alternate layers of eggplant, spaghetti sauce, sausage mixture and cheese; ending with mozzarella.

Bake at 350F for 35 to 40 minutes.

Per serving: *Calories - 343; Total Fat - 12.6g;*
Saturated Fat - 3.9g; Cholesterol - 39.5mg

Per serving with no-fat cheese: *Calories - 283; Total Fat - 2.7g;*
Saturated Fat - .9g; Cholesterol - 49.5mg

FIVE HOUR "BEEF" STEW

Yield: 6 servings

1 pound turkey thighs, skinned, boned
and cut into large bite-size pieces
1 16-ounce can tomatoes
6 carrots, cut into 3-inch pieces
1 rutabaga (1 pound), cut into
1-inch cubes
1 pound white onions, peeled
1¼ cups mushroom soup, see
page 118

1 tablespoon kosher salt
3 packets sugar substitute
3 tablespoons tapioca
¼ cup dry vermouth
¼ teaspoon black pepper
1 garlic clove, pressed
1 bay leaf
1 16-ounce can whole Irish potatoes,
or 2 fresh potatoes, quartered

In a medium-size roasting pan combine all ingredients, except Irish potatoes. Bake, covered, in a 250F oven for 5 hours, stirring once or twice. Add the Irish potatoes 40 minutes before stew is done. If using fresh potatoes, put in stew 1 hour before completion time.

Per serving: Calories - 314; Total Fat - 6.8g;
Saturated Fat - 2.1g; Cholesterol - 65.2mg

HUNGARIAN GOULASH
(A 1,000 year old dish, popular the world over)

Yield: 4 servings

2 tablespoons BAC*OS (bacon
  flavored bits)
1 tablespoon canola oil
1 cup chopped onion
1 small bell pepper, chopped
¾ pound turkey thigh meat,
  skinned, boned and cubed
1½ cups low-sodium beef broth

1 tablespoon paprika
1 teaspoon salt (opt.)
½ teaspoon garlic powder
¼ teaspoon pepper
⅛ teaspoon dried marjoram
½ cup white wine
1 tablespoon cornstarch
½ teaspoon paprika

In a Dutch oven, slowly cook the BAC*OS in the oil until lightly browned. Remove with a slotted spoon, and reserve. Add the onion and pepper; cook, covered, over low heat until tender. Remove vegetables and keep warm.

Spray pan with vegetable oil spray; add the meat and cook on low heat being sure to cook on all sides.

Add broth and the next 5 ingredients. Stir in the vegetable mixture. Slowly add the wine; bring to a boil. Reduce heat, cover, and simmer for 2 hours. Remove meat with a slotted spoon. Thicken liquid by adding a paste of cornstarch and water. Stir constantly, over low heat, until thickened.

Return meat to kettle. Add paprika and cook for 5 minutes longer.

Per serving: *Calories - 268; Total Fat - 10.8g;*
                   Saturated Fat - 2.4g; Cholesterol - 72mg

MOUSSAKA

Yield: 6 servings

2 eggplants, weighing about
 ¾ pound each
2 small onions, chopped
1 pound freshly-ground turkey
Vegetable oil spray
¼ teaspoon pepper
1 tablespoon chopped parsley
1 teaspoon salt (opt.)
¼ cup red wine
½ teaspoon dried oregano
1 cup grated cheddar cheese
 alternative, divided
¼ cup mozzarella cheese
 alternative, or non-fat cheese
¼ cup egg substitute
½ cup fresh bread crumbs, divided

Vegetable oil spray
1 16-ounce can tomatoes,
 chopped
1 8-ounce can no-salt tomato
 sauce
2 packets sugar substitute, or
 4 teaspoons sugar
1 teaspoon dried basil
3 tablespoons liquid Butter Buds,
 see page 48
3 tablespoons cornstarch
1½ cups skim milk, warmed
Pepper, to taste
Dash of nutmeg
¼ teaspoon cinnamon
½ cup egg substitute

Peel eggplants; cut into ½-inch slices. Sprinkle with salt and set on plate; weight down with another plate for 30 minutes.

Cook turkey and onion in vegetable oil spray until meat loses its color. Add next 5 ingredients; simmer until liquid is nearly absorbed. Stir in ¾ of the cheddar and all the mozzarella. After the cheese melts, remove from heat; cool slightly; add egg and half the bread crumbs. Sprinkle the remaining bread crumbs in the bottom of a 3-quart casserole.

Pat the eggplant dry with paper towels. Place the eggplant on a sprayed non-stick cookie sheet. Spray the eggplant and broil for 3 minutes, about 4 inches from heat; turn, spray and broil 3 minutes longer. In a bowl, combine the tomatoes, sauce, sugar substitute and basil. Fill casserole with alternating layers of eggplant, meat mixture and tomato sauce mixture, starting and ending with eggplant.

Add Butter Buds to a saucepan. Dissolve cornstarch in milk; add milk to saucepan, whisking until thickened. Add pepper, nutmeg and cinnamon; remove pan from heat.

Mix 2 tablespoons milk mixture into the egg substitute; return to sauce; mix well; pour over casserole. Top with remaining cheese. Bake in 350F oven for 1 hour, or until top is golden.

Per serving: *Calories - 389; Total Fat - 13.5g;*
                   Saturated Fat - 3.9g; Cholesterol - 60mg

MEXICAN FLAVORED STUFFED PEPPERS

Yield: 4 servings

4 large green peppers
¾ pound turkey sausage,
  see page 87
1 medium onion, chopped
1 cup whole kernel corn
½ cup grated cheddar
  cheese alternative
1 teaspoon chili powder

½ cup chili sauce
1 teaspoon worcestershire-wine
  sauce
¼ teaspoon black pepper
¼ cup corn muffin mix
2½ tablespoons liquid Butter Buds,
  see page 48
Paprika

Cut peppers in half lengthwise; remove seeds and ribs. Drop into lightly salted boiling water for 4 minutes. Drain on paper towels.

Set out a 13x9x2-inch baking dish.

In a 12-inch non-stick sprayed skillet, cook the onions and turkey sausage until meat loses its color and the onions are softened. Stir in the rest of the ingredients, except the corn muffin mix and the Butter Buds.

Fill the peppers with the meat mixture. Sprinkle with a layer of corn muffin mix. Drizzle each pepper half with a teaspoon of Butter Buds, dust with paprika and bake at 350F for 40 minutes.

Per serving: *Calories - 297; Total Fat - 7.9g;*
                     Saturated Fat - 1.9g; Cholesterol - 64.3mg

PASTA PIZZA

Yield: 4 servings

4 ounces vermicelli, cooked with
no salt, drained
¼ cup freshly-grated parmesan
cheese
¼ cup egg substitute
¾ pound freshly-ground turkey
1 garlic clove, pressed
½ cup onion, chopped
¼ cup bell pepper, chopped
1 6-ounce can tomato paste

1 8-ounce can stewed tomatoes,
undrained and coarsely chopped
2 teaspoons sugar or 1 packet
sugar substitute
1 teaspoon dried oregano
½ teaspoon garlic powder
½ cup 1% fat cottage cheese
4 ounces shredded mozzarella
cheese alternative, or grated
non-fat mozzarella

Put vermicelli into a mixing bowl; mix in the parmesan cheese. Add the egg substitute; mix well. Spoon mixture into a deep 10-inch sprayed pie plate. Form pasta into a pie shell shape, spreading evenly across the bottom and up the sides. Microwave on HIGH, uncovered, for 3 minutes, or until set. Set aside.

Break up ground turkey into a 2-quart casserole; stir in garlic, onion and pepper. Cover with plastic wrap or microwave wrap and microwave on HIGH for 5 minutes, stirring twice. Add tomato paste, tomatoes, sugar and seasonings; mix well. Cover and microwave on HIGH for 3½ to 4 minutes, stirring once.

Spread cottage cheese over "pie shell". Top with the meat sauce; cover with plastic wrap or microwave wrap and microwave on HIGH for 6 minutes. Sprinkle with the mozzarella cheese; microwave, uncovered, on HIGH for about 1 minute, or until cheese begins to melt. Let stand for 10 minutes.

Per serving: *Calories - 424; Total Fat - 13.1g;*
Saturated Fat - 5.3g; Cholesterol - 77.8mg

STUFFED SHELLS

Yield: 8 servings

32 jumbo pasta shells
15-ounces no-fat ricotta cheese
½ pound 1% fat cottage cheese
2 cups shredded mozzarella
   cheese alternative, or non-fat
½ cup egg substitute
2 garlic cloves, pressed
½ teaspoon salt (opt.)

Dash of pepper
½ teaspoon dried basil
½ teaspoon garlic powder
1 tablespoon chopped parsley
6 saltines, crushed
2 16-ounce jars marinara sauce
¼ cup freshly-grated parmesan
   cheese

Cook shells per package instructions. Rinse with cold water, drain; let cool.

In a large bowl combine remaining ingredients, except for marinara sauce and parmesan cheese. Fill shells with the ricotta mixture. At this time the shells may be placed on a cookie sheet and frozen; package them and keep frozen until needed.

Spread a thin layer of marinara sauce in a 13x9x2-inch baking dish. Arrange shells in a single layer; top with the remaining sauce; sprinkle with the parmesan. Cover the dish with foil and bake at 350F for 25 to 30 minutes.

Remove foil and bake for 10 minutes more. Let stand for 5 minutes. Serve.

Per serving: *Calories - 385; Total Fat - 12.5g;*
                 Saturated Fat - 5.3g; Cholesterol - 16.3mg

"BEEF" ALA BING

Yield: 6 servings

1 cup uncooked elbow macaroni
1 teaspoon dried basil
1 onion, coarsely chopped
2 garlic cloves, pressed
2 stalks celery, sliced
2 bell peppers, coarsely chopped
1 tablespoon olive oil
Dried Italian seasoning, to taste

Salt (opt.) and pepper, to taste
¾ pound freshly-ground turkey
1 16-ounce can tomatoes
1 8-ounce can no-salt tomato sauce
1½ packets sugar substitute, or
   1 tablespoon sugar
½ cup shredded mozzarella cheese
   substitute, or no-fat mozzarella

Cook macaroni as directed, adding the basil to the water; drain and set aside.

In a large covered skillet, saute onions, garlic, celery and peppers in the olive oil until softened. Season with Italian seasoning, salt and pepper. Remove vegetables; keep warm.

Add turkey to skillet and break it up. Cook over moderate heat, stirring constantly, until no longer pink. Reduce heat and add vegetables, macaroni, tomatoes and tomato sauce. Break up tomatoes and mix well. Add sugar substitute, more Italian seasoning and the cheese; mix well.

Simmer, covered, for 15 minutes. Remove from heat and let stand for 3 to 4 hours, or better yet, overnight. Reheat before serving.

Per serving: *Calories - 245; Total Fat - 7.6g;*
                   Saturated Fat - 1.8g; Cholesterol - 43.7mg

SOSATIES (NEAR EAST SKEWERED "LAMB")

Yield: 2 servings

1 tablespoon olive oil	¼ teaspoon salt (opt.)
1 medium onion, chopped	Dash cayenne pepper
1 garlic clove, minced	½ pound boned turkey thighs,
½ cup low-sugar apricot	skinned and cut into large
preserves	chunks for skewering
1 tablespoon brown sugar	1 pound small white onions
¾ teaspoon cider vinegar	1 large green bell pepper
2 teaspoons hot curry powder	10 large mushrooms

In a medium saucepan, brown the onion in the oil. Add next 7 ingredients; mix well and simmer for 10 minutes, uncovered. Remove from heat and cool. Place the turkey in a shallow dish; cover with the onion mixture. Refrigerate, covered, for 48 hours. Stir occasionally.

Peel onions; parboil for 10 minutes. Add pepper, cut into 1x2-inch pieces, and cook for 5 minutes more.

Place turkey pieces on a skewer; set aside. Mix the vegetables and mushrooms into the marinade, thinned with a little water; let sit for ½ hour. With a slotted spoon, lift vegetables onto a square of heavy-duty aluminum foil. Add 4 ice cubes; wrap and seal.

Place vegetables and the skewered meat on a gas grill set on medium; close hood and cook for 15 minutes, turning meat every 5 minutes and basting with the marinade. Turn vegetable package once halfway through the cooking time.

Per serving: *Calories - 492; Total Fat - 12.5g;*
Saturated Fat - 3.3g; Cholesterol - 96mg

ORANGE "LAMB", GREEK STYLE

Yield: 4 servings

¾ pound skinned, boned turkey
thighs, cut into bite-size pieces
⅓ cup flour for dredging
2 shallots, minced
1 medium onion, sliced
1 stalk celery, coarsely chopped
1 garlic clove, minced
1 tablespoon olive oil
¾ cup white wine

¾ cup orange juice
Salt (opt.) and pepper, to taste
1 tablespoon chopped parsley
1 bay leaf
½ orange peel
2 teaspoons sugar
1 tablespoon minced parsley
1 navel orange, peeled and cut into
sections, membranes removed

Dredge the meat in flour, shaking off excess. In a small Dutch oven, cook the vegetables in the olive oil over low heat until they are tender. Transfer to a small bowl. Add the meat and cook over medium heat, adding more oil, if necessary, until cubes are cooked on all sides. Add wine and orange juice; bring to boil. Reduce heat. Return vegetables to the kettle; season mixture with salt and pepper. Add parsley, bay leaf and orange peel. Simmer covered, over low heat, for 1 hour.

In a small stainless steel saucepan, over low heat, cook the sugar, stirring constantly, until it is carmelized. Add ½ cup cooking liquid in a stream, stirring constantly, until the mixture is smooth. Add the sugar mixture to the casserole; cook, covered, for 1 hour more.

With a slotted spoon, transfer meat to a bowl; keep warm. Strain the liquid into a saucepan, pressing the vegetables against sides of strainer. Cook down, over medium heat, for 5 minutes. Return liquid and meat to the Dutch oven; add parsley and orange sections. Bring to a rolling boil; turn stove off and let kettle cool down, covered, for 5 minutes. Remove bay leaf and orange peel.

Per serving: *Calories - 317; Total Fat - 9.9g;*
                  Saturated Fat - 2.6g; Cholesterol - 72mg

"BEEF" LOAF ALA NORTH STREET

Yield: 4 servings

Vegetable oil spray
1 medium onion, chopped
1 pound freshly-ground turkey
¼ cup egg substitute
¼ cup chili sauce or 2 tablespoons
   Salsa, see page 233
1 8-ounce can tomato sauce

1 slice Swiss cheese alternative,
   diced
¼ teaspoon garlic powder
⅛ teaspoon pepper
1 teaspoon dried thyme
1 tablespoon chopped parsley
½ cup seasoned bread crumbs

In a small non-stick skillet over low heat, soften the onion in the vegetable oil spray.

In a large bowl, mix all ingredients together. Place in a sprayed loaf pan with high sides, and bake 50 to 60 minutes at 350F.

Per serving: *Calories - 308; Total Fat - 7.4g;*
                   Saturated Fat - 2.4g; Cholesterol - 88mg

BARBEQUED "PORK"

Yield: 16 servings

4 pounds turkey thighs, skinned
¼ cup water
1 tablespoon white wine

4 cups Barbeque Sauce,
   see page 223
16 hamburger rolls

Place first 3 ingredients in a medium size roasting pan; cover. Bake at 250F for 2 hours. Baste with barbeque sauce. Reduce heat to 200F and bake for another 2 hours. Turn oven off and let rest in oven for 30 minutes. Cool until meat can be handled.

With your fingers, shred meat into a large saucepan. Add Barbeque Sauce and mix well. Warm desired amount of mixture slowly and serve as barbeque sandwiches on the hamburger rolls. Stack it high. This is a great meal.

Remainder may be frozen in appropriate size containers for future use.

Per serving: *Calories - 411; Total Fat - 12g;*
                   Saturated Fat - 3.5g; Cholesterol - 96mg

"VEAL" MARSALA WITH MUSHROOMS

Yield: 4 servings

¾ pound turkey medallions cut
from the breast
¼ cup flour, mixed with salt and
pepper, to taste
6 tablespoons liquid Butter Buds,
see page 48
1 tablespoon olive oil

½ pound mushrooms, thinly sliced
2 green onions, thinly sliced
1 garlic clove, pressed
½ cup Marsala wine
⅓ cup low-sodium beef broth
1 teaspoon lemon juice
4 ounces spinach noodles

Flatten the medallions slightly between 2 sheets of wax paper. Coat them liberally with the flour mixture. In a non-stick skillet over medium heat, saute the medallions in 4 tablespoons of the Butter Buds and the oil until they are just cooked through. Transfer them to a platter and keep warm.

In a separate, covered, non-stick skillet, saute the mushrooms, green onion and garlic in the remaining Butter Buds for 3 to 4 minutes, or until the mushrooms are tender.

Meanwhile, in the first skillet, add the Marsala, broth and lemon juice; deglaze the pan. Cook down by ⅓ or until the sauce thickens to the consistency of gravy. Add the mushroom mixture, mix well, and simmer for 5 minutes. Pour mushroom mixture over turkey medallions, and serve with the spinach noodles, cooked as directed.

Per serving: *Calories - 371; Total Fat - 10.8g;*
Saturated Fat - 1.8g; Cholesterol - 59mg

"VEAL" OSCAR

Yield: 4 servings

This is one you won't believe, and without the expense of veal and crab!

½ pound imitation crabmeat,
  shredded
2 tablespoons liquid Butter Buds,
  see page 48
8 medallions, cut from turkey
  breast meat, about 1 pound

3 tablespoons liquid Butter Buds,
  see page 48
1 package frozen asparagus pieces,
  cooked and drained
1 cup Bearnaise Sauce, see page 224

In a covered saucepan, warm crabmeat in Butter Buds; set aside and keep warm. Between 2 sheets of wax paper, flatten the medallions slightly to about ¼-inch thick.

In a large non-stick skillet, cook the medallions in the 3 tablespoons of Butter Buds over medium heat. When they are just cooked through, remove from the skillet; arrange on a heated platter. Place about 5 pieces of asparagus over each medallion. Divide the crabmeat among them.

Add 3 tablespoons of water to the skillet; deglaze the pan. Pour over the medallions. Top with heated Bearnaise Sauce.

Per serving: *Calories - 331; Total Fat - 10.9g;*
                    Saturated Fat - 1.7g; Cholesterol - 88.8mg

"VEAL" STUFFED MANICOTTI

Yield: 3 servings

6 manicotti shells
2 tablespoons liquid Butter Buds,
　see page 48
1 small onion, finely chopped
½ green or red bell pepper,
　finely chopped
1 garlic clove, pressed
6 ounces freshly-ground turkey
1 teaspoon black pepper
¼ teaspoon garlic powder

1 cup spaghetti sauce, see page
　234, or use commercially bottled
1 teaspoon dried basil
1½ teaspoons dried oregano
2 tablespoons chopped parsley
1 packet sugar substitute, or
　2 teaspoons sugar
½ cup 1% fat cottage cheese
½ cup shredded mozzarella cheese
　alternative, or no-fat, divided

Cook manicotti as directed. In a covered, non-stick 10-inch skillet, over low heat, saute the onions, pepper and garlic in the Butter Buds. When the vegetables begin to soften, add the turkey meat, black pepper and garlic powder. Cover, and continue cooking, stirring occasionally, until meat loses its color.

Add spaghetti sauce, oregano and basil; mix well, cover and simmer 10 minutes, stirring occasionally.

In a small bowl, mix the parsley, sugar substitute, cottage cheese and ¼ cup of the mozzarella. Add cheese mixture to the sauce; mix well and simmer until the cheese is melted. Let cool.

Stuff shells with ⅔ of the meat sauce; place in sprayed shallow baking dish just large enough to hold the shells. Pour remaining sauce over; sprinkle with remaining cheese.

Bake, covered with foil, at 350F for 20 minutes. Remove foil and continue cooking for 5 minutes more. Let stand for 5 minutes before serving.

Per serving:　　*Calories - 352; Total Fat - 13.5g;*
　　　　　　　　Saturated Fat - 3.3g; Cholesterol - 50mg

POULTRY

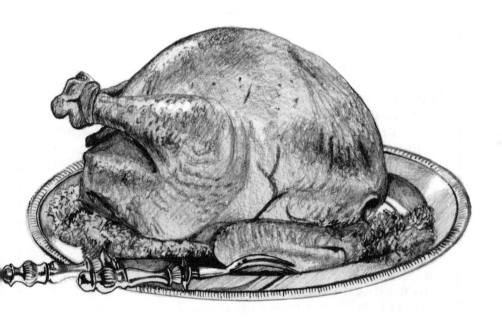

POULTRY

We never seem to tire of poultry, especially chicken. In fact, we don't even miss the lack of skin anymore. (Remember — skin is a no-no.) There are so many different ways to prepare chicken, it was difficult to cull down our recipe collection to those we put in **THE HEALTHY HEART GOURMET.**

Chicken is inexpensive and has reasonable fat and cholesterol levels. Enjoy the variety of recipes we have prepared for you, and know they are good for you.

Do try the Cornish game hen recipes and those recipes made from our low-fat champion - **turkey.**

BROILER'S SAUTERNE

Yield: 4 servings

½ cup sauterne	½ teaspoon salt (opt.)
½ tablespoon olive oil	1 teaspoon freshly-grated ginger
1 tablespoon capers, drained	1 broiler/fryer, cut up and skinned,
and crushed	wing tips discarded

Mix the first 5 ingredients together; pour mixture over chicken; refrigerate for 24 hours, turning several times.

Place the chicken on heavy-duty aluminum foil on grill, over low heat, for 20 minutes. Brush with the marinade and turn chicken every 2 minutes for even cooking.

Remove foil and grill 10 minutes longer, again turning and basting every 2 minutes. Chicken is done when juices run clear when pricked with a fork.

Per serving: *Calories - 200; Total Fat - 7.4g;*
Saturated Fat - 1.8g; Cholesterol - 81.5mg

BROCCOLI-CHICKEN STEW

Yield: 6 servings

12 chicken thighs, skinned, boned
and halved, about 1½ pounds
1 tablespoon canola oil
1 garlic clove, pressed
1 envelope (0.8 ounce) lite Italian
salad dressing mix
1 teaspoon salt (opt.)
4 cups low-sodium chicken broth
½ cup white wine
1 tablespoon worcestershire sauce

¼ cup catsup
3 packets sugar substitute
4 medium potatoes, cut into
¾-inch cubes
1 green bell pepper, cut into strips
16-ounce bag frozen whole boiling
onions
10 ounces fresh or frozen broccoli,
cut into bite-size pieces
2 cups sliced mushrooms

In a 4½-quart Dutch oven, slowly brown the chicken pieces in the oil and garlic. Remove the chicken and drain fat.

In the same pan, mix the salad dressing and the next 6 ingredients over low heat. Add the chicken pieces, potatoes and peppers. Bring to a boil; reduce heat, cover and simmer for 30 minutes. Add onions, broccoli and mushrooms. Cover and simmer for 10 minutes more, or until the vegetables are done to your liking.

Serve in soup bowls with soft dinner rolls, see page 95.

Note: The gravy may be thickened by adding a cornstarch and water paste. Stir constantly until it thickens.

Per serving: *Calories - 414; Total Fat - 15g;*
Saturated Fat - 3.7g; Cholesterol - 98.7mg

BUZZED CHICKEN
Yield: 4 servings

2 onions, diced
3 tablespoons liquid Butter Buds,
  see page 48
1 broiler/fryer, cut up and skinned,
  wing tips discarded

Salt (opt.) and pepper, to taste
½ cup skim milk
1 tablespoon cornstarch
2 tablespoons brandy
1 teaspoon hot curry powder

In a covered, non-stick skillet just large enough to hold the chicken pieces, soften onions in the Butter Buds. Add the chicken; sprinkle with salt and pepper; simmer, covered, for 30 minutes, turning pieces once.

Remove chicken to a serving dish; keep warm.

Dissolve cornstarch in the milk; add to the skillet with the brandy and curry powder. Bring near a boil, whisking constantly until sauce thickens. Pour over chicken.

Per serving: *Calories - 254; Total Fat - 7.8g;*
                    Saturated Fat - 1.8g; Cholesterol - 82mg

CHICKEN BREASTS IN SHALLOT BUTTER
Yield: 2 servings

1 large shallot, minced
3 tablespoons liquid Butter Buds,
  see page 48

1 tablespoon white wine
2 boned/skinned chicken breast
  halves, cut into ½-inch slices

In a covered, non-stick skillet, saute the shallot in the Butter Buds until soft. Add the wine and the chicken pieces; saute gently until just done. Place chicken on platter; pour remaining sauce over.

Per serving: *Calories - 194; Total Fat - 7g;*
                    Saturated Fat - 1.2g; Cholesterol - 73mg

CHICKEN BREASTS WITH MUSTARD SAUCE
Yield: 4 servings

4 chicken breast halves, skinned
  and boned
½ cup white wine
6 shallots, minced
¼ cup chopped parsley

½ pound mushrooms, sliced
½ teaspoon dried tarragon
¼ cup drained capers
3 tablespoons Dijon mustard
Black pepper to taste

Flatten the chicken breasts slightly between 2 sheets of wax paper. Pour wine into a heavy skillet just large enough to hold the chicken. Add the shallots, parsley, mushrooms, tarragon and capers; cook over medium heat for 2 minutes. Add chicken, mustard and pepper. Cook, uncovered, for 8 to 10 minutes. Add more wine, if needed.

Remove chicken from pan; keep warm. Smooth out sauce by stirring well; pour over chicken.

Per serving: *Calories - 192; Total Fat - 4g;*
               Saturated Fat - .9g; Cholesterol - 73mg

SWEET/SOUR CHICKEN
Yield: 4 servings

1 broiler/fryer, cut up and skinned,
  wing tips discarded
1 small can crushed pineapple,
  in its own juices
2 tablespoons cornstarch
¾ cup sugar

½ cup lite soy sauce
¼ cup vinegar
1 garlic clove, pressed
½ teaspoon ground ginger
¼ teaspoon pepper

Arrange chicken in a 13x9x2-inch baking dish. Drain pineapple, reserving 2 tablespoons juice. In a saucepan, combine the reserved juice and remaining ingredients. Cook over medium heat, stirring constantly, until thick and bubbly. Pour over chicken.

Bake in a 325F oven for 30 minutes, basting several times. Turn chicken pieces, and spread with pineapple. Spoon sauce over all, and continue baking and basting another 30 minutes, or until tender.

Per serving: *Calories - 370; Total Fat - 5.7g;*
               Saturated Fat - 1.6g; Cholesterol - 81.5mg

CHICKEN IN CREAM SAUCE

Yield: 4 servings

1 broiler/fryer, cut up and skinned,
  wing tips discarded
1 onion sliced
1 tablespoon canola oil
2½ cups cream of mushroom
  soup, see page 118

1 teaspoon crushed dried tarragon
1 tablespoon hot curry powder
¼ cup red wine
Salt (opt.) and pepper, to taste
4 ounces uncooked noodles

Saute chicken and onion slices in a large skillet in oil until softened. Add remaining ingredients except noodles, lower heat and simmer, covered, for 45 minutes.

Cook noodles as directed. Serve chicken over noodles.

Per serving: *Calories - 385; Total Fat - 12g;*
                   Saturated Fat - 2.8g; Cholesterol - 84.3mg

CHICKEN AND RICE CASSEROLE

Yield: 4 servings

1 garlic clove, pressed
1 small onion, chopped
1 small green pepper, chopped
2 tablespoons liquid Butter Buds,
  see page 48
1¼ cups cream of mushroom
  soup, see page 118

2 teaspoons curry powder
2 cups, cubed cooked chicken
2 cups cooked long grain rice
½ cup seasoned bread crumbs
2 tablespoons freshly-grated
  parmesan cheese
Dash of paprika

In a 1-quart covered saucepan over low heat, saute the garlic, onion and pepper in the Butter Buds. When soft, add the soup, curry powder and chicken. Mix well.

In a 2-quart sprayed casserole, put a layer of the chicken mixture; then a layer of rice. Repeat layers, ending with the chicken mixture.

Top the casserole with bread crumbs and cheese. Sprinkle with paprika and bake, uncovered, at 350F for 30 to 35 minutes, or until bubbly.

Per serving: *Calories - 407; Total Fat - 10.3g;*
                   Saturated Fat - 3.3g; Cholesterol - 65.8mg

CHICKEN MARENGO

Yield: 4 servings

1 broiler/fryer, cut up and skinned,
wing tips discarded
⅓ cup all-purpose flour
1 teaspoon salt (opt.)
¼ teaspoon pepper
½ teaspoon dried tarragon
Vegetable oil spray
1 tablespoon olive oil
1 garlic clove, pressed

3 tablespoons chopped onion
4 tomatoes, skinned and quartered
1 cup sauterne
Bouquet garni (parsley, dried thyme
and bay leaf) in cheesecloth bag
2 tablespoons liquid Butter Buds,
see page 48
1 cup sliced mushrooms
¼ cup sliced green olives (opt.)
2 tablespoons cornstarch

Coat chicken evenly with the next 4 ingredients which have been mixed in a plastic bag. In a large skillet, heat the garlic in the vegetable oil spray. Add the olive oil and the chicken; cook until browned. Add the onion, tomatoes, wine and bouquet garni. Cover and simmer for 30 minutes, or until chicken is tender.

Remove chicken from the skillet; cool and bone. In a small covered skillet, saute the mushrooms in the Butter Buds for 4 minutes. Add to the chicken along with the olives. Dispose of the bouquet garni and gradually add a mixture of the cornstarch and water to the pot liquor, stirring constantly until it thickens.

Return the chicken mixture to the sauce; cover, and simmer for about 10 minutes. Arrange the chicken on a platter; pour sauce over.

Per serving: *Calories - 338; Total Fat - 11g;*
Saturated Fat - 2.3g; Cholesterol - 81.5mg

CHICKEN STIR FRY

Yield: 4 servings

3 tablespoons lite soy sauce
2 teaspoons cornstarch
2 tablespoons sauterne
1 teaspoon freshly-grated
   ginger-root
1 teaspoon sugar
½ teaspoon salt (opt.)
½ teaspoon crushed red pepper
1 tablespoon peanut oil
2 garlic cloves, halved
4 slices ginger-root

2 medium green peppers, cut
   into thick slices
3 ounces peapods (snow peas)
4 green onions, cut into 1-inch
   pieces
½ cup pecan halves (opt.)
4 chicken breast halves, skinned,
   boned and cut into thin slices
¼ teaspoon sesame oil
1 cup long grain rice, cooked as
   directed

Mix the first 7 ingredients together. Set aside.

Add ½ teaspoon oil to a preheated wok or large heavy skillet, set on high. Fry a piece of garlic and ginger until they begin to brown; discard. Add the green peppers, peapods and onions. Stir fry until crisp tender. Remove to a bowl and keep warm.

Add more oil, garlic and ginger. Again discard garlic and ginger. Add the pecans; fry until golden. Remove to the holding bowl. Repeat the seasoning process; add half the chicken, cooking until just done.   Remove; cook remaining chicken again after seasoning the oil.

Lower heat; return all the vegetables and chicken to the wok. Add the soy sauce mixture; stir until thick and bubbly. Mix in the sesame oil. Serve over hot rice.

Per serving: *Calories - 511; Total fat - 16.8g;*
                    Saturated Fat - 2.5g; Cholesterol - 73mg

CHICKEN WITH PORT WINE SAUCE
Yield: 2 servings

SAUCE

½ cup port wine
1½ tablespoons minced shallots
1½ teaspoons lime juice
1½ teaspoons orange juice

⅛ teaspoon black pepper
Pinch each dried thyme, salt (opt.)
  and cayenne pepper
½ cup Veloute Sauce, see page 235

In a small saucepan, combine the above ingredients, except the Veloute Sauce. Bring to a boil; reduce by half. Pour mixture into the warmed Veloute Sauce; mix well and keep warm.

2 chicken breast halves, skinned
  and boned
¼ cup flour
⅛ teaspoon pepper

¼ teaspoon salt (opt.)
Vegetable oil spray
3 tablespoons liquid Butter Buds,
  see page 48

Dredge the chicken in a plastic bag containing a mixture of the flour, salt and pepper. In a non-stick skillet sprayed with the vegetable oil, cook the chicken in the Butter Buds over low heat, turning once. Cook about 7 minutes on each side.

Pour one half the sauce on a warm serving platter. Arrange the chicken on top and pour the remaining sauce over all.

Per serving: *Calories - 335; Total Fat - 8.9g;*
            Saturated Fat - 1.5g; Cholesterol - 73.5mg

CHUCK'S CHICKEN

Yield: 4 servings

1 broiler/fryer, cut up and skinned,
  wing tips discarded
2 tablespoons olive oil
¼ cup chopped green onions
12 very small white onions
¼ cup brandy

2 garlic cloves, pressed
½ teaspoon salt (opt.)
¼ teaspoon black pepper
¾ cup white wine
½ pound mushrooms, sliced

Pat chicken dry, and in a non-stick skillet brown in the oil. Remove from pan; set aside. Saute the green and white onions until lightly browned.

Place chicken on top of browned vegetables. Warm brandy; pour over chicken and ignite. Shake pan until flames are extinguished.

Mix garlic, salt and pepper together. Sprinkle over chicken; add mushrooms. Cover and simmer for 40 minutes, or until chicken is done.

Per serving: *Calories - 328; Total Fat - 9.4g;*
                Saturated Fat - 2.2g; Cholesterol - 81.5mg

CRISPY BAKED CHICKEN

Yield: 4 servings

1 broiler/fryer, cut up and skinned,
  wing tip discarded

¼ to ⅓ cup fat and cholesterol-
  free mayonnaise
½ to ¾ cup seasoned bread crumbs

Coat the chicken pieces lightly with the mayonnaise. Roll in the bread crumbs and arrange in a shallow baking dish.

Bake at 400F for 15 minutes.

Reduce heat to 300F; continue baking for 25 to 30 minutes, or until juices run clear when pricked with a fork.

Per serving: *Calories - 263; Total Fat - 6.6g;*
                Saturated Fat - 1.9g; Cholesterol - 82.5mg

FLORIDA CHICKEN

Yield: 4 servings

¼ cup egg substitute
2 tablespoons water
1 cup seasoned bread crumbs
⅓ cup freshly-grated parmesan cheese
¼ cup chopped parsley
½ teaspoon salt (opt.)

Pepper, to taste
1 broiler/fryer, cut up and
  skinned, wing tips discarded
¼ cup liquid Butter Buds,
  see page 48
1 garlic clove, pressed

In a shallow bowl, mix egg substitute with the water and dip chicken pieces to coat. Mix crumbs with next 4 ingredients. Dip chicken pieces into crumb mixture; coat well.

Arrange chicken in a shallow, sprayed, roasting pan. Mix the Butter Buds with garlic and pour over all. Bake at 350F for 50 to 60 minutes, until tender and cooked through. Do not turn chicken. Baste frequently with the pan drippings.

Per serving: *Calories - 393; Total Fat - 15.8g;*
                  Saturated Fat - 6.2g; Cholesterol - 99.3mg

MASKED CHICKEN

Yield: 4 servings

2 garlic cloves, pressed
1 small onion, chopped
¼ teaspoon cayenne pepper
½ teaspoon cardamom, peeled
  and crushed
½ teaspoon cumin
¼ teaspoon saffron threads

1 tablespoon liquid Butter Buds,
  see page 48
Juice of ½ lemon
1 tablespoon chopped parsley
Pinch of powdered ginger
1 broiler/fryer, cut up and
  skinned, wing tips discarded
¾ cup bread crumbs

Place all ingredients, except chicken and bread crumbs, in a blender. Blend into a paste.

Spray a baking dish just large enough to hold the chicken pieces. Make diagonal slashes in the chicken pieces; spread the paste over all. Coat with bread crumbs and bake in a 400F oven for 20 to 25 minutes, or until done.

Per serving: *Calories - 257; Total Fat - 7.3g;*
                  Saturated Fat - 2g; Cholesterol - 82.5mg

SOUR CREAM CHICKEN

Yield: 4 servings

1 cup mock sour cream, see page 51
1 tablespoon lemon juice
1 teaspoon celery salt
½ teaspoon salt (opt.)
1 teaspoon paprika
⅛ teaspoon pepper

1 tablespoon worcestershire-
   wine sauce
1 broiler/fryer, cut up and
   skinned, wing tips discarded
¾ cup seasoned bread crumbs
2 tablespoons liquid Butter Buds,
   see page 48

Combine first 7 ingredients. Roll the chicken in the sour cream mixture. Pour the remaining sauce over the chicken; refrigerate, covered, overnight. Roll in crumbs; cover and refrigerate for 2 hours more.

Place in a sprayed baking pan. Drizzle with Butter Buds and bake at 325F for 1 hour 15 minutes.

Per serving: *Calories - 222; Total Fat - 8g;*
                    Saturated Fat - 2.7g; Cholesterol - 88.5mg

STUFFED ROASTED CHICKEN

Yield: 6 servings

1 roasting chicken (4 to 4½
pounds), cleaned

STUFFING

2 stalks celery, finely chopped
1 medium onion, finely chopped
1 teaspoon dried thyme, crushed
3 tablespoons liquid Butter Buds,
see page 48
8 slices stale bread, cubed
1 teaspoon salt (opt.)

¼ teaspoon pepper
⅔ to 1 cup low-sodium chicken
bouillon
1 tablespoon white wine
¼ cup egg substitute
2 tablespoons chopped parsley

In a covered non-stick skillet, over low heat, saute the celery, onions and thyme in the Butter Buds. Meanwhile, in a large bowl, combine the bread cubes with remaining ingredients. Add sauteed vegetables; mix well.

Fill the cavity of the chicken with the dressing, and sew or truss up opening. If the cavity is too small, bake the excess dressing in a small, sprayed baking dish, covered, for 35 minutes at 350F.

Make a basting sauce by mixing together:

⅓ cup orange juice
¼ teaspoon seasoning and
browning sauce

Brush the chicken with the basting sauce; sprinkle with pepper. To assure moist breast meat, place breast side down in open roasting pan and bake at 350F for about 45 minutes, basting once or twice. Turn chicken breast side up, baste, and continue roasting another 50 to 60 minutes, again basting once or twice. Chicken is done when its juices run clear when pricked with a fork.

Per serving: *Calories - 310; Total Fat - 12.7g;*
Saturated Fat - 3.4g; Cholesterol - 72.8mg

TURKEY-BROCCOLI CASSEROLE

Yield: 6 servings

2 packages frozen broccoli spears,
cooked, drained, cut into bite-size
pieces
2 cups cooked, turkey meat, cubed
2 tablespoons liquid Butter Buds,
see page 48
⅛ teaspoon salt (opt.)
Pepper, to taste
1 tablespoon lemon juice

1¼ cups cream of mushroom
soup, see page 118
½ cup skim milk
½ cup fat and cholesterol free-
mayonnaise
½ cup white wine
⅓ cup grated cheddar cheese
alternative

In a large baking dish, arrange the broccoli to cover the bottom; place turkey pieces on top. Drizzle with Butter Buds; sprinkle with salt, pepper and lemon juice.

Mix the remaining ingredients together and pour over the turkey. Bake at 325F for 35 to 40 minutes.

Per serving: *Calories - 244; Total Fat - 6.5g;*
                Saturated Fat - 1.7g; Cholesterol - 54mg

BAKED STUFFED CORNISH GAME HENS
Yield: 4 servings

2 Cornish game hens, cleaned,
  rinsed and patted dry
2 tablespoons chopped celery
¼ cup chopped onion
2 tablespoons liquid Butter Buds,
  see page 48

1½ cups herb stuffing mix
2 tablespoons liquid Butter Buds,
  see page 48
½ cup hot water
2 tablespoons white wine

In a covered, non-stick skillet, over low heat, saute the celery and onion in 2 tablespoons Butter Buds until softened. Combine with the next 4 ingredients. Stuff the hens, and sew or truss the opening.

Put in a baking dish just large enough to hold the hens, and bake at 350F for 50 to 60 minutes, basting occasionally with the following sauce:

¼ cup liquid Butter Buds,
  see page 48
2 tablespoons brown sugar

2 tablespoons lime juice
2 tablespoons white wine
2 teaspoons lite soy sauce

Per serving: *Calories - 501; Total Fat - 12g;*
                 Saturated Fat - 2.2g; Cholesterol - 135mg

CORNISH HENS WITH LONG GRAIN & WILD RICE

Yield: 4 servings

1 6-ounce package mixed long
  grain and wild rice
1 cup water
2 tablespoons liquid Butter Buds,
  see page 48
1 medium onion, finely chopped
1 tablespoon cornstarch
2 cups low-sodium chicken broth
½ cup sliced mushrooms

1 10-ounce package frozen peas,
  thawed
2 Cornish game hens, halved,
  cleaned and patted dry
1 tablespoon liquid Butter Buds,
  see page 48
Salt (opt.) and pepper, to taste
½ teaspoon dry mustard

Combine rice, its seasonings and the water in a 2-quart saucepan. Cover and cook for 12 minutes, or until water is absorbed.

In a covered saucepan, over low heat, saute the onions in Butter Buds. Dissolve cornstarch in broth. Pour broth into saucepan, stirring constantly until it thickens. Stir in the rice, mushrooms and peas. Remove from heat.

Rub hens with a mixture of Butter Buds, salt, pepper and dry mustard. Arrange the rice mixture in a sprayed 12x8x2-inch baking dish. Place the hens on top of rice and cover. Bake at 350F for 1 hour and 15 minutes, or until the rice is done and the hens are tender.

Per serving: *Calories - 391; Total Fat - 8.4g;*
                    Saturated Fat - 2.2g; Cholesterol - 135mg

LAZY LEFT OVER TURKEY

Yield: 4 servings

1 medium onion, chopped
1 garlic clove, pressed
½ green bell pepper, chopped
3 tablespoons liquid Butter Buds,
  see page 48
2 tablespoons reduced-calorie
  apricot preserves

1 tablespoon white wine
¼ teaspoon ground nutmeg
Salt (opt.) and pepper, to taste
½ cup sliced mushrooms
2 cups cooked turkey meat, cubed
1 can cream of chicken soup
½ cup skim milk

In a medium covered saucepan, over low heat, saute the vegetables in the Butter Buds until softened. Add the remaining ingredients, and simmer for about 20 minutes, stirring occasionally. Serve over rice or pasta.

Per serving: *Calories - 285; Total Fat - 8g;*
                   Saturated Fat - 2g; Cholesterol - 82.3mg

TURKEY CASSEROLE

Yield: 6 servings

½ cup onion-garlic croutons
⅓ cup skim milk
1¼ cups cream of celery soup,
  see page 117
1 tablespoon white wine
⅓ cup mock sour cream, see page 51
2 cups cooked turkey, cut into bite-
  size pieces

1 cup frozen peas
½ small onion, chopped
¼ cup mango chutney, see page 52,
  or commercially-bottled chutney
Salt (opt.) and pepper, to taste
1 cup onion-garlic croutons, crushed
⅓ cup liquid Butter Buds,
  see page 48

Place the ¾ cup croutons in a 1½-quart sprayed casserole. Set aside. In a large mixing bowl, combine the milk, soup, wine and sour cream. Stir well.

Add turkey, thawed peas, onion, chutney, salt and pepper. Pour into casserole. Sprinkle with the 1 cup crushed croutons, and drizzle with the Butter Buds. Bake, uncovered, for 45 minutes at 300F.

Per serving: *Calories - 259; Total Fat - 7.3g;*
                   Saturated - 1.4g; Cholesterol - 54mg

TURKEY TETRAZZINI

Yield: 4 servings

4 ounces uncooked spaghetti,
  broken into thirds
1 teaspoon Italian seasoning
1 teaspoon parsley, chopped
2 cups cooked turkey or chicken,
  cubed
½ cup sliced mushrooms
1¼ cups cream of mushroom
  soup, see page 118

¾ cup Instant Chicken Gravy,
  see page 227
Salt (opt.) and pepper, to taste
¼ cup seasoned bread crumbs
2 tablespoons liquid Butter Buds,
  see page 48
¼ cup freshly-grated parmesan
  cheese
Paprika

Cook spaghetti with Italian seasoning and parsley added to the water.

In a large bowl, combine the next 6 ingredients; mix well. Blend in the spaghetti and place in a 1½-quart sprayed casserole. Cover with bread crumbs, and drizzle with the Butter Buds, parmesan and paprika.

Bake at 350F for 20 to 25 minutes.

Per serving: *Calories - 433; Total Fat - 11.4g;*
                Saturated Fat - 4.3g; Cholesterol - 90.8mg

SEAFOOD

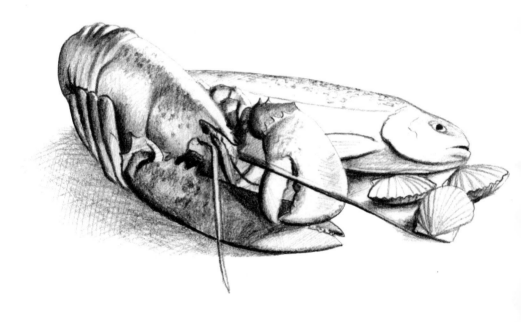

SEAFOOD

Seafood is good for you with finfish and bivalves topping the list. Shrimp carry a fair amount of cholesterol, so eat them in moderation. Fresh fish are best, but the new "flash-freezing" methods are proving quite acceptable.

Sauces beautifully enhance the subtleness of many fish. Try them!

Surimi, the imitation crabmeat, shrimp and lobster have opened many new doors for low-fat, inexpensive main entrees, salads and side dishes for "meatless" meals.

If you haven't been a fresh salmon or tuna fan, do give yourself a real treat. You won't be unhappy!

When we mention "white" fish in this book we mean those common white fish fillets available in most any good fish market-----Cod, Haddock, Orange Ruffy, Snapper, Grouper and the like.

BAKED BLUE FISH

Yield: 4 servings

1 pound blue fish fillets, skinned	**¼ cup gin**
¼ cup liquid Butter Buds,	**Salt (opt.) and pepper, to taste**
see page 48	

Line a shallow baking pan with aluminum foil. Place fish in pan.

Mix gin and Butter Buds together; pour over fish. Sprinkle with salt and pepper. Bake, uncovered, at 400F for 20 to 25 minutes, or until fish flakes easily.

Per serving: Calories - 308; Total Fat - 8.5g;
*   Saturated Fat - 1.4g; Cholesterol - 82.8mg*

CRAB IMPERIAL

Yield: 4 servings

1 pound imitation crabmeat,	**¼ teaspoon salt (opt.)**
chopped	**¼ cup egg substitute**
2 tablespoons liquid Butter Buds,	**½ cup fat and cholesterol-free**
see page 48	**mayonnaise**
½ teaspoon worcestershire-wine	**1 tablespoon sauterne**
sauce	**2 slices Swiss cheese alternative,**
1 tablespoon cream-style horseradish	**grated**

In a medium bowl, mix all ingredients together, except the Swiss cheese. Put mixture into 4 sprayed ramekins or small oven-proof dishes.

Sprinkle tops with grated cheese; bake at 300F for 35 minutes, or until hot and bubbly.

Per serving: Calories - 221; Total Fat - 8.8g;
*   Saturated Fat - 1.5g; Cholesterol - 20.9mg*

GOURMET FILLET OF FISH

Yield: 4 servings

1 pound white fish fillets
1 tablespoon grated onion
½ teaspoon salt (opt.)
⅛ teaspoon black pepper
1 large tomato, peeled and cut
   into small pieces

1 tablespoon white wine
3 tablespoons liquid Butter Buds,
   see page 48
2 tablespoons sweet pickle relish
½ cup shredded Swiss cheese
   alternative

Cut fillets into serving pieces; place in single layer on a sprayed baking pan just large enough to hold them. Sprinkle fish with onion, salt and pepper. Cover with tomato pieces. Pour wine mixed with Butter Buds on top.

Broil about 4 inches from the heat for 8 to 10 minutes, or until fish flakes easily when tested with a fork.

Remove from oven; spread with relish, then sprinkle with cheese. Broil 2 minutes longer, or until cheese melts.

*Per serving: Calories - 215; Total Fat - 5.7g;
            Saturated Fat - 1.2g; Cholesterol - 84mg*

POACHED FISH WITH HORSERADISH SAUCE
Yield: 4 servings

1 pound white fish fillets
Cheesecloth to wrap fish
Boiling water to cover fish
⅓ cup sauterne

1 small onion, chopped
2 tablespoons parsley, chopped
½ teaspoon salt (opt.)
⅛ teaspoon black pepper

Wrap fillets in the cheesecloth; place in a 10-inch skillet with a tight-fitting cover. Add next 6 ingredients. Cover and simmer for 10 minutes or until the fish flakes when tested with a fork.

SAUCE

¾ cup mock sour cream,
  see page 51

½ teaspoon lemon juice
2 tablespoons cream-style
  horseradish

Blend the sauce ingredients together. Rest at room temperature. Remove fish from cloth; place on serving dish; nap with sauce.

Per serving: *Calories - 195; Total Fat - 1.9g;*
            Saturated Fat - 1g; Cholesterol - 89.3mg

WHITE FISH WITH CAPER SAUCE

Yield: 4 servings

2 tablespoons shallots, minced
2 tablespoons white wine vinegar
1 tablespoon lemon juice
Salt (opt.) and pepper, to taste
2 teaspoons drained capers
¼ cup egg substitute

3 tablespoons liquid Butter Buds,
   see page 48
1 tablespoon chopped parsley
1 pound white fish fillets
3 tablespoons liquid Butter Buds,
   see page 48

In a saucepan, combine the first 4 ingredients; bring to a boil; reduce to about 2 tablespoons.

Place mixture in a blender with the capers, and puree. Add the egg substitute, Butter Buds and parsley; blend well. Return sauce to pan; keep warm. Be careful not to scramble egg substitute.

Place the fillets and Butter Buds in a non-stick skillet, over low heat, and cook, covered, until they flake easily when tested with a fork. Place fish on a serving platter and pour sauce over.

Per serving: *Calories - 190; Total Fat - 5g;*
                    Saturated Fat - .5g; Cholesterol - 84mg

BAKED HADDOCK AU GRATIN

Yield: 4 servings

1 pound haddock fillets, or
  other white fish fillets
1 tablespoon lemon juice
⅛ teaspoon paprika
Salt (opt.) and pepper, to taste
1 tablespoon liquid Butter Buds,
  see page 48
1 tablespoon cornstarch

½ cup skim milk, warmed
½ cup shredded mozzarella
  cheese alternative
1 tablespoon white wine
¼ cup bread crumbs
2 tablespoons liquid Butter Buds,
  see page 48

Cut fish into serving pieces; place in a sprayed shallow baking dish. Sprinkle with lemon juice, paprika, salt and pepper.

Add Butter Buds to a saucepan over medium heat. Dissolve the cornstarch, salt and pepper in the milk. Add milk to saucepan, whisking constantly until sauce is thick and bubbly. Stir in cheese until it melts. Add wine; pour sauce over fillets.

Sprinkle with crumbs; drizzle with the remaining Butter Buds, and bake at 350F for 20 minutes, or until fish flakes easily when tested with a fork.

Per serving: Calories - 265; Total Fat - 8.4g;
*   Saturated Fat - 2g; Cholesterol - 85mg*

COMPANY LOBSTER

Yield: 4 servings

¾ pound cooked lobster meat
  coarsely chopped, or ¾ pound
  chopped imitation lobster
¼ cup liquid Butter Buds,
  see page 48
2 tablespoons cornstarch
1 cup skim milk, warmed

½ teaspoon salt (opt.)
½ teaspoon paprika
Few grains cayenne pepper
1 tablespoon lemon juice
2 tablespoons finely-chopped
  parsley
2 tablespoons white wine

In a covered saucepan over low heat, saute the lobster in the Butter Buds until heated through. Remove from pan; keep warm. Dissolve cornstarch in milk. Add to pan with next 3 ingredients; cook, whisking constantly, until the mixture thickens. Add the lemon juice, parsley and wine; mix well. Remove from heat and add the lobster meat; mix well.

Divide the mixture into 4 sprayed ramekins; top with a mixture of the following:

12 saltine crackers, crumbled
¼ cup grated parmesan cheese

Finally, drizzle the top with 2 tablespoons liquid Butter Buds, and bake at 450F for 10 to 12 minutes, or until the tops are golden.

Per serving: *Calories - 275; Total Fat - 9.8g;*
                   Saturated Fat - 3.3g; Cholesterol - 76mg

Per serving with imitation lobster:
                   Calories - 274; Total Fat - 9.3g;
                   Saturated Fat - 3.2g; Cholesterol - 30mg

KING MACKEREL

Yield: 4 servings

4 king mackerel steaks, about
¾ pound total
1 tablespoon lime juice
1 tablespoon fat and cholesterol-
free mayonnaise

2 tablespoons fresh-cut chives
1 teaspoon dillweed
Salt (opt.) and pepper, to taste

Sprinkle both sides of steaks with lime juice; let rest for 10 minutes. Spread with the mayonnaise; sprinkle with the chives, dillweed, salt and pepper.

Grill 10 minutes per inch thickness. Turn frequently for even cooking.

Per serving: *Calories - 229; Total Fat - 15g;*
              Saturated Fat - 3.6g; Cholesterol - 64mg

OYSTER STEW

Yield: 4 servings

2 tablespoons liquid Butter Buds,
see page 48
½ cup chopped onion
1 dozen oysters
3 cups warmed skim milk

Salt (opt.) and white pepper,
to taste
Cayenne pepper, to taste
2 tablespoons liquid Butter Buds,
see page 48

In a covered, non-stick skillet, saute the onions in the Butter Buds until soft.

Remove the oysters from their shells, reserving the liquid. Poach them in their own liquid for about 3 minutes, or until their edges begin to curl. Add the milk, onion, salt, pepper and cayenne. Mix well and simmer for 5 minutes, or until done.

Add the 2 tablespoons Butter Buds. Combine well, and serve.

Per serving: *Calories - 127; Total Fat - 4g;*
              Saturated Fat - .7g; Cholesterol - 26mg

POMPANO EN PAPILLOTE

Yield: 4 servings

SAUCE

½ cup imitation crabmeat,
coarsely chopped
½ cup cooked shrimp, chopped

1 cup thick White Sauce,
see page 235
¼ cup white wine

Mix the first 3 ingredients together in a saucepan; heat thoroughly. Add the wine; set aside to cool, then refrigerate.

4 15x12-inch pieces of parchment
paper
Vegetable oil spray
4 pompano fillets, about 3 ounces
each (flounder works well)

½ teaspoon salt (opt.)
⅛ teaspoon pepper

Fold each piece of parchment paper in half, lengthwise; crease sharply. With scissors, trim each piece into a large heart shape. Place open hearts on baking sheet and spray the right side with vegetable oil, leaving the edge unoiled.

Place fillets on the oiled sides near crease. Sprinkle with salt and pepper. Divide the crab sauce among the fillets. Fold left side of heart over the right. Starting with the rounded edge of each heart, pleat and crimp edges together to seal. At the lower end, twist paper tightly.

Bake at 375F about 20 minutes, or until papers are puffed and lightly browned. Before serving cut a cross in the top of each papillote to release steam. Warn your guests of escaping steam as they open their papillote.

Per serving: *Calories - 286; Total Fat - 12.3g;*
Saturated Fat - 4.3g; Cholesterol - 88mg

BLENDER SALMON MOUSSE

Yield: 4 servings

1 tablespoon liquid Butter Buds,
  see page 48
1 shallot, minced
¾ cup 1% fat cottage cheese
2 tablespoons skim milk
¼ teaspoon sugar
2 tablespoons lemon juice
1 envelope unflavored gelatin
1 small onion, chopped
½ cup boiling water

½ cup fat and cholesterol-free
  mayonnaise
½ teaspoon paprika
1½ tablespoons fresh dill, or
  1½ teaspoons dried
¼ cup chili sauce
8 drops Tabasco sauce
1 7-ounce can pink salmon, drained,
  skin and larger bones removed
3 drops red food coloring

In a small covered skillet, saute the shallot in the Butter Buds until softened.

Blend the shallot in blender with remaining ingredients.

Pour into a sprayed 1-quart decorative mold and refrigerate. A fish-shaped mold is perfect.

Serve on a bed of lettuce.

NOTE: This recipe also makes a great appetizer spread for 15 to 20 people. Serve with crackers.

Per serving: *Calories - 177; Total Fat - 4.1g;*
             Saturated Fat - 1.1g; Cholesterol - 24.5mg

BROILED SALMON WITH BEARNAISE SAUCE

Yield: 2 servings

2 salmon steaks - 1-inch thick	¼ teaspoon dried thyme
1 teaspoon olive oil	Salt (opt.) and pepper, to taste
1 tablespoon minced shallots	¼ cup Bearnaise Sauce,
1 teaspoon lemon juice	see page 224

Place steaks in a shallow glass dish. Mix the next 5 ingredients together; pour over salmon and marinate for 1 hour, turning once.

On a grill, cook the drained steaks on high for 1 minute on each side. Reduce heat to medium, and cook for 8 to 10 minutes, turning every 2 minutes for even cooking. Baste with marinade at each turning. Transfer the salmon to a serving dish, remove skin, carefully, and top the steaks with warmed Bearnaise Sauce.

Per steak: *Calories - 260; Total Fat - 12.9g;*
                  Saturated Fat - 2.1g; Cholesterol - 56mg

POACHED SALMON WITH DILL SAUCE

Yield: 4 servings

4 salmon steaks, about	1 tablespoon flour
1-inch thick	2 teaspoons Dijon mustard
1 small onion, sliced	1 teaspoon dill seeds
½ lime, sliced	¼ teaspoon grated lime rind
1 bay leaf	Dash of white pepper
¼ teaspoon salt (opt.)	1 teaspoon lime juice
¾ cup skim milk	¼ cup egg substitute

Place salmon in 10-inch skillet. Add enough water to cover. Add onion, lime slices and bay leaf; sprinkle with salt and bring to boil. Cover, reduce heat, and simmer 8 minutes, or until fish flakes when tested with a fork.

Combine milk and flour in a saucepan, whisking constantly, until thickened. Add mustard, dill seeds, lime rind and pepper. Cook over medium heat and stir in lime juice and egg substitute. Serve immediately over salmon steaks.

Per serving: *Calories - 210; Total Fat - 6.7g;*
                    Saturated Fat - 1.3g; Cholesterol - 42.8mg

BUBBLY BAKED SCALLOPS

Yield: 4 servings

1 medium onion, minced
1 shallot, minced
2 tablespoons liquid Butter Buds,
   see page 48
2 slices bread
½ cup skim milk
1 pound bay scallops, rinsed and
   patted dry with paper towels
½ cup Bechamel Sauce,
   see page 225

1 tablespoon chopped parsley
½ teaspoon worcestershire-wine
   sauce
1 tablespoon white wine
¼ teaspoon dry mustard
Salt (opt.) and pepper, to taste
¼ cup fresh bread crumbs
Paprika
2 tablespoons liquid Butter Buds,
   see page 48

In a covered saucepan, over low heat, saute the onion and shallot in the Butter Buds until softened. Remove from heat.

Soak the bread slices in the milk. Squeeze the excess from the bread; add bread to onion mixture. Add the scallops and the next 6 ingredients.

Divide the mixture among 4 sprayed ramekins. Sprinkle each with bread crumbs, dust with paprika, and drizzle with Butter Buds. Bake in 375F oven for 12 to 15 minutes.

NOTE: You may use sea scallops, halved or quartered.

Per serving: *Calories - 221; Total Fat - 5.3g;*
                Saturated Fat - .8g; Cholesterol - 16mg

SCALLOP NEWBURG

Yield: 4 servings

1 pound bay scallops whole, or
   sea scallops halved or quartered
4 tablespoons liquid Butter Buds,
   see page 48
1 tablespoon lemon juice
4 tablespoons liquid Butter Buds,
   see page 48

4 tablespoons cornstarch
⅔ cup skim milk, warmed
4 tablespoons white wine
Salt (opt.) and white pepper to taste
Paprika
⅓ cup egg substitute

In a covered medium, non-stick skillet, cook the scallops in 4 tablespoons Butter Buds for 2 minutes. Add the lemon juice, and cook for 1 minute more.

In the top part of a medium-size double boiler, directly on the burner over medium heat, warm 4 tablespoons Butter Buds. Dissolve cornstarch in the milk. Slowly add the milk to the saucepan, whisking constantly until the sauce thickens. Add the wine and then the scallops. Season well with the salt, pepper and paprika; mix well.

Place on top of double boiler over simmering water; simmer until ready to serve. Be careful sauce doesn't become too thick. Stir in more warmed milk, if necessary.

Just before serving, remove pan from hot water and cool slightly. Put 3 tablespoons of sauce in a bowl with the egg substitute; mix well. Place egg mixture in the newburg and mix well. Serve over toast points.

In place of scallops you may substitute imitation crab, real crabmeat, lobster, shrimp or white fish chunks. Or try combinations. You can't go wrong.

*Per serving: Calories - 216; Total Fat - 6.3g;
                   Saturated Fat - .6g; Cholesterol - 15.2mg*

SCRUMPTIOUS SCAMPI

Yield: 4 servings

1 teaspoon olive oil
¼ cup liquid Butter Buds,
  see page 48
¾ pound large raw shrimp,
  peeled, tail segment left on

2 garlic cloves, pressed
1 tablespoon chopped parsley
1 tablespoon white wine
1½ teaspoons lemon juice
Pepper, to taste

In a large, non-stick skillet, heat the oil and the Butter Buds; add shrimp. Mix well with the oil. Lower heat, cover and cook until done, stirring occasionally for about 5 minutes. Don't overcook.

Remove shrimp to a platter; keep warm. Pour drippings into a small saucepan; add remaining ingredients. Cook over medium heat for 2 minutes. Pour over shrimp and serve immediately.

Per serving: *Calories - 134; Total Fat - 5.3g;*
                  Saturated Fat - .6g; Cholesterol - 110mg

NEW ENGLAND SWORDFISH

Yield: 4 servings

1 swordfish steak, about 1 pound
1 cup mock sour cream, see page 51
Salt (opt.), pepper and paprika,
  to taste
1 tablespoon lemon juice

2 tablespoons liquid Butter Buds,
  see page 48
1 tablespoon worcestershire-wine
  sauce
2 tablespoons chopped parsley

Wipe swordfish on both sides with paper towel. Place fish on rack and broil for 5 minutes. Remove from oven, turn over, and spread with the mock sour cream. Sprinkle with seasonings. Set oven for 425F. Return swordfish to oven, and bake for 12 to 15 minutes, or until fish flakes easily.

Mix and heat the remaining ingredients; pour over fish and serve.

Per serving: *Calories - 189; Total Fat - 8.2g;*
                  Saturated Fat - 2.7g; Cholesterol - 64.3mg

SHRIMP AND CRAB DELIGHT

Yield: 2 servings

4 ounces medium shrimp
6 ounces beer, at room
 temperature
2 tablespoons liquid Butter Buds,
 see page 48
¼ cup finely-chopped green
 bell pepper
¼ cup finely-chopped onion
½ cup finely-chopped celery
¼ pound imitation crabmeat,
 coarsely chopped
½ cup fat and cholesterol-
 free mayonnaise

1½ teaspoons worcestershire-wine
 sauce
1 tablespoon sherry
¼ teaspoon salt (opt.)
Dash of white pepper
1 tablespoon cornstarch
½ cup fresh bread crumbs
1 tablespoon liquid Butter Buds,
 see page 48
Paprika

Boil shrimp in beer for 1 minute. Rinse in cold water, peel, devein and cut into small pieces.

In a covered, non-stick skillet, over low heat, soften the vegetables in the Butter Buds. Combine the next 7 ingredients in a medium-size bowl. Add vegetables and mix well. Place mixture in a 20-ounce sprayed casserole or 2 10-ounce sprayed ramekins.

Cover the top with the bread crumbs; drizzle with the Butter Buds and paprika.

Bake at 350F for 35 minutes.

Per serving: *Calories - 381; Total Fat - 6.4g;*
                   Saturated Fat - .9g; Cholesterol - 84.5mg

SHRIMPLY DELICIOUS

Yield: 4 servings

BETTER THAN SCAMPI!!

4 tablespoons liquid Butter Buds,
  see page 48
1 garlic clove, pressed
¾ pound shrimp, shelled, with
  tail segment left on
Salt (opt.) and white pepper
  to taste

1 tablespoon chopped parsley
1 tablespoon chopped fresh dill,
  or 1 teaspoon dried
1 tablespoon chopped fresh basil,
  or 1 teaspoon dried
3 tablespoons brandy, warmed

In a large, covered non-stick skillet, over low heat, saute garlic in Butter Buds. Don't overcook.

Add the shrimp; cook over medium heat. While stirring constantly, add the salt, pepper, parsley, dill and basil. When shrimp are cooked (about 5 minutes) remove pan from heat; pour brandy over shrimp. Ignite and shake pan until flames are extinguished. Serve immediately.

Per serving: *Calories - 165; Total Fat - 4.1g;*
                   Saturated Fat - .5g; Cholesterol - 110mg

TUNA WITH GREEN PEPPERCORN SAUCE

Yield: 4 servings

¾ cup Green Peppercorn
  Sauce, see page 228

¾ pound tuna steak
  Vegetable oil spray

In a saucepan, prepare Green Peppercorn Sauce; keep warm.

Spray tuna with the vegetable oil spray and over medium heat, cook on a gas grill for 6 to 7 minutes per inch thickness, or until cooked to your state of doneness. Turn every minute for even cooking. Tuna is best a little underdone. Serve napped with the sauce.

Per serving: *Calories - 353; Total Fat - 13.3g;*
                   Saturated Fat - 3g; Cholesterol - 84mg

TUNA CURRY CASSEROLE

Yield: 4 servings

1 10-ounce package frozen
baby Lima beans
1 garlic clove, halved
1 7-ounce can tuna, packed
in water, drained
1¼ cups cream of mushroom
soup, see page 118
¼ cup fat and cholesterol-
free mayonnaise
¼ cup mock sour cream,
see page 51
2 tablespoons cornstarch

1 tablespoon lemon juice
1 teaspoon hot curry powder
¼ teaspoon pepper
1 tablespoon white wine
½ small box corn muffin mix
2 tablespoons freshly-grated
parmesan cheese
3 tablespoons liquid Butter Buds,
see page 48
¼ cup toasted, slivered almonds,
see page 49 (opt.)

Cook Lima beans with garlic per package directions until beans begin to soften, about 10 minutes. Drain, discard garlic. Arrange beans in bottom of sprayed 1½-quart casserole. Layer with tuna and then a mixture of the next 8 ingredients.

Top with the dry corn muffin mix; add cheese. Drizzle with Butter Buds.

Top with the almonds, if desired, and bake at 325F for 45 minutes.

Per serving: *Calories - 289; Total Fat - 7.3g;*
Saturated Fat - 2.5g; Cholesterol - 37mg

VEGETABLES

VEGETABLES

Vegetables, like poultry, can be prepared in so many interesting and creative ways that with us, they are always a new experience. With the great varieties of fresh vegetables now available throughout the year in most good markets, frequent duplication of recipes is far from a necessity.

We find that we often use vegetable dishes as the focal point of a meal rather than a side dish. If you do use vegetables as the main course, be sure to check the combinations which make up a complete protein. These are found on page 27.

As stated earlier, this book is like an insurance policy on your heart and health. Vegetables are at the top of the list in vitamins, minerals and fiber, and at the bottom of the list in calories, fats and cholesterol. Eat hearty and live longer!

COMPANY GREEN BEANS
Yield: 4 servings

2 9-ounce packages frozen French-
  style green beans
½ cup chopped onion
1 cup sliced mushrooms
4 tablespoons liquid Butter Buds,
  see page 48

4 tablespoons blanched, toasted
  slivered almonds, see page 49
Salt (opt.) and pepper, to taste
½ cup mock sour cream,
  see page 51

Cook the beans per package instructions. Drain well. Over low heat, in a covered, non-stick skillet, saute onion and mushrooms in the Butter Buds. Add the cooked beans, almonds, salt and pepper. Finally, fold in the sour cream, and reheat. Do not boil.

Per serving: *Calories - 87; Total Fat - 3.3g;*
             Saturated Fat - .8g; Cholesterol - 3.5mg

TOM'S BAKED BEANS
Yield: 6 servings

This has been adapted from an original recipe created by a Wampanoag Indian who lived on Martha's Vineyard Island.

1 pound dried navy beans
¼ cup BAC*OS (bacon
  flavored bits)
½ teaspoon baking soda
2 medium onions, quartered
½ cup sugar
1 tablespoon brown sugar

¼ cup molasses
½ teaspoon salt (opt.)
½ teaspoon pepper
1 teaspoon dry mustard
¼ teaspoon paprika
Reserved bean liquid

Place beans in a large saucepan: cover with water, plus 2 inches. Bring to a boil; simmer for 1 hour, covered. Strain beans through a colander, reserving liquid. Place beans in the bottom of a bean pot. Add the remaining ingredients, except for the reserved liquid, and mix together slowly by lifting from the bottom. Add enough reserved liquid to just cover beans. Cover and bake in a 250F oven for 7 hours. Check occasionally; press beans down. Add reserved liquid, or water, if needed.

Per serving: *Calories - 371; Total Fat - 1.9g;*
             Saturated Fat - Tr; Cholesterol - 0

BLACK BEANS

Yield: 10 servings

1 pound dried black beans
1 large onion, diced
1 large green bell pepper, diced
5 garlic cloves, minced
¼ cup olive oil
¼ cup sliced olives
  (green with pimento)

¼ cup white wine
3 tablespoons vinegar
1 bay leaf
1 teaspoon dried oregano
½ teaspoon salt (opt.)
½ teaspoon pepper
¼ teaspoon ground cumin

Cover beans with water, plus 2 inches. Soak overnight.

In a small skillet, saute the onion, pepper and garlic in the olive oil until soft. Stir mixture into beans. Add remaining ingredients, mixing well. Cover; bring to a boil; reduce heat, and simmer 3 to 4 hours, or until beans are cooked. Add more water, if needed.

Remove and discard the bay leaf. Serve with Saffron Rice, see page 214. Place rice on a platter; top with beans; garnish with chopped green or white onions. Freezes well.

Per serving: *Calories - 203; Total Fat - 6.6g;*
               Saturated Fat - .9g; Cholesterol - 0

HARVARD BEETS

Yield: 4 servings

1 tablespoon cornstarch
⅓ cup sugar
½ teaspoon salt (opt.)
½ cup cider vinegar
1 teaspoon minced onion

2 tablespoons liquid Butter Buds,
  see page 48
1 16-ounce can sliced beets,
  liquid reserved

In a 1-quart saucepan, combine the cornstarch, sugar, salt and vinegar. Cook over medium heat, stirring until sauce becomes thick and clear. Add onion, 2 tablespoons reserved beet juice and Butter Buds. Stir until smooth. Add beets, and simmer, uncovered, until heated through. If sauce becomes too thick, add more beet juice.

Per serving: *Calories - 127; Total Fat - 1.4g;*
               Saturated Fat - Tr; Cholesterol - 0

BROCCOLI CASSEROLE

Yield: 4 servings

1 10-ounce package frozen
broccoli spears
1 small onion, finely chopped
¼ cup chopped pecans or
walnuts (opt.)
1 cup Bechamel Sauce, see page 225
Salt (opt.) and pepper, to taste

½ cup packaged herbed stuffing
mix
2 tablespoons liquid Butter Buds,
see page 48
¼ cup shredded mozzarella
cheese alternative
Paprika, to taste

Cook broccoli spears as directed. Drain, and chop into ¼-inch pieces. Add onion and nuts. Pour the Bechamel Sauce over. Season with salt and pepper.

Place mixture in a sprayed 1-quart baking dish. Sprinkle with stuffing mix; drizzle with the Butter Buds. Bake, uncovered, at 375F for 25 minutes. Add the cheese and paprika; bake another 5 minutes, or until cheese is bubbly.

Per serving: *Calories - 156; Total Fat - 4.7g;*
Saturated Fat - .9g; Cholesterol - 1.5mg

NUTTY BRUSSELS SPROUTS

Yield: 4 servings

3 tablespoons liquid Butter Buds,
see page 48
3 tablespoons cornstarch
1 ¾-cups warm low-sodium
chicken broth
¾ cup nonfat dry milk

¼ teaspoon nutmeg
1 ounce chopped pecans
1+ pounds Brussels sprouts, trimmed
and cooked until crisp tender
1 cup herbed stuffing mix

Place Butter Buds in a medium saucepan over medium heat. Dissolve cornstarch in broth. Add to the saucepan, whisking constantly until it thickens. Still whisking, add the dry milk; bring to a boil. Remove from heat; stir in the nutmeg and nuts.

Place the cooked Brussels sprouts in a sprayed 1½-quart casserole; pour sauce over. Top with the stuffing mix. Bake in a 400F oven for 10 to 15 minutes, or until the topping is lightly browned.

Per serving: *Calories - 327; Total Fat - 8.5g;*
Saturated Fat - .9g; Cholesterol - 5mg

CARROT PUDDING

Yield: 4 servings

1 cup carrots, peeled, sliced,
cooked and drained
1 tablespoon chopped onion
¼ cup liquid Butter Buds,
see page 48
Pinch of cinnamon

1 packet sugar substitute
1½ teaspoons cornstarch
½ teaspoon baking powder
½ teaspoon salt (opt.)
½ cup skim milk
½ cup egg substitute

Combine all ingredients, except egg substitute, in a blender. Blend until smooth. Add the egg substitute, and mix thoroughly. Pour into a sprayed 1-quart casserole; bake at 350F for 40 to 45 minutes.

Per serving: *Calories - 70; Total Fat - 2.7g;*
Saturated Fat - Tr; Cholesterol - Tr

RUM CARROTS

Yield: 4 servings

1 pound baby carrots, washed,
trimmed and cut into small
barrel shapes
2 tablespoons liquid Butter Buds,
see page 48
½ teaspoon salt (opt.)
¼ teaspoon pepper

½ teaspoon ground or crushed
coriander
2 tablespoons light rum
2 tablespoons water
1 teaspoon lemon juice
1 tablespoon chopped parsley

In a small saucepan, mix all ingredients. Let stand, stirring occasionally, for 1 hour.

Cook, covered, over low heat, stirring occasionally, for 25 minutes or until carrots are crisp tender.

Per serving: *Calories - 57; Total Fat - 1.4g;*
Saturated Fat - Tr; Cholesterol - 0

COMPANY CAULIFLOWER

Yield: 8 servings

1 large head cauliflower, separated
  into flowerets
3 tablespoons liquid Butter Buds,
  see page 48
¾ cup small bread cubes

2 cups Mornay Sauce, see page 231
1 tablespoon lemon juice
¼ cup white wine
¾ cup shredded cheddar or Swiss
  cheese alternative

In a large saucepan with a little salted water, cook cauliflower 8 to 10 minutes, or until crisp tender; drain. In a non-stick skillet over low heat, cook the bread cubes in the Butter Buds until golden.

Add the wine and lemon juice to the Mornay Sauce. In a 2-quart, sprayed casserole, arrange one half the flowerets; cover with one half the sauce. Repeat the process. Sprinkle top with cheese. Arrange bread cubes around the border of the casserole.

Bake at 350F for 30 minutes, or until top is lightly browned.

Per serving: *Calories - 116; Total Fat - 5.4g;*
Saturated Fat - 1.5g; Cholesterol - 2.9mg

HEART-SAFE SOUTHERN STYLE COLLARD GREENS

Yield: 4 servings

1 tablespoon BAC*OS (bacon
  flavored bits)
1 tablespoon olive oil
1 garlic clove, finely minced
1 dried hot chili pepper pod (opt.)

1 pound collard greens, washed
2 teaspoons brown sugar
½ teaspoon celery salt
Black pepper, to taste

Remove ribs from greens; slice leaves into strips. In a large kettle, over medium heat, saute the BAC*OS in the olive oil until they begin to brown. Add garlic and pepper pod. Saute 1 minute. Add collards to pan. Cover. Stir occasionally.

When greens begin to cook down, add sugar, celery salt and black pepper. Lower heat and cook for about 45 minutes, or until desired doneness is reached. Remove pepper pod.

Per serving: *Calories - 104; Total Fat - 4.1g;*
Saturated Fat - .6g; Cholesterol - 0

MA'S BAKED CORN

Yield: 4 servings

1 16-ounce can cream-style corn
Salt (opt.) and pepper to taste
1 teaspoon sugar or ½ packet
   sugar substitute

16 saltine crackers, crumbled
¼ cup liquid Butter Buds,
   see page 48
½ cup skim milk

Spray a 9x5x3-inch loaf pan. Put one half of the corn in the bottom of pan. Lightly sprinkle with salt, pepper and one half of the sugar. Put one half of the crumbled saltines on top; drizzle with one half of the Butter Buds. Repeat process. Pour milk over all. Bake at 350F for 45 minutes.

Per serving: *Calories - 195; Total Fat - 5g;*
                  Saturated Fat - .6g; Cholesterol - 4.6mg

ITALIAN EGGPLANT

Yield: 2 or 3 servings

1 medium eggplant, peeled,
   cut into ¾-inch cubes
¼ cup chopped onion
2 tablespoons chopped green pepper
Vegetable oil spray
1 small tomato, peeled and
   coarsely chopped
1 tablespoon freshly-grated
   parmesan cheese

½ teaspoon Italian seasoning
⅛ teaspoon garlic powder
⅛ teaspoon lemon-pepper
   seasoning
5 saltines, crumbled
1 ounce shredded cheddar cheese
   alternative
Paprika

Cook eggplant in small amount of boiling water 4 to 5 minutes or until tender.

In a non-stick medium skillet, saute onion and green pepper in vegetable oil spray until tender. Add eggplant and next 6 ingredients; mix well.

Spoon mixture into a sprayed 20-ounce casserole. Top with cheese; sprinkle with paprika.

Bake at 350F for 20 minutes.

Per serving: *Calories - 190; Total Fat - 5.1g;*
                  Saturated Fat - 2.1g; Cholesterol - 8mg

CURRIED LIMA BEANS

Yield: 4 servings

1 medium onion, finely chopped
3 tablespoons liquid Butter Buds,
  see page 48
3 tablespoons cornstarch
2 cups skim milk, warmed
1 teaspoon lemon juice

1½ teaspoons curry powder
Salt (opt.) and white pepper,
  to taste
2 cups frozen Lima beans, cooked
  until crisp tender

In a covered saucepan, over low heat, saute the onions in the Butter Buds until softened. Dissolve the cornstarch in the milk. Gradually add milk to the onions, whisking constantly, until the mixture thickens. Add the lemon juice, curry, salt and pepper; simmer for 3 to 4 minutes.

Drain the Lima beans; place in serving dish. Pour the sauce over the beans.

Per serving: *Calories - 202; Total Fat - 2.7g;*
                   Saturated Fat - Tr; Cholesterol - 2mg

CHEESE MUSHROOMS

Yield: 4 servings

1 pound mushrooms, sliced
¼ cup chopped onion
1 garlic clove, minced
1 teaspoon olive oil
1 tablespoon white wine
1 tablespoon freshly-grated
  parmesan cheese

2 tablespoons grated mozzarella
  cheese alternative
1 tablespoon chopped parsley
½ teaspoon salt (opt.)
⅛ teaspoon dried oregano
½ cup seasoned bread crumbs

In a large, non-stick skillet, saute the sliced mushrooms, onion and garlic in the olive oil until the onion is softened. Add the wine and simmer for 1 minute. Add the cheeses, parsley, salt, oregano and enough bread crumbs to absorb most of the liquid. Be careful not to make it too dry. Mix well.

Divide mixture among 4 small sprayed ramekins. Sprinkle tops with more bread crumbs; bake in 400F oven for 15 to 20 minutes, or until tops are lightly browned.

Per serving: *Calories - 109; Total Fat - 3.8g;*
                   Saturated Fat - 1.3g; Cholesterol - 3.4mg

HOT AND SWEET ONIONS
Yield: 2 servings

1 large sweet onion, peeled, cut into ¼-inch slices	¼ teaspoon salt (opt.)
1 tablespoon honey	¼ teaspoon paprika
¼ teaspoon dry mustard	¼ teaspoon lemon pepper

Place onion slices in center of sprayed sheet of heavy-duty aluminum foil. Combine honey and mustard; pour over onions. Sprinkle with remaining ingredients.

Seal the foil, allowing room for expansion. Place on grill, and cook, on low, for 30 minutes.

Per serving: *Calories - 108; Total Fat - Tr;*
                   Saturated Fat - Tr; Cholesterol - 0

PASTA SAUTE
Yield: 4 servings

½ pound cooked and chilled linguine or Angel's hair pasta	¼ teaspoon salt (opt.)
2 tablespoons light corn oil spread	Pepper, to taste
1 large garlic clove, pressed	2 tablespoons freshly-grated parmesan cheese
	Paprika

Over medium heat, melt spread in a large, non-stick skillet. Add the garlic, and saute for 1 minute. Add the pasta, and continue sauteing, stirring frequently. Cook until pasta begins to brown.

Transfer to a serving dish; add salt, pepper and cheese; mix well. Sprinkle with paprika, and serve immediately.

Per serving: *Calories - 178; Total Fat - 6.6g;*
                   Saturated Fat - 2.4g; Cholesterol - 5.5mg

SEA SHELLS FLORENTINE

Yield: 4 servings

8-ounces sea shells, cooked and
drained
1 package frozen, chopped spinach,
cooked and well drained
1¼ cups cream of mushroom soup,
see page 118
¼ cup skim milk

⅛ teaspoon nutmeg
¼ cup mock sour cream, see
page 51
2 tablespoons liquid Butter Buds,
see page 48
2 tablespoons freshly-grated
parmesan cheese

In a medium saucepan, place the drained spinach. Stir in soup, milk and nutmeg. Cook over low heat, stirring occasionally. When warmed through, stir in mock sour cream; heat thoroughly.

Toss the hot, cooked shells with the Butter Buds. Spoon the spinach mixture into a wide serving bowl. Top with the shells; sprinkle with grated cheese.

Per serving: *Calories - 327; Total Fat - 6.2g;*
Saturated Fat - 2.2g; Cholesterol - 9.2mg

DILLED ENGLISH PEAS

Yield: 4 servings

2 cups cooked English peas,
fresh, if available
4 tablespoons mock sour cream,
see page 51

1 teaspoon lemon juice
2 teaspoons dried dill or
2 tablespoons fresh
Salt (opt.) and pepper, to taste

In a saucepan, blend all ingredients well over low heat. Do not boil!

Per serving: *Calories - 45; Total Fat - Tr;*
Saturated Fat - Tr; Cholesterol - 1.8mg

OVEN FRENCH FRIES

Yield: 2 servings

2 medium, thin-skin potatoes, washed, unpeeled

1 tablespoon canola oil
¼ teaspoon garlic powder

Cut the potatoes into ½-inch strips resembling French fries. Pat dry and toss in a bowl with the oil and garlic.

Spread them on a well-sprayed cookie sheet and place in 475F oven for 35 minutes. It is not necessary to turn the potatoes.

If browner, crispier potatoes are desired, turn the strips and place under the broiler for a couple of minutes.

Per serving: *Calories - 281; Total Fat - 7.2g; Saturated Fat - Tr; Cholesterol - 0*

SPECIAL MASHED POTATOES

Yield: 4 servings

4 large potatoes, peeled, boiled and drained
¼ cup skim milk
Lemon juice, to taste
Salt (opt.) and pepper to taste
¼ cup finely-chopped onion
3 tablespoons finely-chopped green bell pepper
1 garlic clove, pressed

2 tablespoons liquid Butter Buds, see page 48
1 tablespoon chopped parsley
¼ cup seasoned bread crumbs
2 tablespoons liquid Butter Buds, see page 48
¼ cup shredded mozzarella cheese alternative

Mash the potatoes with the milk, lemon juice, salt and pepper. In a small covered, non-stick skillet, over low heat, saute the onion, green pepper and garlic in the Butter Buds until softened. Add the parsley, and stir mixture into the mashed potatoes.

Place the potato mixture in 4 sprayed ramekins; cover with bread crumbs; drizzle with Butter Buds and top with cheese. Bake in oven at 400F for 12 minutes.

Per ramekin: *Calories - 226; Total Fat - 4.4g; Saturated Fat - .8g; Cholesterol - .6mg*

POTATO CASSEROLE

Yield: 4 servings

6 servings instant mashed
  potatoes
¼ cup egg substitute
½ teaspoon dry mustard
6 to 8 drops Tabasco sauce

½ teaspoon onion powder
¼ cup freshly-grated parmesan
  cheese
¼ cup skim milk
Paprika

Prepare potatoes as directed. Use enough milk to make potatoes very moist. Add remaining ingredients; mix well. Place in a sprayed 1-quart casserole. Sprinkle with additional cheese; dust with paprika.

Bake at 350F for 30 to 40 minutes.

Per serving: *Calories - 244; Total Fat - 11.1g;*
                  Saturated - 4.4g; Cholesterol - 14.3mg

QUICK BAKED POTATOES ON A GRILL

Yield: 2 servings

Pierce 2 potatoes with a fork; cook on HIGH in the microwave for 5 minutes. Set each potato on a square of heavy-duty foil. Place a pat of light corn oil spread on each potato, and sprinkle with garlic powder and pepper, to taste. Wrap and seal the potatoes.

Place on grill over medium heat and cook for 15 minutes. Turn and cook for 15 minutes more, or until tender.

Per serving;   *Calories - 248; Total Fat - 2.9g;*
                  Saturated Fat - .7g; Cholesterol - 0

POTATO SLICES ON THE GRILL
Yield: 4 servings

Scrub 4 potatoes. Pat dry; cut, unpeeled, into ½-inch thick slices. Place slices in sprayed wire fish basket; brush slices with melted light corn oil spread mixed with salt, pepper and garlic powder, to taste.

Grill on low for 30 minutes turning every 5 minutes and basting with the spread mixture. Be careful not to burn the potatoes.

Per serving: *Calories - 241; Total Fat - 2.3g;*
                   Saturated Fat - .6g; Cholesterol - 0

RICE PILAF
Yield: 4 servings

1 cup minced onion
1 medium green bell pepper, chopped
3 tablespoons light corn oil spread
1 cup long grain rice
2 cups low-sodium chicken broth

¼ teaspoon saffron strands, softened in a small amount of hot water
Salt (opt.) and pepper to taste
2 tablespoons freshly-grated parmesan cheese

In a large, non-stick skillet, saute the onion and green pepper in the spread until softened. Add the rice; stir until rice begins to turn a golden color.

Add the chicken broth. Bring to a boil, stirring constantly. Remove from heat, and add the saffron, salt and pepper. Mix well. Transfer the rice mixture to a sprayed 2-quart casserole. Cover, and bake at 350F for 25 to 30 minutes, or until liquid is absorbed and rice is tender.

Sprinkle cheese on top and bake, uncovered, for 5 minutes more.

Per serving: *Calories - 327; Total Fat - 9.1g;*
                   Saturated Fat - 3.2g; Cholesterol - 6mg

SAFFRON RICE

Yield: 4 servings

1 small onion, chopped
1 garlic clove, minced
1 small bell pepper, finely
  chopped
1 tablespoon liquid Butter Buds,
  see page 48

2 cups water
½ teaspoon saffron, softened
  in a small amount of hot water
1 bay leaf
1 cup long grain rice
1 teaspoon salt (opt.)

In a medium saucepan, saute onions, garlic and pepper in olive oil until softened. Add water, saffron and bay leaf; bring to a boil. Add rice and salt; reduce heat. Cover, and simmer about 20 to 25 minutes.

Per serving: *Calories - 220; Total Fat - .9g;*
                 Saturated Fat - Tr; Cholesterol - 0

HILLSINGER SAUERKRAUT

Yield: 4 servings

1 garlic clove, minced
1 large onion, chopped
2 tablespoons liquid Butter Buds,
  see page 48
1 green bell pepper, sliced
1 16-ounce can sauerkraut, well
  rinsed and drained
¼ cup sauterne

1 (8¾-ounce) can no-salt
  tomatoes, chopped
1 teaspoon ground ginger
3 packets sugar substitute or
  2 tablespoons sugar
Dried basil, oregano and pepper
  to taste

Over low heat in a medium, covered saucepan, saute the garlic and onions in the Butter Buds until soft. Add the pepper and sauerkraut; mix well and cook for 5 minutes, stirring frequently.

Add the remaining ingredients, and simmer for 20 minutes. Let pan cool and stand for 2 hours. Reheat before serving. Serve with smoked turkey sausage cooked on the grill.

Per serving, without sausage: *Calories - 85; Total Fat - 1.8g;*
                                     Saturated Fat - Tr; Cholesterol - 0

SUMMER SQUASH CASSEROLE
Yield: 4 servings

1½-pounds summer squash,
   washed
1 small onion, finely chopped
3 tablespoons liquid Butter Buds,
   see page 48
¾ cup cream of celery soup,
   see page 117
¼ teaspoon salt (opt.)
Dash of pepper

¼ cup egg substitute
½ teaspoon sugar
¼ cup fresh bread crumbs
1 tablespoon freshly-grated
   parmesan cheese
3 tablespoons liquid Butter Buds,
   see page 48
Paprika

Slice squash and cook in a medium saucepan with a small amount of lightly salted water. Drain well; mash down and drain again. Mix next 7 ingredients with squash. Pour into a sprayed 1½-quart casserole.

In a small bowl, combine the bread crumbs and cheese. Sprinkle over the top of casserole. Drizzle the Butter Buds over the top, and dust with paprika.

Bake at 350F for 40 to 45 minutes.

Per serving: *Calories - 146; Total Fat - 6.3g;*
                          Saturated Fat - 1.3g; Cholesterol - 3.1mg

BAKED STUFFED TOMATOES

Yield: 4 servings

4 large tomatoes
1 tablespoon grated parmesan
 cheese
1 ounce mozzarella cheese
 alternative
2 sweet pickles, finely chopped
1 tablespoon sugar

½ teaspoon salt (opt.)
1 teaspoon Italian seasoning
½ teaspoon dry mustard
¼ teaspoon garlic powder
Black and cayenne pepper,
 to taste
¼ cup seasoned bread crumbs

Cut the tops off tomatoes, and scoop out the meat into a medium size bowl. Do not remove the meat on the side walls. Dry the tomato shells, lightly salted, upside down in an 8x8x2-inch sprayed baking dish at 400F for 5 minutes.

Mix all the ingredients except bread crumbs with the tomato meat.

Stuff the tomatoes with the tomato/cheese mixture; sprinkle the bread crumbs on top. Place in the sprayed baking dish; bake at 400F for 20 minutes.

Per serving: *Calories - 166; Total Fat - 2.7g;*
               Saturated Fat - 1.1g; Cholesterol - 5.8mg

MARINATED TOMATOES

Yield: 4 servings

4 medium tomatoes, sliced
2 tablespoons olive oil
¼ cup red wine vinegar
1 tablespoon chopped parlsey
½ teaspoon salt
Pinch of dried oregano

Pinch of dried thyme
½ teaspoon dried basil, or
1½ teaspoons fresh
¼ teaspoon black pepper
¼ teaspoon sugar

Place the tomatoes in a shallow dish. Mix remaining ingredients in a small bowl; pour over tomatoes. Cover and refrigerate overnight.

Per serving, drained: *Calories - 90; Total Fat - 3.7g;*
                    Saturated Fat - 1g; Cholesterol - 0

SPICY WHITE TURNIPS

Yield: 6 servings

2 pounds white turnips, peeled and cut into ½-inch cubes	1 teaspoon cornstarch
	2 teaspoons warm water
4 large shallots, minced	1 tablespoon white wine
4 tablespoons liquid Butter Buds, see page 48	¼ teaspoon salt (opt.)
	Cayenne pepper, to taste
1¼ cups low sodium beef broth	

Over low heat, in a medium, covered saucepan, saute the turnips and shallots in the Butter Buds until they begin to soften. Add the beef broth and cook, covered, over low heat for 10 minutes, or until the turnips are tender.

Make a paste with the cornstarch and water; Mix into saucepan; cook, stirring constantly, until liquid thickens.

Add the white wine, salt and pepper; simmer for 3 to 4 minutes longer.

Per serving: *Calories - 44; Total Fat - 2.8g;*
                   Saturated Fat - Tr; Cholesterol - 0

VEGETABLE MEDLEY

Yield: 2 servings

2 potatoes, peeled and cut into ½-inch dice	1 garlic clove, pressed
	1 cup frozen peas
⅓ cup liquid Butter Buds, see page 48	1 tablespoon chopped parsley
	3 large mushrooms, coarsely chopped
1 small red bell pepper, cut into ½-inch pieces	Salt (opt.) and pepper, to taste

Over low heat in a medium-sized, covered non-stick skillet, saute the potatoes in the Butter Buds for 5 minutes, stirring occasionally. Add the garlic and red pepper. Cook, covered, for another 5 minutes, stirring occasionally. Add remaining ingredients, and continue cooking for 10 minutes more, or until done, stirring occasionally.

Per serving: *Calories - 250; Total Fat - 7.6g;*
                   Saturated Fat - .7g; Cholesterol - 0

BAKED ZUCCHINI

Yield: 4 servings

2 or 3 small zucchini, about
  1 pound, washed
1 cup Bechamel Sauce, see page 225
½ cup fresh bread crumbs
1 tablespoon parsley, minced
¼ teaspoon dried basil

¼ teaspoon dried oregano
½ teaspoon garlic powder
3 tablespoons liquid Butter Buds,
  see page 48
1½ ounces shredded mozzarella
  cheese alternative

In a wide saucepan, in a small amount of boiling water, cook whole zucchini until tender, but firm. Halve the zucchini lengthwise, and arrange them, cut side up, in a sprayed 9-inch square baking dish. Cover the zucchini with the Bechamel Sauce.

Mix the bread crumbs with the next 4 ingredients; saute in Butter Buds for 3 to 4 minutes. Sprinkle crumb mixture over zucchini and cover with mozzarella. Bake at 350F for 25 minutes, or until bubbly.

Per serving: *Calories - 137; Total Fat - 5.2g;*
                  Saturated Fat - 1g; Cholesterol - 2.1mg

ZESTY ZUCCHINI
Yield: 4 servings

2 medium zucchini, peeled
and cut into ½-inch cubes
1 small onion, chopped
1 garlic clove, pressed
2 tablespoons liquid Butter Buds,
see page 48

Paprika, salt (opt.) and pepper,
to taste
½ cup mock sour cream, see
page 51
½ teaspoon crushed dried dill weed
½ tablespoon flour

In a medium saucepan, boil zucchini in a little salted water until crisp tender. Drain and set aside.

In a covered saucepan, over low heat, saute onion and garlic in the Butter Buds until soft. Add the drained zucchini, paprika, salt and pepper; mix well. Heat the mock sour cream and dill until bubbly. Mix in flour; stir until thickened. Mix into the zucchini mixture and serve.

Per serving: *Calories - 60; Total Fat - 2g;*
Saturated Fat - .6g; Cholesterol - 3.5mg

SUGAR/BUTTER PARSNIPS
Yield: 4 servings

1 pound parsnips, scraped and
cut into 3-inch julienne strips
3 tablespoons liquid Butter Buds,
see page 48
2 tablespoons brown sugar
2 tablespoons orange juice

1 teaspoon lemon juice
Seeds from 2 cardamom pods,
crushed
Dash of freshly-grated nutmeg,
or powdered
Salt (opt.) and pepper, to taste

In a medium saucepan with a small amount of water, cook the parsnips until tender (about 5 minutes); drain well.

In a large non-stick skillet, melt the sugar in the Butter Buds. Add the parsnips and cook over medium heat, stirring constantly until glazed. Add the remaining ingredients; mix well. Cover and cook over low heat, for 4 to 5 minutes more.

Per serving: *Calories - 114; Total Fat - 2.2g;*
Saturated Fat - Tr; Cholesterol - 0

STUFFED ZUCCHINI

Yield: 4 or more servings

What to do with that enormous zucchini growing in your garden?

1 very large zucchini, 2 to 2½
  pounds
Lemon juice, dried thyme,
  salt (opt.) and pepper
2 medium onions, chopped
1 medium bell pepper, chopped
3 tablespoons liquid Butter Buds,
  see page 48

½ cup seasoned bread crumbs
2 tablespoons liquid Butter Buds,
  see page 48
1 large tomato, cut into small,
  thin wedges

Slice a wedge out of the long side of the zucchini. Shave the other side slightly, so that it will stand without rolling. Remove seeds and discard. Sprinkle the inside of the zucchini with the lemon juice, thyme, salt and pepper.

In a covered, non-stick skillet, over low heat, saute the onions and bell pepper in the Butter Buds until softened. Add the bread crumbs; mix well.

Fill the squash with the mixture. Drizzle with Butter Buds. Add the tomato wedges; replace top of zucchini.

Bake at 350F for 1¼ to 1½ hours. Keep your eye on it. Size of squash will determine the actual baking time. Slide a sharp knife along side of wedge and into flesh on far side to determine doneness.

Per serving for 4:   *Calories - 126; Total Fat - 4.2g;*
                         Saturated Fat - Tr; Cholesterol - .6mg

SAUCES

SAUCES

A good sauce is worth every second of time spent on its creation. In today's world, people are beginning to shy away from sauces because they are notoriously "heavy" with creams, butter and other high-fat products. Our sauces keep the old-fashioned flavor but are definitely not heavy.

Vegetables stand on their own merit, but add an interesting sauce and they take on a whole new dimension. Broiled or grilled beef or fresh tuna steak constitutes a real treat, but spoon Green Peppercorn Sauce over either one and you have something truly heavenly. Lean cuts of meat tend to be a little tough, so marinate and tenderize with a marinade and add new flavor.

THE HEALTHY HEART GOURMET leads the way in heart-safe sauces. However, remember even these sauces are to be used in moderation. In other words, don't completely cover up the flavor of the food underneath. Fat intake, even vegetable oils, still should remain at or below 30%. Use to enhance foods, not to disguise them.

HOUSE DRESSING

Yield: About ½ cup

¼ cup catsup
¼ cup fat and cholesterol-
   free mayonnaise
½ teaspoon sugar

1 teaspoon cream-style
   horseradish
¼ teaspoon lemon juice

Mix all ingredients together; chill until salad is served. Keeps well in the refrigerator.

Excellent with cold roast beef too!

*Per tablespoon: Calories - 19; Total Fat - Tr;
            Saturated Fat - Tr; Cholesterol - 0*

TOM'S BARBEQUE SAUCE

Yield: About 2 cups

½ cup catsup
¾ cup water
½ cup red wine vinegar
1 packet sugar substitute
1 tablespoon prepared mustard
2 tablespoons liquid Butter Buds,
   see page 48

2 tablespoons worcestershire sauce
½ teaspoon black pepper
½ teaspoon salt (opt.)
¼ teaspoon cayenne pepper
1½ teaspoons liquid smoke
1 medium onion, chopped
1 thick lemon slice

Mix all ingredients together in a 1-quart saucepan. Bring to a boil and simmer, uncovered, for 20 minutes.

*Calories - 276; Total Fat - 7g;
Saturated Fat - .5g; Cholesterol - 0*

BASTING SAUCE FOR BEEF AND TURKEY

Yield: About 1/3 cup

2 tablespoons finely-chopped
 onion
1 garlic clove, pressed
¼ cup liquid Butter Buds,
 see page 48

1 tablespoon worcestershire sauce
2 tablespoons red wine
Black pepper, to taste
Tabasco sauce, to taste

Over low heat in a covered saucepan, soften the onions and garlic in the Butter Buds. Add remaining ingredients and simmer for 10 minutes. Remove from heat. Let stand for about 1 hour.

Reheat sauce. Brush on meat about ½ hour before cooking. Be sure to cover all surfaces. Brush meat with sauce frequently while cooking.

Calories - 158; Total Fat - 10.4g;
Saturated Fat - .8g; Cholesterol - 0

BEARNAISE SAUCE

Yield: About 1 cup

1 sprig fresh tarragon, chopped,
 or 1 heaping teaspoon dried
1 sprig parsley, chopped
1 shallot, minced
2 or 3 black peppercorns, crushed

2 tablespoons tarragon wine vinegar
6 tablespoons liquid Butter Buds,
 see page 48
⅓ cup egg substitute
Cayenne pepper, to taste

Place first 5 ingredients in a small saucepan. Heat over medium high heat until reduced almost to a paste.

Lower heat and add the Butter Buds, whisking constantly. Remove from heat; cool slightly. Add the egg substitute, whisking briskly. Add cayenne to taste, mix well and serve.

Calories - 222; Total Fat - 15.7g;
Saturated Fat - 1.2g; Cholesterol - 0

BECHAMEL SAUCE
Yield: About 1½ cups

1 tablespoon finely-chopped onion
2 tablespoons liquid Butter Buds,
   see page 48

2 tablespoons cornstarch
1 cup skim milk, warmed

Over medium heat in a covered medium saucepan, saute the onion in the Butter Buds until softened. Dissolve the cornstarch in the warm milk. Slowly add the milk to the saucepan, whisking constantly until the liquid thickens. Be patient! A good, smooth sauce takes time.

If desired, substitute meat, fish or vegetable stock in place of milk to further enhance your choice of entree.

Calories - 216; Total Fat - 5.8g;
Saturated Fat - .7g; Cholesterol - 4mg

BEER MARINADE
Yield: About 2 cups

12 ounces light beer,
   at room temperature
1 tablespoon canola oil
1 garlic clove, minced
3 whole cloves

½ small onion, minced
2 tablespoons lemon juice
1 teaspoon sugar
¼ teaspoon salt (opt.)
½ teaspoon dried thyme

In a medium bowl, mix the beer and oil together. Add the other ingredients; mix well. Let stand for 1 hour. Use as a marinade for meat and turkey.

Calories - 269; Total Fat - 14g;
Saturated Fat - .9g; Cholesterol - 0

BROWN SAUCE
Yield: About 1⅓ cups

3 tablespoons liquid Butter Buds,
  see page 48
2 tablespoons finely-chopped onion

2 tablespoons cornstarch
1 cup strong beef bouillon,
  or beef broth

In a small, covered saucepan, saute the onion in the Butter Buds until soft. Dissolve the cornstarch in the bouillon. Slowly add the bouillon to the saucepan, whisking constantly until the sauce is smooth and thickened.

Calories - 181; Total Fat - 8.6g;
Saturated Fat - 1g; Cholesterol - Tr

CAPER AND SHALLOT BUTTER SAUCE
Yield: About ⅓ cup

1 tablespoon liquid Butter Buds,
  see page 48
2 shallots, minced
1 teaspoon capers, drained

¼ teaspoon lemon juice
1 tablespoon white wine
1 tablespoon liquid Butter Buds,
  see page 48

Put 1 tablespoon Butter Buds, the shallots and capers in a small covered saucepan over medium heat. When bubbling add the lemon juice and wine. Cook until the shallots are soft. Add the other tablespoon of Butter Buds and remove from heat. Serve over fish or white meat.

Calories - 86; Total Fat - 5.2g;
Saturated Fat - Tr; Cholesterol - 0

CHEESE SAUCE FOR VEGETABLES
Yield: About 1½ cups

2 tablespoons liquid Butter Buds,
  see page 48
2 tablespoons cornstarch
1 cup skim milk, warmed

2 slices Swiss cheese alternative,
  cubed
¼ teaspoon salt (opt.)
Dash pepper

Place Butter Buds in a small saucepan over medium heat. Dissolve the cornstarch in the warmed milk. Gradually add milk to saucepan, whisking constantly until thick and bubbly. Add cheese, salt and pepper. Whisk until cheese melts and sauce is smooth.

Calories - 318; Total Fat - 13.2g;
Saturated Fat - 3g; Cholesterol - 4mg

INSTANT CHICKEN GRAVY
Yield: About 1¼ cups

2 tablespoons liquid Butter Buds,
  see page 48
2 tablespoons cornstarch
1 cup chicken stock, or low-
  sodium bouillon

¼ teaspoon ground sage
White pepper, to taste
2 tablespoons white wine
1 tablespoon chopped parsley

Place Butter Buds in a saucepan over medium heat. Dissolve cornstarch in warmed stock. Slowly add stock to saucepan, whisking constantly, until liquid begins to thicken. Add the sage, pepper and wine. Stir in the parsley; simmer for about 10 minutes.

If a darker color is desired, add a couple drops of Seasoning and Browning Sauce.

Calories - 188; Total Fat - 6.7g;
Saturated Fat - .8g; Cholesterol - 1mg

COCKTAIL SAUCE

Yield: About ¾ cup

½ cup catsup
3 to 4 tablespoons cream-
style horseradish

1 tablespoon lemon juice
Tabasco sauce, to taste

Mix all ingredients together in a small bowl. Cover and refrigerate for at least 1 hour.

Calories - 156; Total Fat - .8g;
Saturated Fat - Tr; Cholesterol - 0

CREAM SAUCE FOR BROCCOLI

Yield: About ½ cup

⅓ cup mock sour cream,
see page 51
½ tablespoon cream-style
horseradish

½ tablespoon Dijon mustard
Salt, to taste (opt.)

Combine all ingredients in a small saucepan; heat thoroughly. Pour over cooked broccoli or green beans.

Calories - 56; Total Fat - 1.7g;
Saturated Fat - 1.2g; Cholesterol - 8.4mg

GREEN PEPPERCORN SAUCE

Yield: About ¾ cup

¼ cup liquid Butter Buds,
see page 48
¼ cup finely-chopped parsley
2 teaspoons green peppercorns,
drained and bruised

1 teaspoon lemon juice
¼ teaspoon Dijon mustard
2 teaspoons worcestershire-wine
sauce
2 tablespoons dry vermouth

In a saucepan, mix all ingredients together. Bring to a boil. Simmer for a few minutes, covered. Serve with beef or fresh tuna.

Calories - 146; Total Fat - 10.4g;
Saturated Fat - .8g; Cholesterol - 0

HOLLANDAISE SAUCE

Yield: About 1 cup

½ cup liquid Butter Buds,
   see page 48
½ cup egg substitute
2 teaspoons lemon juice

White pepper, to taste
Pinch of salt (opt.)
1 tablespoon cornstarch

In top of a double boiler over hot, but not boiling, water, put in ¼ cup Butter Buds and the egg substitute, whisking constantly; add remaining Butter Buds.

Add the lemon juice, pepper and salt. Mix cornstarch with enough warm water to make a paste. Whisk into sauce and stir constantly until the sauce thickens. Be patient. The results are worth it. Use over vegetables and eggs.

Calories - 316; Total Fat - 21g;
Saturated Fat - 1.6g; Cholesterol - 0

HORSERADISH SAUCE

Yield: About 1¼ cups

1 cup White Sauce,
   see page 235
3 tablespoons cream-style
   horseradish

1 tablespoon Dijon mustard
⅛ teaspoon white pepper

Warm White Sauce. Add the remaining ingredients, one at a time, whisking constantly. Let stand until needed. Serve warm. Great with meat or vegetables.

Calories - 216; Total Fat - 7.2g;
Saturated Fat - 1.5g; Cholesterol - 6mg

JALAPENO BUTTER SAUCE

Yield: About ½ cup

2 Jalapenos, seeded and finely
  chopped (wear rubber gloves)
1 large shallot, minced
¼ cup liquid Butter Buds,
  see page 48

1 tablespoon white wine
1 tablespoon finely-chopped
  parsley

In a small, covered saucepan, over low heat, soften the peppers and shallot in the Butter Buds. Add wine and parsley; simmer 4 to 5 minutes. Serve warm over beef or turkey.

Calories - 139; Total Fat - 10.5g;
Saturated Fat - .8g; Cholesterol - 0

LEMON BUTTER

Yield: About ½ cup

⅓ cup liquid Butter Buds,
  see page 48
½ teaspoon seasoned salt

2 tablespoons lemon juice
Tabasco sauce, to taste

Heat all ingredients in a small saucepan, stirring occasionally. Great over green vegetables or whitefish!

Calories - 160; Total Fat - 13.9g;
Saturated Fat - 1.1g; Cholesterol - 0

MADEIRA CREAM SAUCE

Yield: About 1 cup

½ cup Madeira wine
½ cup liquid Butter Buds,
  see page 48

2 tablespoons mock sour cream,
  see page 51
1 tablespoon cornstarch

Over medium high heat, in a small saucepan, reduce the wine by half. Lower heat and stir in the Butter Buds. Cook; reducing a little more. Reduce heat and add sour cream, whisking until smooth. Add a paste of cornstarch and warm water. Whisk until sauce is smooth and thickened. Use over seafood.

Calories - 371; Total Fat - 21.3g;
Saturated Fat - 2.1g; Cholesterol - 3.5mg

MORNAY SAUCE

Yield: About 1 cup

1 cup Bechamel Sauce,
  see page 225
½ tablespoon freshly-grated
  parmesan cheese

½ tablespoon grated Swiss
  cheese alternative
1 tablespoon liquid Butter Buds,
  see page 48

In a saucepan, heat the Bechamel Sauce over low heat, whisking constantly. Add the 2 cheeses. Whisk until smooth.

Remove from heat, and whisk in the Butter Buds. Serve immediately.

Calories - 261; Total Fat - 12.2g;
Saturated Fat - 2.4g; Cholesterol - 11.5mg

MUSTARD SAUCE

Yield: About 2 cups

2 tablespoons chopped onion
¼ cup liquid Butter Buds,
 see page 48
3 tablespoons cornstarch
¾ cup skim milk, warmed
¾ cup chicken broth or
 low-sodium bouillon

1 tablespoon lemon juice
1½ tablespoons Dijon mustard
1 teaspoon sugar or ½ packet
 sugar substitute
½ teaspoon salt (opt.)

In a medium, covered saucepan or in the top of a double boiler, cook the onion in the Butter Buds until soft. Dissolve cornstarch in milk. Gradually add milk and then chicken broth to the saucepan, whisking constantly until mixture is smooth and thickened. Stir in remaining ingredients. Serve immediately over hot cooked vegetables, or keep warm in a double boiler until needed.

Calories - 360; Total Fat - 13.3g;
Saturated Fat - 1.4g; Cholesterol - 3.8mg

ONION-RUM SAUCE

Yield: 1¾ cups

1 small onion, finely chopped
2 tablespoons liquid Butter Buds,
 see page 48
2 tablespoons cornstarch
1¼ cups skim milk, warmed

1 tablespoon minced parsley
¼ teaspoon salt (opt.)
¼ teaspoon pepper
¼ cup egg substitute
1 tablespoon light rum

In a small, covered saucepan, heat the onion in the Butter Buds until softened. Dissolve the cornstarch in the milk. Gradually add the milk to the saucepan, whisking constantly until the mixture begins to thicken. Add the parsley, salt and pepper.

Remove from heat. Mix about ¼ cup of mixture into the egg substitute. Return egg mixture to the sauce; mix well. Stir in rum and let sit for 2 minutes. Serve over hot vegetables.

Calories - 364; Total Fat - 6g;
Saturated Fat - .8g; Cholesterol - 5mg

PIZZA SAUCE

Yield: About 4 cups

1 16-ounce can tomatoes,
  coarsely chopped
1 15-ounce can no-salt
  tomato sauce
1 8-ounce can no-salt
  tomato sauce
¾ teaspoon salt (opt.)

½ teaspoon celery seed
½ teaspoon onion powder
¼ teaspoon garlic powder
½ teaspoon dried oregano
½ teaspoon dried basil
¼ teaspoon ground rosemary
2⅓ tablespoons sugar

Mix all ingredients together in a 2-quart saucepan and cook gently, covered, for 30 minutes. Remove cover and cook for 1 hour longer. Freezes well.

Per cup: *Calories - 166; Total Fat - 5.5g;*
               Saturated Fat - Tr; Cholesterol - 0

SALSA

Yield: About 2½ cups

3 large tomatoes, skinned
  and chopped
1 chili pepper, seeded and
  finely chopped (wear
  rubber gloves)
3 Jalapenos, seeded and finely
  chopped (wear rubber gloves)

3 garlic cloves, pressed
1 medium onion, finely chopped
Dash of cayenne pepper
1 tablespoon finely-chopped parsley
½ teaspoon cumin
½ teaspoon salt (opt.)
1 teaspoon sugar

In a medium bowl, mix all ingredients well. Adjust seasonings for heat, sweetness, pepper, etc. Refrigerate for several hours. Keeps well.

Serve with tortilla chips or with Mexican dishes.

Calories - 175; Total Fat - 1.6g;
Saturated Fat - Tr; Cholesterol - 0

SHALLOT BUTTER FOR ASPARAGUS

Yield: About ⅔ cup

3 tablespoons finely-chopped
  shallots
3 tablespoons water

¼ cup liquid Butter Buds,
  see page 48
Pepper to taste

In a small saucepan, combine the shallots and water. Bring to a boil; reduce heat and cook until liquid is reduced by half.

Add Butter Buds, whisking rapidly. Add freshly ground pepper. Serve over cooked asparagus.

Calories - 123; Total Fat - 10.5g;
Saturated Fat - .8g; Cholesterol - 0

SPAGHETTI SAUCE

Yield: 16 servings

2 tablespoons olive oil
2 large onions, chopped
4 stalks celery, chopped
2 green peppers, chopped
5 garlic cloves, pressed
1 tablespoon dried basil
1 pound freshly-ground turkey
¼ teaspoon garlic powder
3 28-ounce cans Italian tomatoes

2 6-ounce cans tomato paste
2 large bay leaves
½ teaspoon chili powder
2 teaspoons Kosher salt
½ teaspoon black pepper
3 tablespoons sugar
2 teaspoons fennel seed, crushed
1½ tablespoons dried oregano

In a large, covered Dutch oven, saute the vegetables in the olive oil with basil until they are opaque. Remove from kettle.

Cook turkey, seasoned with a little garlic powder, until the meat is no longer pink. Break up meat as it cooks.

Return the vegetables to the kettle. Add remaining ingredients, breaking up the tomatoes, and simmer, covered, for 4 hours. **Freezes well.**

Per serving: Calories - 110; Total Fat - 3.6g;
Saturated Fat - .8g; Cholesterol - 21.8mg

VELOUTE SAUCE

Yield: About 1¼ cups

2 tablespoons liquid Butter Buds,
** see page 48**
2 tablespoons cornstarch

1 cup chicken stock, or 1 cup
** chicken bouillon**

Place the Butter Buds in a small saucepan over medium heat. Dissolve cornstarch in bouillon. Slowly add the bouillon to the saucepan, whisking constantly, until the sauce is smooth and thickened.

Calories - 166; Total Fat - 6.7g;
Saturated Fat - .8g; Cholesterol - 1mg

WHITE SAUCE

Yield: About 1¼ cups

2 tablespoons liquid Butter Buds,
** see page 48**
2 tablespoons cornstarch

1 cup skim milk, warmed
Salt (opt.) and white pepper,
** to taste**

Place Butter Buds in a small saucepan over medium heat. Dissolve cornstarch in the milk. Gradually add milk to saucepan, whisking constantly until sauce is smooth and thickened. Add salt and white pepper; cook for 1 minute more, whisking constantly.

Calories - 213; Total Fat - 5.7g;
Saturated Fat - .7g; Cholesterol - 4mg

TOM'S TURKEY GRAVY

Yield: About 7 cups

2 fresh turkey necks
5 cups water
1 large onion, quartered
2 celery ribs, coarsely chopped
1 large carrot, coarsely chopped
1 tablespoon beau monde seasoning
½ teaspoon freshly-ground
  black pepper

¾ cup liquid Butter Buds,
  see page 48
¾ cup cornstarch
½ cup skim milk, warmed
¼ teaspoon white pepper
¼ teaspoon salt (opt.)
1 additional teaspoon beau monde
  seasoning

Place first 7 ingredients in a covered Dutch oven. Bring to a boil and simmer for 2 hours and 30 minutes. Strain liquid and refrigerate overnight. Skim all fat from top of liquid, and discard.

Reheat the stock in the Dutch oven. In a small saucepan mix the cornstarch with some of the warmed stock and make a paste. Stir paste back into stock and whisk, constantly, until smooth and thickened. Add the Butter Buds and warmed milk, again whisking constantly. Add the seasonings, cover and simmer for 5 minutes. If it is too thick add more warmed milk. To thicken add more cornstarch mixed with a little warm water.

This necessarily must be made a couple days ahead of time. Don't worry, the aging only enhances the flavor. May be frozen in small containers for later use.

Per 1/4 cup serving: *Calories - 36.9; Total Fat - 1.4g;*
                      Saturated Fat - .2g; Cholesterol - 2mg

DESSERTS

DESSERTS

Most people love desserts. So do we, but we have them rarely, thus keeping them a special happening.

As desserts go, ours are not only heart-safe, but are relatively low in calories. For company, our favorite is the Bread Pudding, still warm from the oven, dripping in its creamy Hot Whiskey Sauce P.241. The Happy Heart Cheesecake P.242 is also a big hit and with only 210 calories, 5 grams of fat and 3 milligrams of cholesterol per serving could almost be considered a low-calorie-diet food. ENJOY!

APPLE KRISP

Yield: 12 servings

7 to 9 green cooking apples,
  peeled and sliced
¼ cup sugar
½ teaspoon cinnamon
1 cup flour
1 teaspoon baking powder

¾ cup sugar
½ teaspoon salt
½ teaspoon cinnamon
1 whole egg
½ cup liquid Butter Buds,
  see page 48

Place apples in an 8x8x2-inch baking pan. Sprinkle with sugar and cinnamon.

In a medium-size mixing bowl, combine the next 5 ingredients. Add the egg and mix with a fork until mixture becomes crumbly. Place mixture over the apples. Pour Butter Buds over crumbs. Bake at 375F for 35 to 40 minutes.

Per serving: *Calories - 277; Total Fat - 4.1g;*
                   Saturated Fat - .6g; Cholesterol - 26.7mg

APPLESAUCE

Yield: 3 pints

10 to 12 green cooking apples
Dash of salt

½ cup sugar
½ teaspoon cinnamon

Wash apples, quarter and core. Place in a large kettle with water to top of apples. Add salt; bring to a boil. Simmer, covered, 20 to 30 minutes, or until apples are soft. Add more water if needed.

Place a Foley Food Mill over a 2-quart mixing bowl. Mill the apples by filling the mill 2/3 full and turning until only the skins remain. Discard skins. Repeat process until all apples are milled.

Add sugar and cinnamon to the apples. Mix well. If applesauce is a little too green, swirl in 2 or more drops of red food coloring.

Per ½ cup: *Calories - 113; Total Fat - .5g;*
                 Saturated Fat - Tr; Cholesterol - 0

BABY-SAFE BLUEBERRY DESSERT
Yield: 4 servings

1 cup Zwieback (about 12),
   crushed
¼ cup sugar, or 6 packets
   sugar substitute
¼ teaspoon cinnamon

3 tablespoons liquid Butter Buds,
   see page 48
2 cups well-drained blueberries,
   fresh or frozen

Mix the dry ingredients together in a medium bowl. Add the Butter Buds; mix well. Place 1 cup berries in a sprayed 1-quart casserole. Sprinkle with half the Zwieback mixture. Put another cup berries on top; add remaining crumbs. Press down; bake in a 350F oven for 30 minutes.

The flavors are much better if made 1 day ahead.

Per serving: *Calories - 200; Total Fat - 4.5g;*
                   Saturated Fat - Tr; Cholesterol - 0

BREAD PUDDING WITH HOT WHISKEY SAUCE
Yield: 6 servings

3 slices stale cinnamon bread   Baked custard, see page 243
2 tablespoons liquid Butter Buds,
  see page 48

Spray bottom and sides of an 8½x4½x2½-inch glass loaf pan. Break the bread into pan. Drizzle with Butter Buds and pour the uncooked custard on top. Set loaf pan in a larger pan with paper towels in the bottom and about ¾-inch hot water.

Bake at 350F for 55 to 60 minutes or until knife inserted into the custard comes out clean.

WHISKEY SAUCE

2 tablespoons sugar   ½ teaspoon vanilla
2 teaspoons cornstarch   Few grains of nutmeg
½ cup boiling water   Few grains of salt
3 packets sugar substitute   2 tablespoons rye whiskey or
1 tablespoon liquid Butter Buds, bourbon
  see page 48

In a small saucepan, mix sugar and cornstarch together. Over medium high heat add water gradually, whisking constantly. Cook for 1 minute after thickening. Remove from heat; stir in the remaining ingredients.

Pour sauce over servings of warm pudding.

Per serving: *Calories - 222; Total Fat - 2g;*
               Saturated Fat - Tr; Cholesterol - 2mg

HAPPY HEART CHEESECAKE

Yield: 10 servings

CRUST

1 cup graham cracker crumbs, about 14 crackers	**¼ cup melted light corn oil spread**

Mix graham cracker crumbs with the spread; press the mixture into the bottom and onto the sides of a sprayed 10½-inch springform pan.

FILLING

3 cups 1% fat cottage cheese	**⅓ cup flour**
¾ cup egg substitute	**¼ cup fresh lemon juice**
¾ cup skim milk	**1 tablespoon grated lemon rind**
¾ cup sugar	

In a large blender or food proccesor, beat the cottage cheese until creamy. Add the egg substitute, ¼ cup at a time, then the milk, beating well after each addition. Mix the sugar and flour together; add to cheese mixture; beat smooth. Add remaining ingredients, beating until smooth.

Pour mixture into the prepared cracker crust; bake at 300F for 1½ hours, or until set. Cool for several hours, then add your favorite topping.

Per serving: *Calories - 210; Total Fat - 5g;*
Saturated Fat - 1.5g; Cholesterol - 3.3mg

For a large gathering, use 56 foil-lined mini-muffin cups. Place a vanilla wafer in the bottom of each cup. Fill with the cheesecake mixture; place on cookie sheets and bake at 300F for 1 hour.

Cool; top with lite pie filling. Refrigerate until needed or freeze for later use.

Per cheesecake: Calories - 50; Total Fat - .7gr.
Saturated Fat - Tr; Cholesterol - .6mg

BAKED CUSTARD
Yield: 6 servings

¾ cup egg substitute
½ cup sugar
¼ teaspoon salt

3 cups skim milk, warmed
1 teaspoon vanilla
Nutmeg

Beat egg substitute, sugar and salt with a rotary beater. Pour milk slowly over egg substitute, beating with a whisk to keep smooth. Add vanilla. Pour into 6 small sprayed custard cups. Sprinkle with nutmeg. Set in shallow pan on sheet of paper towel. Pour in about ¾ inch hot water in the pan.

Bake at 350F for about 55 minutes. Test doneness by inserting a clean knife blade into the custard. If it comes out clean, custard is done.

Per serving: *Calories - 119; Total Fat - Tr;*
                    Saturated Fat - Tr; Cholesterol - 2mg

MARY SMITH'S CHOCOLATE CAKE
Yield: 9 servings

1½ cups all-purpose flour
1 cup sugar
3 tablespoons cocoa
1 teaspoon baking soda

1 teaspoon cider vinegar
1 teaspoon vanilla
6 tablespoons canola oil
1 cup water

In an 8-inch square pan, sift the dry ingredients together. Make a depression in the center and add the remaining ingredients. Mix with a whisk until completely mixed and moist. Be sure all lumps are gone.

Bake at 350F for 35 minutes.

Per serving: *Calories - 242; Total Fat - 9.7g;*
                    Saturated Fat - .7g; Cholesterol - 0

LIGHT DELIGHT DESSERT

Yield: 4 servings

1 cup boiling water
1 3-ounce package sugar-
    free strawberry jello
1 10-ounce package frozen
    sweetened strawberries, thawed

1 8-ounce can crushed pineapple,
    in its own juices, drained
1 banana, mashed
¾ cup mock sour cream,
    see page 51

Mix all ingredients together except the sour cream. Place half the mixture in the bottom of a 1½-quart casserole dish. Refrigerate until set. Spread the mock sour cream over the chilled gelatin; pour remaining gelatin on top. Chill and serve.

Per serving: *Calories - 111; Total Fat - 1.2g;*
               Saturated Fat - .8g; Cholesterol - 5.3mg

HOT WATER GINGERBREAD

Yield: 12 servings

7 tablespoons canola oil
½ cup sugar
1 cup light molasses
½ teaspoon ground cloves
½ teaspoon cinnamon
½ teaspoon ground ginger

½ teaspoon salt (opt.)
¼ cup egg substitute
1 cup boiling water
2½ cups all-purpose flour
2 teaspoons baking soda

Combine first 7 ingredients together in a mixing bowl; mix well. Add the egg substitute; mix well. Add boiling water; mix well. Add flour mixed with baking soda; beat with an electric hand mixer until smooth.

Pour into sprayed 9x9x2-inch baking pan. Bake at 350F for 30 to 35 minutes.

Per serving: *Calories - 258; Total Fat - 8.4g;*
               Saturated Fat - .6g; Cholesterol - 0

KEY LIME PIE

Yield: 8 servings

FILLING

1 cup sugar
6 tablespoons cornstarch
1½ cups water
8 packets sugar substitute

1 egg yolk
¼ cup egg substitute
⅓ cup bottled key lime juice

In a saucepan, mix the sugar and cornstarch. Gradually add the water over medium heat and cook, stirring constantly, until mixture comes to a boil and thickens. Bubble the mixture for 1 minute. Remove from heat; cool slightly. Add sugar substitute, egg yolk, egg substitute and lime juice. Mix well and set aside.

CRUST

⅓ cup light corn oil spread   1½ cups graham cracker crumbs

Melt the spread in a 9-inch pie pan. Combine with the graham cracker crumbs; press into bottom and up sides of pie pan. Bake at 350F for 10 minutes. Set aside to cool for at least 10 minutes. Pour pie filling into baked crust.

TOPPING

3 large egg whites   4 tablespoons sugar
¼ teaspoon cream of tartar

In a large bowl, beat egg whites and the cream of tartar until frothy. Add the sugar, a little at a time, beating constantly. When mixture is stiff and holds peaks, mound onto the pie filling and level. Reform peaks with the back side of a spoon.

Bake in a 425F oven for 4 to 5 minutes, or until top is lightly browned.

Per serving: *Calories - 301; Total Fat - 8g;*
                    Saturated Fat - 2g; Cholesterol - 34.3mg

LEMON LOAF

Yield: 8 servings

1 cup sugar	½ teaspoon salt (opt.)
⅓ cup light corn oil spread	1½ teaspoons baking powder
Rind of one lemon, grated	½ cup skim milk
½ cup egg substitute	⅓ cup sugar
1½ cups all-purpose flour	Juice of 1 small lemon

In a large mixing bowl, beat sugar and spread with an electric mixer. Add lemon rind; mix well. Beat in egg substitute.

Sift flour, salt and baking powder together and add to sugar mixture alternately with milk, beginning and ending with flour, beating continuously. Pour into a well-sprayed 8½x4½x2½-inch loaf pan. Bake at 350F for 50 to 60 minutes.

Dissolve the ⅓ cup of sugar in the lemon juice; pour over hot loaf. Allow to cool in pan. Remove from pan and slice.

Per serving: *Calories - 274; Total Fat - 5.6g;*
Saturated Fat - 1.4g; Cholesterol - Tr;

ONE CRUST PIE CRUST

Yield: 1 8 to 9½-inch pie crust

1¼ cups all-purpose flour	⅓ cup light corn oil spread
½ teaspoon salt	3 to 4 tablespoons ice water

Sift flour and salt together in a large mixing bowl. Cut the spread into the flour until it resembles coarse meal. Add the water, one tablespoon at a time, and mix lightly, but thoroughly. Form the pastry into a ball and chill for at least 15 minutes before using.

Roll out on floured countertop.

Per crust: *Calories 952; Total Fat - 44g;*
Saturated Fat - 10.9g; Cholesterol - 0

PINEAPPLE FILLED CAKE

Yield: 12 servings

1 8-ounce can crushed pineapple
  in its own juice, undrained
½ cup sugar
2 teaspoons cornstarch
12 packets sugar substitute
½ cup light corn oil spread
1 cup sugar

1 teaspoon vanilla
½ cup egg substitute
1 whole egg
2 cups all-purpose flour, sifted
  with 1 teaspoon baking powder
1 tablespoon sugar

In a saucepan, cook the pineapple, sugar and cornstarch over low heat, stirring until thickened. Remove from heat and stir in the sugar substitute.

In a large mixing bowl, cream the corn oil spread, sugar and vanilla together. Add the egg substitute and whole egg slowly, while continuing to beat the mixture. Gradually add the sifted flour and baking powder.

Spread half the batter into a sprayed 8-inch square pan and cover with the pineapple mixture. Add remaining batter and sprinkle with the tablespoon of sugar.

Bake in 350F oven for 30 minutes, or until done.

Per serving: *Calories - 252; Total Fat - 6g;*
            Saturated Fat - 1.5g; Cholesterol - 17.8mg

PINEAPPLE/LEMON FREEZER DESSERT

Yield: 10 servings

1 12-ounce can evaporated
  skimmed milk
1 7-ounce jar marshmallow creme
1 6-ounce can frozen lemonade,
  thawed, undiluted

1 8-ounce can crushed pineapple
  in its own juice, well drained
1 20-ounce package frozen
  sweetened stawberries

Pour evaporated milk into a large, deep bowl; place in freezer for about 45 minutes, or until the edges begin to freeze.

In the meantime, in a smaller bowl, beat the marshmallow and lemonade together with an electric mixer set at medium speed. Beat until mixture is smooth.

With mixer at high, beat the chilled milk until stiff; slowly pour in the marshmallow mixture. Continue to beat until very thick.

Fold in the drained pineapple. Pour into a 12x8x2-inch baking dish and freeze for several hours.

Serve topped with the strawberries, which have been slightly mashed.

Per serving: *Calories - 126; Total Fat - 1.4g;*
                   Saturated Fat - .6g; Cholesterol - Tr

POMME GRATINEE

Yield: 6 servings

1 cup water
3 tablespoons sugar, or 4½
  packets sugar substitute
2 dessert apples, red or golden
  delicious, quartered and seeded

1 piece vanilla bean
¾ pound cooking apples
1 teaspoon light corn oil spread

In a saucepan, combine water and sugar. Add quartered dessert apples and vanilla bean. Poach gently until tender and clear. Set aside.

Peel and slice cooking apples. Rub pan with corn oil spread. Place apples in pan, cover and cook over medium high heat until soft. Do not add any water. Remove dessert apples from syrup; place on dish. Beat cooking apples until smooth. Add the syrup to applesauce and return to heat. Continue to cook down, and stir until thickened. Pour into sprayed 8-inch glass pie plate. Arrange the apple quarters on top.

TOPPING

1 egg white
1 tablespoon sliced almonds

2 tablespoons powdered sugar

In a medium bowl whisk egg white, adding 1 tablespoon powdered sugar gradually until thick. Fold in almonds and spread over apples. Dust with remaining powdered sugar; bake in 375F oven for 5 minutes, or until lightly browned.

Per serving: *Calories - 121; Total Fat - 2.1g;*
                Saturated Fat - Tr; Cholesterol - 0

PUMPKIN PIE

Yield: 8 servings

1 16-ounce can pumpkin or
  squash
¼ cup sugar
½ cup light brown sugar
½ cup egg substitute
½ teaspoon salt (opt.)

½ teaspoon ground ginger
2 teaspoons cinnamon
⅛ teaspoon ground cloves
1½ cups evaporated skimmed
  milk

Combine all ingredients in a deep bowl. Beat well with a rotary beater.

Make a 9½-inch pie shell. See page 246. Pour mixture into pie shell.

Bake at 425F for 15 minutes. Reduce heat to 350F and continue baking for about 45 minutes more. Pie is done when a knife blade inserted into center of pie comes out clean.

Per serving: *Calories - 283; Total Fat - 7.2g;*
                   Saturated Fat - 2.2g; Cholesterol - 0

TWO WEEK MEAL PLANNER

Chicken + Rice	Fish		
5 Salmon with Bearnaise	**6** Veal + Shrimp	**7** Pasta Casserole	
12 Walpole Veal	**13** Beef Loaf ala North St	**14** Tuna Steak	
19	**20**	**2**	

TWO WEEK MEAL PLANNER

This section has been added as an answer to innumerable requests. People **want** to eat healthy, but they also **want** help in planning their daily and weekly meals. We offer two full weeks of planned meals using **THE HEALTHY HEART GOURMET** as a base. In addition to the 14 days of menus, we have added some suggestions which will make your shopping and meal preparation easier.

We have chosen meals that vary in style and flavor, using foodstuffs available in most supermarkets. These meals are balanced nutritionally and provide you with a safe fat from calories percentage of 30% or less. However, consider adding a second vegetable or salad to round out your meals.

A positive note about meal planning is that you will shop only once a week. This eliminates most of the impulse buying the markets are sure to throw at you daily. First, learn the floor plan in your supermarket. After choosing your weekly meals, write a shopping list following that plan. **"STICK TO YOUR LIST!!"** Once you get the hang of it, you will find that meal planning and shopping done weekly, rather than daily, will save you time, money and much frustration.

We have not included appetizers, desserts or drinks. For most people appetizers are reserved for more formal meals or special holidays.

THE HEALTHY HEART GOURMET has an extended dessert section. Most are relatively low in fat but, because of their sweetness, some have a higher dose of calories than we personally care to eat on a regular basis. Desserts in our house are a rare treat.

Drinks with meals have been left to individual choice. Just be sure you and your family have the proper amount of milk daily. (See the **MILK GROUP** beginning on page 17.) Be careful of the high caffeine found in some sodas, tea and coffee. Use caffeine-free, when possible. If you enjoy a beer with dinner, but don't want the alcohol, try one of the new non-alcoholic beers. You'll be surprised how much they have improved. Finally, don't forget the old standby — **WATER**. No fat, no calories!

We have listed 14 different breakfasts. These offer you a chance to break the habit of eating the same thing every morning.

We have also offered a couple of meatless meals. Don't knock them. Give them a try. They could open up a whole new, healthier way of eating for you. For those who are leaning towards a vegetarian diet **THE HEALTHY HEART GOURMET** has 9 Entrees to add to your collection, besides many meatless luncheon salads.

WEEK #1

	BREAKFAST	LUNCH	DINNER
Day 1 Fat - 23%	Juice, 4 oz. No Problem Pancakes♥ - P.80, with lite syrup or fruit topping	Baked Burgers - P.71 French Green Bean Salad♥ - P.124 Fresh or frozen strawberries	Broiled Salmon with Bearnaise Sauce - P.193 Vegetable Medley - P.217
Day 2 Fat - 22%	Juice, 4 oz. Egg substitute and vegetable omelet, Toasted English muffin with spread	Eggplant Subs - P.75 Lettuce wedges with oil-free dressing Fresh apple, sliced	Veal and Shrimp Extraordinary - P.137 Dilled English Peas - P.210; steamed new potatoes with Butter Buds
Day 3 Fat - 20%	½ grapefruit Cold cereal with skim milk and fresh fruit	Man-size Open-Face Sandwiches - P.79 Sliced frozen or fresh peaches	Pasta Casserole - P.80 Sweet/Sour Spinach Salad - P.127 Corn on the cob with liquid Butter Buds
Day 4 Fat - 28%	Juice, 4 oz. Plain Bagel with light cream cheese and a sigh of jam	Shrimp Pasta Salad♥ - P.82 Low-fat bread sticks Navel orange sections	Chicken in Cream Sauce P.169 Steamed broccoli Rice Pilaf - P.213
Day 5 Fat - 20%	½ grapefruit Cheese alternative melted on toast Fresh apple, sliced	Cream of Brussels Sprouts Soup - P.105♥ Casserole Bread♥ - P.94, with spread Banana	Spaghetti with sauce♥ - P.234 Green salad with oil-free dressing Garlic bread with spread

♥ = Make a day or two ahead

WEEK #1 cont'd.

	BREAKFAST	LUNCH	DINNER
Day 6 **Fat - 22%**	Juice, 4 oz. Hot cereal with warmed skim milk Fresh fruit	Egg Salad Sandwiches ❤ P.76 Cucumber pickles Carrot Sticks Fresh pear, sliced	Tuna Curry Casserole - P.199 Steamed cauliflower Soft Dinner Rolls❤- P.95, with spread
Day 7 **Fat - 26%**	Juice, 4 oz. French Toast - P.77, with lite syrup or powdered sugar	Bacon-Cheese-Relish Dip❤ in Pita Bread - P.57 Sugar-free Jello with fruit cocktail❤	Swedish Meatballs❤ - P.65 Mashed potatoes Rum Carrots - P.205

WEEK# 2

	BREAKFAST	LUNCH	DINNER
Day 1 **Fat - 30%**	½ grapefruit Poached Eggs with Bearnaise Sauce - P.76-served on ½ toasted English muffin	Italian Submarine Sandwich - P.78 Fresh apple, sliced	Gourmet Fillet of Fish - P.185 Lima Bean Salad❤ - P.124 Pasta Saute - P.209
Day 2 **Fat - 29%**	Juice, 4 oz. Weekend Waffles❤ with lite syrup or fruit topping - P.85	Tabbouleh in Pocket Bread❤ - P.89 Mixed sliced fruit	Stuffed Roasted Chicken P.176* Mashed potatoes Instant Chicken Gravy - P.227; Company Green Beans - P.202

❤ = Make a day or two ahead

WEEK #2 cont'd.

	BREAKFAST	LUNCH	DINNER
Day 3 **Fat - 30%**	Juice, 4 oz. Peanut Butter♥ on toast - P.50 Banana	Crab and Rice Salad♥ - P.74 Sliced tomatoes and Cucumbers	Black Beans♥ - P.202 Saffron Rice - P.214 Southern Style Collards P. 206; Jamaican Corn Muffins - p.96, with spread.
Day 4 **Fat - 26%**	Juice, 4 oz. Western style omelet with egg substitute and Canadian Bacon	Taco Salad - P.83 Fresh Pear, sliced	Walpole Veal - P.139 served over eggless noodles Broccoli Casserole - P.204
Day 5 **Fat - 21%**	Fresh Fruit Salad Grits with Cheese Alternative	Carrot Soup♥ - P.106 Zucchini Muffins - P.98♥, with spread.	"Beef" Loaf Ala North Street P.159 Baked Potato Nutty Brussels Sprouts - P.204
Day 6 **Fat - 20%**	Juice, 4 oz. ½ bagel with ½ slice Canadian Bacon and 1 slice fat-free cheese, broiled	Vegetable Pasta Salad♥ - P.84 Harmless Deviled Eggs♥ - P.60 No-fat French bread with spread	Grilled Tuna Steak with Green Peppercorn Sauce P.198 Oven French Fries - P.211; Spicy White Turnips - P.217
Day 7 **Fat - 28%**	Juice, 4oz. Italian Sausage♥ - P.87, cooked and served in English muffin	Luncheon Jello Salad♥ P.78 Tomato wedges with no-fat no-cholesterol mayonnaise Soft bread sticks	Chicken and Rice Casserole - P.169* Sweet/Sour Cabbage Salad♥ - P.121 Mayonnaise Muffins - P.97, with spread

♥ = Make a day or two ahead

The low-fat, cholesterol and calories in these meals offer you the opportunity to have desserts. Any recipe from the dessert section of this book will be fine, if eaten in moderation. **NO SECOND HELPINGS.** We expect you will adjust each serving to fit your own daily caloric allowance, as determined by your physician or dietitian.

WEEK #1 - Leisurely breakfasts are scheduled for the weekend, as are the first 3 lunches. Lunches days 4 through 7 can easily be carried to work. Buy extra shrimp for dinner, day 2. Cook and freeze excess for lunch day 4. Make 1½ cups mock sour cream, on day 2, for the week. Buy enough fresh ground turkey for Baked Burgers, Spaghetti Sauce & Swedish Meatballs. Buy enough fresh mushrooms for days #1,2 & 3.

WEEK #2 - *Freeze chicken, cubed, for dinner day 7. Make pasta for Pasta Saute 1 day ahead. It's better after refrigerating. Buy enough tomatoes for dinner day 1 and lunches days 1-4 and 7. Buy enough ground turkey for lunch day 4, dinner day 5 and breakfast day 7. Cook enough rice for lunch day 3 to cover dinner day 7. Make 1 cup mock sour cream for the week.

EXTENDED MEAL PLAN OFFER

We are offering **Meal Planners 3 & 4.** The two planners will provide an entire month of healthy meals planned just for you. Also available is a new **Formal Meal Planner** which includes two **5** course meals for four to six people — including wines selected by wine expert, Gary Kenfield.

THE HEALTHY HEART GOURMET
3716 North A-1-A
Vero Beach, FL 32963

Please send me_____copies of week 3 & 4 **Weekly Meal Planner** at $2.95

Please send me_____copies of the two meal **Formal Meal Planner** at $1.95

Enclosed is my check/money order for $_____

Name_____

Address_____

City_____State_____Zip_____

THE HEALTHY HEART GOURMET
3716 North A-1-A
Vero Beach, FL 32963

Please send me ___ copies of **THE HEALTHY HEART GOURMET** at $14.95, plus $2.50 s/h for the first book and $1.50 s/h for each additional book. Florida residents must add $.90 sales tax per book.

Enclosed is my check/money order for $_____

Name_____

Address_____

City_____State_____Zip_____

☎ MC/VISA 24 hours per day 1-800-444-2524 ☎

✂--

THE HEALTHY HEART GOURMET
3716 North A-1-A
Vero Beach, FL 32963

Please send me ___ copies of **THE HEALTHY HEART GOURMET** at $14.95, plus $2.50 s/h for the first book and $1.50 s/h for each additional book. Florida residents must add $.90 sales tax per book.

Enclosed is my check/money order for $_____

Name_____

Address_____

City_____State_____Zip_____

☎ MC/VISA 24 hours per day 1-800-444-2524 ☎

HEALTHY HEART NOTES